BARTH ON THE DESCENT INTO HELL

The Christian confession that Jesus Christ descended into hell has been variously misunderstood or simply neglected by the Church and dogmatic theology. This work is a significant retort to dogmatic forgetfulness and ecclesial misunderstanding. It succeeds in this by offering a close reading and critical analysis of Karl Barth's treatment of the descent into hell and its relation to his extraordinary theology of the atonement.

The reach of David Lauber's work is extended by placing Barth in conversation with Hans Urs von Balthasar's innovative theology of Holy Saturday. In revealing and unexpected ways, this book casts light upon the ecumenical breadth of Barth's theology. It is a valuable interpretation of significant facets of Barth's doctrine of God, reflection upon the passion of Jesus Christ, and ethics. In addition, Lauber offers a constructive theological proposal for how the descent into hell affects the theological interpretation of Scripture, the Trinitarian being and activity of God, and the non-violent and authentic shape of Christian life and witness before our enemies.

Barth Studies

Series editors:

Revd Professor John Webster, University of Oxford;
Dr Hans-Anton Drewes, Karl Barth-Archiv, Basel;
Professor George Hunsinger, Center for Barth Studies, Princeton

The work of Barth is central to the history of modern western theology and remains a major voice in contemporary constructive theology. His writings have been the subject of intensive scrutiny and re-evaluation over the past two decades, notably on the part of English-language Barth scholars who have often been at the forefront of fresh interpretation and creative appropriation of his theology. Study of Barth, both by graduate students and by established scholars, is a significant enterprise; literature on him and conferences devoted to his work abound; the Karl Barth Archive in Switzerland and the Center for Barth Studies at Princeton give institutional profile to these interests. Barth's work is also considered by many to be a significant resource for the intellectual life of the churches.

Drawing from the wide pool of Barth scholarship, and including translations of Barth's works, this series aims to function as a means by which writing on Barth, of the highest scholarly calibre, can find publication. The series builds upon and furthers the interest in Barth's work in the theological academy and the church.

Other titles in the series:

Ecclesial Mediation in Karl Barth
John Yocum

The Ascension in Karl Barth
Andrew Burgess

Barth on the Descent into Hell

God, Atonement and the Christian Life

DAVID LAUBER
Wheaton College, USA

ASHGATE

Published by
Ashgate Publishing Limited
Gower House
Croft Road
Aldershot
Hants GU11 3HR
England

Ashgate Publishing Company
Suite 420
101 Cherry Street
Burlington, VT 05401-4405
USA

Ashgate website: http://www.ashgate.com

British Library Cataloguing in Publication Data
Lauber, David
    Barth on the Descent into Hell : God, Atonement and the
    Christian Life. – (Barth Studies)
    1. Jesus Christ – Descent into hell   2. Barth, Karl, 1886–1968
    – Views on Jesus Christ's descent into hell   3. Balthasar,
    Hans Urs von, 1905– – Views on Jesus Christ's descent into hell
    I. Title
    232.9'67

Library of Congress Cataloging-in-Publication Data
Lauber, David, 1966–
    Barth on the Descent into Hell: God, Atonement, and the Christian Life /
    David Lauber.
        p. cm. – (Barth Studies)
    Includes bibliographical references.
    1. Jesus Christ – Descent into hell.   2. Barth, Karl, 1886–1968.
    3. Balthasar, Hans Urs Von, 1905–   I. Title.   II. Series.
    BT470.L38 2003
    232.96'7 – dc22
                                                                        2003057768

ISBN 0 7546 3341 1

Typeset by Setsystems Ltd, Saffron Walden, Essex

Printed and bound in Great Britain by MPG Books Ltd, Bodmin, Cornwall

Contents

Acknowledgements

This study is a slightly revised version of my Princeton Theological Seminary dissertation. I owe a debt of gratitude to professors, mentors and readers who helped me conceive this project and who encouraged and guided me through its research and writing. I am grateful to David Willis, Bruce McCormack, James Buckley and Daniel Migliore.

My parents, Marilyn and Richard Lauber, provided a home conducive to Christian nurture and theological curiosity, and modelled the essential interconnection between Christian belief and practice. Their encouragement and support of me and this project have been invaluable; for this I will always be grateful.

Finally, my warmest thanks are reserved for Dawn. I am grateful for her support, encouragement, patience and sacrifice during the process that has resulted in this book. Her consistent confidence in my own abilities and work eased the challenge of my research and writing. The loving atmosphere created by her, along with Caroline, Andrew and Bradley, provided much-needed refreshment and diversion. For these and for all those things unmentioned I give thanks.

Permissions

I am grateful to The Continuum International Publishing Group and to Ignatius Press for their kind permission to include multiple and lengthy excerpts from major works by Barth and Balthasar.

Selections from Hans Urs von Balthasar. *Mysterium Paschale: The Mystery of Easter*. Translated by Aidan Nichols, O.P. Edinburgh: T. & T. Clark. Reprinted with the permission of The Continuum International Publishing Group.

Selections from Karl Barth. *Church Dogmatics*, volume II, part 1. The Doctrine of God. Translated by T. H. L. Parker, W. B. Johnson, H. Knight and J. L. M. Haire. Edinburgh: T. & T. Clark, 1957. Reprinted with the permission of The Continuum International Publishing Group.

Selections from Karl Barth. *Church Dogmatics*, volume II, part 2. The Doctrine of God. Translated by G. W. Bromiley, J. C. Campbell, Ian Wilson, J. Strathearn McNab, H. Knight, and R. A. Stewart. Edinburgh: T. & T. Clark, 1957. Reprinted with the permission of The Continuum International Publishing Group.

Selections from Karl Barth. *Church Dogmatics*, volume IV, part 1. The Doctrine of Reconciliation. Translated by G. W. Bromiley. Edinburgh: T. & T. Clark, 1956. Reprinted with the permission of the Continuum International Publishing Group.

Selections from Karl Barth. *Church Dogmatics*, volume IV, part 2. The Doctrine of Reconciliation. Translated by G. W. Bromiley. Edinburgh: T. & T. Clark, 1958. Reprinted with the permission of The Continuum International Publishing Group.

Excerpts from Hans Urs von Balthasar. *Theo-Drama: Theological Dramatic Theory*, volume IV, *The Action*. Translated by Graham Harrison. San Francisco: Ignatius Press, 1994. Reprinted with permission of Ignatius Press, San Francisco, CA.

Abbreviations

C   Karl Barth. *Credo: A Presentation of the Chief Problems of Dogmatics with Reference to the Apostle's [sic] Creed.* trans. James Stathearn McNab. London: Hodder & Stoughton, 1936.

CD   Karl Barth. *Church Dogmatics.* Edinburgh: T. & T. Clark, 1956–75.

MP   Hans Urs von Balthasar. *Mysterium Paschale: The Mystery of Easter.* Edinburgh: T. & T. Clark, 1990.

TD   Hans Urs von Balthasar. *Theo-Drama: Theological Dramatic Theory.* San Francisco: Ignatius Press, 1989–98.

For Dawn

CHAPTER ONE

Karl Barth: Jesus Christ's death in God-abandonment as the descent into hell

It is a serious matter to be threatened by hell, sentenced to hell, worthy of hell, and already on the road to hell. On the other hand, we must not minimize the fact that we actually know of only one certain triumph of hell – the handing-over of Jesus – and that this triumph of hell took place in order that it would never again be able to triumph over anyone. We must not deny that Jesus gave Himself up into the depths of hell not only with many others but on their behalf, in their place, in the place of all who believe in Him. (*CD* II/2, p. 496)

The issue that drives this study is Karl Barth's precise and consistent exploration of and emphasis on the wrath of God that Jesus Christ suffered in his passion on our behalf and in our place. The argument that I will offer is that an understanding of Barth's emphasis on the substitutionary suffering of Jesus Christ is incomplete without paying attention to the often overlooked and misunderstood confession of the Church that Jesus descended into hell. As the above passage indicates, Barth affirms that Jesus enters into the depths of hell as the culmination of his life and passion, which is lived and endured *pro nobis* – on our behalf and in our place. Further, it is precisely in giving himself over to the depths of hell that Jesus is victorious and triumphs over hell. God indeed unleashes his wrath and punishment on Jesus Christ, who identifies with the rejected, even to the point of being distinguished uniquely as *the* Rejected. In this event, moreover, we encounter the profound mystery of the suffering love of God. As God exposes Jesus to his righteous wrath, he exposes himself to this wrath. To affirm that Jesus Christ is *the* Rejected of God entails that 'God makes Himself rejected in [Jesus Christ], and has Himself alone tasted to the depths all that rejected means and necessarily involves' (*CD* II/2, p. 496).

The explication and analysis of the function of the doctrine of the descent into hell in Barth's treatment of Jesus Christ's passion will contribute to a comprehensive understanding of Barth's doctrine of reconciliation, for which the category of substitution or *Stellvertretung* is central. Barth's commitment to a cross-centred theology, which emphasizes the substitutionary character of Jesus Christ's life and work, is seen clearly in the following:

All theology, both that which follows and indeed that which precedes the doctrine of reconciliation, depends upon [the] *theologia crucis*. And it depends upon it under the particular aspect under which we have had to develop it in this first part of the doctrine of reconciliation as the doctrine of substitution (*Lehre von der Stellvertretung*). Everything depends upon the fact that the Lord who became a servant, the Son of God who went into the far country, and came to us, was and did all this for us; that He fulfilled in this way, the divine judgment laid upon Him. There is no avoiding this strait gate. There is no other way but this narrow way. (*CD* IV/1, p. 273)

As this programmatic passage indicates, in answering the question *Cur Deus homo?*, Barth addresses the specific issue of what Jesus Christ did *pro nobis*, for us and for the world – *for us and for our salvation*. Furthermore, as has been well observed, Barth insists that we cannot separate the person and the work of Jesus Christ (*CD* IV/1, pp. 126–7). We must therefore emphasize that the salvific significance of Jesus Christ is constituted by who he is and what he has done on our behalf and in our place. As such, Barth's view cannot simply be described as a strain of 'substitutionary' atonement or 'penal substitution', without qualification. These catch-phrases obscure Barth's concentration on the narrative of Jesus Christ – the narrated history of the unique and particular individual – the one who bears the name Jesus Christ.[1]

In *Church Dogmatics* IV/1, Barth elucidates Jesus Christ's life history by using judicial concepts and by insisting that this particular life and death carry the characteristic of being on our behalf and in our place. Jesus Christ is the judge who is judged in our place. In §59.2, Barth details four essential elements of the passion: Jesus Christ took our place as *Judge*; he took our place as the *judged*; he was *judged* in our place; and he acted *justly* in our place (*CD* IV/1, pp. 211–82). Barth summarizes what took place in and through the person and activity of Jesus Christ as follows:

What took place is that the Son of God fulfilled the righteous judgment on us men by Himself taking our place as man and in our place undergoing the judgment under which we had passed. That is why He came amongst us. In this way, in this 'for us,' He was our Judge against us. That is what happened when the divine accusation was, as it were, embodied in His presence in the flesh. That is what happened when the divine condemnation had, as it were, visibly to fall on this our fellow-man. And that is what happened when by reason of our accusation and condemnation it had to come to the point of our perishing, our destruction, our fall into nothingness, our death. Everything happened to us exactly as it had to happen, but because God willed to execute His judgment on us in His Son it all happened in His person, as His accusation and condemnation and destruction. He judged, and it was the Judge who was judged, who let Himself be judged. (*CD* IV/1, p. 222)

---

1   It is clear that Barth would question the validity of such abstract concepts as 'substitutionary atonement' and 'penal substitution' precisely because of his insistence that concepts used in explicating the gospel must be determined by the unique history that is coupled with the unique name Jesus Christ. These concepts also risk reducing God's reconciling activity in Jesus Christ to a mechanical transaction, and as a result, risk separating the work or significance of Jesus Christ from his person or identity.

The task that will occupy us in what follows is an examination of Barth's understanding of the content of the divine condemnation that fell upon Jesus Christ. For Barth, this divine condemnation or judgment includes: perishing, destruction, the fall into nothingness and hell. By exploring the seriousness with which Barth describes the quality of Jesus Christ's crucifixion and death, we will be able to gain a clearer view of his understanding of the atonement. Further, and more particularly, we will readily recognize the importance of Jesus Christ's descent into hell for a comprehensive understanding of the salvific significance of his passion. This seriousness on Barth's part, we may add, is nothing more and nothing less than a reflection of the seriousness with which Scripture both narratively depicts and retrospectively interprets the passion of Jesus Christ. By way of description and analysis, we will gain a clear picture of what exactly Barth affirms and what he dismisses. On the one hand, we will be able to recognize the exact way in which Barth is considered accurately as an heir of St Anselm. On the other hand, we will be able to determine how Barth moves beyond the static, mechanistic and transactional character of common 'satisfaction' and 'penal substitution' theories of the atonement, while retaining an objective emphasis on the vicarious character of Christ's work – something done 'in our place'.[2] I am interested in the particular question of Barth's interpretation of Jesus Christ's death as involving the endurance of God's wrath and judgment in place of sinful humanity and, even more specifically, Barth's understanding of Jesus Christ's death as involving the experience of hell, as he dies the eternal or second death and bears the full weight of God-abandonment and God-forsakenness.

In order to analyse thoroughly Barth's treatment of the descent into hell, I will employ the seminal work on this topic of Hans Urs von Balthasar, the Roman Catholic counterpart to Barth's magisterial work. By exploring how Barth and Balthasar address particular aspects of the doctrine of the descent into hell, we will determine how Balthasar might enhance Barth's treatment of the descent into hell. At the same time, we will see how Barth offers needed restraint to Balthasar's innovative articulation of the descent into hell.

Both Barth and Balthasar articulate an interpretation of Jesus' death that boldly affirms that Jesus Christ saved us from our sins by dying in our place. Perhaps the

---

2 Barth points to the inadequacies of developing atonement theories. He characteristically plays down the significance of his own reflection on the salvific significance of the death of Christ, while at the same time insisting that an adequate treatment of God's reconciliation of humanity through Jesus Christ must include the notion *Stellvertretung*. Barth writes, 'So great is the ruin of the creature that less than the self-surrender of God would not suffice for its rescue. But so great is God, that it is His will to render up Himself. Reconciliation means God taking man's place. Let me add that no doctrine of this central mystery can exhaustively and precisely grasp and express the extent to which God has intervened for us here. Do not confuse my theory of the reconciliation with the thing itself. All theories of reconciliation can be but pointers. But do also pay attention to this "for us": nothing must be deducted from it! Whatever a doctrine of reconciliation tries to express, it *must* say this.' Karl Barth, *Dogmatics in Outline*, trans. G. T. Thomson (New York: Harper & Row, 1959), p. 116.

most significant affirmation held in common by Barth and Balthasar regarding a proper interpretation of the atonement and the passion of Jesus Christ is the conviction that Jesus Christ's atoning death is a complete and perfect work of salvation. This death is in need of nothing further to make it efficacious for human reconciliation and redemption. It does not merely create the condition for the possibility of salvation, nor does it stand in need of completion by the individual believer. The importance of this affirmation is seen in the primary opponents, or better, conversation partners of Barth and Balthasar, i.e. Rudolph Bultmann and Karl Rahner, respectively. It is significant to note that Barth's and Balthasar's constructive soteriologies are driven, to some extent, by a strong polemic against a view of the atonement that minimizes its objective character as a perfect and complete work, which has taken place 'once and for all'. Although both Barth and Balthasar argue extensively and thoroughly against Bultmann and Rahner, it will suffice to mention two brief passages that encapsulate the common position held by them, and the contrasting position held by Bultmann and Rahner. In *Church Dogmatics* IV/1, the content of which Barth attributes to his ongoing intensive debate with Bultmann, Barth affirms the objective and once and for all character of Jesus Christ's saving death, and contrasts this with Bultmann's position. Barth quotes from Bultmann's *The Theology of the New Testament*, 'By Christ there has been created nothing more than the possibility of ζωή, which does, of course, become an assured actuality in those that believe.' To this Barth decisively responds, 'This is the very thing which will not do' (*CD* IV/1, p. 285). In a similar manner, Balthasar criticizes Rahner for minimizing the uniqueness of Jesus Christ's suffering and death as the sin-bearer and for emphasizing the posture that Jesus takes in facing in his death, instead of the pain and suffering of the death itself. For Rahner, according to Balthasar's reading, Jesus Christ does not die in our place and once and for all; rather, Jesus Christ is the perfect example or expression of obedience and love. Balthasar concisely criticizes what he calls Rahner's philosophical or existential interpretation of Jesus Christ's death and his descent into hell. Balthasar insists that 'the (purely philosophical) interpretation of the descent into Hell, which considers it as the "foundation" of a new existential dimension in the radical depths of cosmic being, is neither biblically justified, nor theologically sufficient' (*MP*, p. 147). Although I will not explore completely the arguments against Bultmann and Rahner, it is important to be aware of the similarities between these running debates that shaped the constructive soteriologies of Barth and Balthasar.

The agreement that marks the work of Barth and Balthasar regarding the theologically proper interpretation of the death of Jesus Christ is illustrated clearly in a passage from Balthasar in which his own thought moves directly into and melds with Barth's.

> Can we seriously say that God unloaded his wrath upon the Man who wrestled with his destiny on the Mount of Olives and was subsequently crucified?

Indeed we must. Even in life, Jesus had been the revealer of the whole pathos of God – of his love and his indignation at man's scorning of this love – and now he has to bear the ultimate consequence of his more-than-prophetic mediation. 'What was suffered there on Israel's account and ours was suffered for Israel and for us. [Namely,] The wrath of God that we had merited . . . The reason why the No spoken on Good Friday is so terrible, but why there is already concealed in the Eastertide Yes of God's righteousness, is that he who on the Cross took upon himself and suffered the wrath of God was none other than God's own Son, and therefore the eternal God himself in the unity with human nature that he freely accepted in his transcendent mercy.' (*TD* IV, p. 346)[3]

My concern is the exploration of the content of the wrath of God that Jesus Christ suffered on the cross in our place. It will be through a close reading and analysis of the work of two highly competent, creative, and reputable proponents and reformers of the Anselmian view of the atonement that I will move to the constructive task of proposing how we might best interpret the salvific death of Christ in terms of his bearing the divine condemnation on sin and humans as sinners, primarily through a rehabilitation of the long-neglected clause of the Church's confession that Jesus Christ 'descended into hell'.

Barth's reflection on the Apostles' Creed

In his 1935 lectures delivered at the University of Utrecht on the topic of the chief problems of dogmatics with reference to the Apostles' Creed,[4] Barth centres his reflection on the cross of Jesus Christ. At the outset, in his unfolding of the article, 'God the Father Almighty', Barth underscores his well-known and consistent theme of the necessity of revelation for genuine knowledge of God. This revelation takes place in the concrete particularity of Jesus Christ and especially in his passion. Here we see the prominence of the cross, darkness and hiddenness in Barth's account of God's revelation.

God's revelation in His Son, so far as we understand by that concretely the – to us quite comprehensible – human existence of Jesus Christ, is . . . a way into the *darkness* of God; it is the way of Jesus to Golgotha. If as such it is a way into the light of God, and is therefore really God's *revelation*, then that is because this Jesus on 'the third day rose again from the dead, He ascended into heaven, and sitteth on the right hand of God'. But that is said of Jesus the Crucified. Actually the hidden God here becomes manifest; we are here led right to the limit of what we can conceive in order that *here* (here, where Jesus Himself cries: 'My God, My God, why hast Thou forsaken me?') we may catch the words, 'Behold, your God!' God the Father, as Father of Jesus Christ, is He Who leads His Son into hell and out again. (*C*, p. 21)

---

3   The quotation of Barth is from *CD* II/1, p. 396.
4   These lectures were published in German in 1935 and in an English translation in 1936.

Here we see the centrality of the cross for the life and significance of Jesus Christ, for the actuality of God's revelation and for the reconciled life of the individual believer. Barth insists that it is precisely in God's hiddenness, in the extreme limit of Jesus Christ's death in God-abandonment, that God is fully revealed. We also see that Barth identifies Christ's cry of derelection as his being taken by the Father into hell and his resurrection as the Father's rescue of Jesus from hell. Finally, the quality of Jesus' death determines the quality of Christian discipleship. We must take up our crosses, die with him and acknowledge that our true identities and lives are to be found in Christ – the one who was taken into and removed from hell for us and in our place.

Barth continues these lectures by clarifying this insistence on the centrality of Jesus Christ as the concrete locus both of God's revelation and God's work of reconciliation (*C*, p. 39). God not only reveals himself in the concrete history of Jesus Christ; he also accomplishes the reconciliation of humanity to himself in this particular life history. Barth insists that 'in and with this revelation, our reconciliation is accomplished, this Jesus Christ is *God for us*' (*C*, p. 46). In confessing that God is *for us* in Jesus Christ, Barth affirms that humanity is both granted knowledge of God through God's revelation and humanity is reconciled with God. Reconciliation is accomplished, according to Barth, by God's presence in Jesus Christ and Jesus Christ's suffering and death in our place, which involves the full weight of God's judgment on humanity, the grave burden of God's wrath. Jesus Christ, for Barth, is indeed the one who was led in and out of hell by God. He insists that the guiding issue in reflecting on the revelation of God in Jesus Christ is

> that absolute impossibility, that the Holy One, Whose wrath we have provoked, became man, in order, in spite of everything, to befriend us, to bear this wrath Himself and in our place, accordingly to suffer in our place His own burning wrath, to give satisfaction Himself in our place, in order in that way to be *our* God (and that means, to be *good* for us in a way that we have not deserved and cannot comprehend). (*C*, p. 46)

The reality of Jesus Christ's bearing the full weight of God's judgment on humanity and enduring the full force of God's wrath is an uncompromising suffering. The suffering that Jesus Christ endured cannot be alleviated; it is suffering for which there is no end in sight. This suffering is so real and severe that it can be understood properly only as the concealment of God. In the suffering of Jesus Christ, God empties his wrath on Jesus Christ in such a way that Jesus falls into the hands of his enemies – Jesus suffers at the hands of evil, sin, death and the devil. This suffering is so overwhelming that Jesus Christ is incapable of recognizing the salvation that will be accomplished as a result of his suffering.

> On Good Friday itself – and not only on Good Friday but 'all the time He lived on earth' – the suffering of Jesus, just because it is the suffering of God's wrath against the whole human race, has no frontier, no meaning, no future.

How could He who actually places Himself where the whole human race stands, namely, under the wrath of God – and Jesus *did* place Himself there! – how could He see a frontier, a meaning and a future in what He had there to suffer? The abyss into which sin hurls us, yes us, is just this, that we do not know how deep this abyss is, this suffering *without* frontiers, *without* meaning and *without* future. This burden can only be borne. And Jesus bears it. (*C*, pp. 78–9)

Barth insists that the salvific significance of the suffering of Jesus Christ, in his crucifixion and death, is accessible only retrospectively, only in the light cast by the resurrection of Easter. He strongly affirms the victory present in the suffering and death of Christ, but he maintains that this victory is revealed only in the resurrection. Viewed alone, the cross is shrouded in complete darkness and consists of suffering taken to the limit, suffering that leads to the depths of hell.

Barth addresses the article of the Apostles' Creed that confesses that Jesus Christ 'was crucified, dead, and buried, he descended into hell' as a single unit and points to the dual character of this confession. On the one hand, this phrase describes what Jesus Christ endures in his life and death. On the other hand, it details the significance of this particular life and death for human salvation. That Jesus Christ was crucified, dead and buried and that he descended into hell indicates the gravity of his suffering and the fullness of his identification with sinful humanity, which includes his enduring the consequences of this sin at the hands of God's judgment and wrath. Jesus Christ bears a divine *curse*, for this is what crucifixion manifests (Galatians 3:13). He endures a divine *punishment*, for this is what death entails (Romans 6:23). Finally, he experiences the misery of an *ordeal* allowed by God, for this is what it means that he descended into hell. These qualifications of Jesus Christ's suffering and death as curse, punishment and ordeal demonstrate the uniqueness of this suffering and death. This uniqueness is deter-mined both by the identity of Jesus Christ as the incarnate Son of God and the mission of Jesus Christ as involving the bearing of the world's sin and suffering the judgment of God on this sin in the place of humanity. Barth insists that the violent and painful death of a pure and innocent human being will not and cannot be conceived as curse, punishment and ordeal. This is the case because human beings are incapable of knowing the true nature of sin and the details of the corresponding judgment of God on sin through the implementation of God's wrath. Both the true character of sin and the remedy for this sin as determined by God are revealed only in the suffering and death of Jesus Christ. In fact, the true horror of sin and death is revealed precisely in the remedy for sin – Jesus Christ's death in God-abandonment.

Barth contends that the confession that Jesus Christ was buried points to the genuineness of his humanity. Jesus Christ's burial is directly observable and historically verifiable. As a result, Jesus Christ's particular existence as a human being is confirmed. As Barth wryly claims, 'To say that He was buried is the most unambiguous way in which it is possible to stamp a being as a true actual man. An angel or an idea or the "essence of Christianity" obviously cannot be buried. But Jesus Christ was buried' (*C*, p. 85). Although the burial of Jesus Christ is historically observable and can be affirmed equally by both believer and unbeliever, the quality of Jesus Christ's death as 'curse, punishment and ordeal' is an interpretative claim regarding the significance of the particular death of Jesus Christ. They do not apply to human death in general; rather, they apply exclusively to Jesus Christ. Only Jesus Christ's death may be described accurately as curse and punishment, and, even more pointedly, only Jesus Christ can be said to endure the ordeal. Only Jesus Christ is fully and completely judged and punished by God. Barth asserts the uniqueness of Jesus Christ's death on the cross and his subsequent descent into hell in the following:

> We know nothing of the fact that the inevitable future which burial holds for man means curse, punishment and ordeal above all ordeal: dereliction by God of one sentenced and chastised by God! We know nothing about man's being rightfully and therefore of necessity *killed* by God. *We cannot* know of it. We could not even for a moment bear to know of it. But Jesus Christ *did* know of it. He could know of it and He could bear to know of it; what He did bear on Golgotha, He could bear as curse, punishment and ordeal because He was man like us, but yet as man like us God Himself. (*C*, p. 89)

Although it is accurate, to a point, to describe the death of Jesus Christ as an execution at the hands of the Roman state, and, in addition, as the result of bearing the sin of the world, Barth demands that we press even further. The death of Christ is not merely the consequence of religious and political factors on the historical plane, nor is it simply the natural consequence of human sin; rather, Jesus Christ dies at the hand of God – Jesus Christ is *killed* by God. God determines in his freedom the gravity and character of Jesus' death as curse, punishment and endurance of the ordeal.

The second aspect of this clause of the Apostles' Creed is the redemptive significance that this particular suffering and death has for sinful humanity. That Jesus Christ was crucified leads to an *acquittal*, which is applied to humanity (Colossians 2:14). His death involves the making of a *sacrifice*, which is offered on behalf of the human race (Mark 10:45). And the descent into hell enacts a divine *victory* (1 Peter 3:19 and Revelation 5:5). Again, this view of the suffering and death of Jesus Christ hinges on the uniqueness of his suffering and death, which is the result of his identity and mission as the incarnate Son of God. No mere human suffering and death can be understood properly as 'acquittal, sacrifice and victory'. For Barth, the presence of God in the suffering and death of Jesus Christ leads to the recognition of God's grace in his judgment, acquittal in God's curse, sacrifice in God's punishment, and victory in Jesus Christ's being in subjection to the ordeal.[5]

---

5   Here we see the interrelationship between suffering and victory in the passion of Jesus Christ. This

For our particular purposes, it is significant to see the ramifications of Jesus Christ's going to hell in our place. Barth states:

> if, without ceasing to be God, God in Jesus Christ entered into the ordeal, if Jesus Christ descended into hell and thereby actually doubted Himself as to His being God and man in one, what else can we take that to mean than that He did that also for us and so relieved us of it? It is no longer *necessary* that we go to hell. And we shall no longer require to go to hell in order to ask ourselves there: why has God forsaken us? If we think we have occasion for this question, we should consider that Jesus Christ put it long ago and answered it in our place. How could His way into hell have been other than a victorious way? (*C*, pp. 93–4)

In this passage we see Barth's understanding of the descent into hell as an indication of both the gravity of Christ's suffering – the extremity of his humiliation – as well as the victory for humanity that this suffering and humiliation won. Barth stands squarely within the Reformed tradition and accepts Calvin's view of the descent into hell as an interpretation of the cry of dereliction (*C*, p. 88). At the same time, however, Barth insists that we affirm the triumphant and victorious element of the descent into hell. The descent into hell is a victory because of the severity of Jesus Christ's suffering on the cross. On the cross, Jesus Christ experienced the depth of the abyss into which all humanity ought to be plunged because of sin. This experience effected the elimination and destruction of sin. Jesus Christ bears the world's sin and he bears it away.

It is notable that Barth does not consider the descent into hell to be victorious because it describes an action of the risen Christ. Barth simply does not address alternative interpretations of the descent into hell that suggest that it refers to the victorious and risen Christ descending into the depths of hell in order to carry out an activity, such as proclamation, liberation, or binding of the devil and his

---

is indicated by Barth's insistence that the cross of Christ may be interpreted properly only in the light of the Resurrection. By itself, the cross of Good Friday can be regarded only as utter defeat, but in the light cast by the glory of the Resurrection, the true victorious character of the cross is displayed, and the genuine glory of the cross is brought to light. In his commentary on the Apostles' Creed according to Calvin's catechism, Barth points to the tight relationship between suffering and victory in the cross of Jesus Christ. 'All along the line, these are the two moments: suffering and victory. Not only has Jesus *taken on* our suffering, he has also *taken* it *away*. The message of the cross is not only the message of sorrow and defeat, but even at the same time it is the message of victory and resurrection. If not, it would have no meaning. There is no absolute distinction between the message of Good Friday and that of Easter. For Easter is understood only through Good Friday, and Good Friday only in Easter.' Karl Barth, *The Faith of the Church: A Commentary on the Apostles' Creed According to Calvin's Catechism*, ed. Jean-Louis Leuba, trans. Gabriel Vahanian (New York: Meridian Books, Inc., 1958), p. 90. This anticipates Barth's insistence in *Church Dogmatics* IV/1 that what have been viewed as the two states of Jesus Christ's existence – humiliation and exaltation – are not to be regarded as successive. Rather, they are simultaneous. This will inform our reading of Barth with respect to the descent into hell as being considered both as suffering the ordeal and enacting a divine victory. For Barth's position on the 'two states' see *CD* IV/1, pp. 132–5.

demons. Nonetheless, Barth is clear in his affirmation of the victorious character of the descent into hell. The descent into hell marks a victory for humanity because it describes the suffering and humiliation of Jesus, the extreme to which God is 'for us' – even to the point of true God-forsakenness and God-abandonment.

Barth and the reformed tradition

In order to demonstrate how Barth stands squarely within the Reformed tradition, it is necessary to examine briefly John Calvin's treatment of the descent into hell and subsequent treatments in Reformed confessions. John Calvin treats the descent into hell in book II chapter xvi. 8–12 of the *Institutes of the Christian Religion* within his discussion of the work of Christ, which follows the structure of the Apostles' Creed.[6] In this section, Calvin stresses the importance of this clause of the creed for an understanding of Jesus Christ's redemptive work. 'If it is left out', Calvin writes, 'much of the benefit of Christ's death will be lost.'[7] He begins his interpretation of the descent into hell by refuting two common positions.

First, Calvin disagrees with those who equate the clause about the descent into hell with the previous clause that Christ was buried. This interpretation is unacceptable because there is no reason, according to Calvin, to confuse the clear statement that Christ was buried by following it with the obscure statement that he descended into hell. It is also unlikely, Calvin surmises, that the authors of the Creed would include a superfluous clause, since the Creed is a summary 'in which the chief points of our faith are aptly noted in the fewest possible words'.[8]

Calvin challenges a second common interpretation of the descent into hell, which speaks of Jesus' mission to some 'netherworld' in order to free the Old Testament faithful. Calvin dismisses the notion of 'Limbo', within which the saints of the Old Testament are housed and from which they must be freed by Jesus Christ. Calvin writes, 'This story [Christ's descent to free the patriarchs from prison], although it is repeated by great authors, and even today is earnestly defended as true by many persons, still is nothing but a story. It is childish to enclose the souls of the dead in a prison. What need, then, for Christ's soul to go down there to release them?'[9] In sum, Calvin refutes generally accepted interpretations of the descent into hell that locate the 'event' of the descent into hell as taking place between the crucifixion and the resurrection.

Rather than interpreting the descent into hell sequentially, as a distinct event that takes place after the distinct event of the crucifixion, Calvin interprets the descent into hell as a gloss on the event of the crucifixion. The confession of Jesus

---

6   John Calvin, *Institutes of the Christian Religion*, ed. John T. McNeill, trans. Ford Lewis Battles (Philadelphia: The Westminster Press, 1960), II.xvi.8–12, pp. 512–20.

7   Calvin, *Institutes*, II.xvi.8, p. 513.

8   Ibid., p. 514.

9   Calvin, *Institutes*, II.xvi.9, p. 514.

Christ's descent into hell expresses the gravity of his death by crucifixion. Jesus does not die a mere common physical death; rather, he endures the 'second' death or 'eternal' death. According to Calvin, 'It was expedient at the same time [of his bodily death] for him to undergo the severity of God's vengeance, to appease his wrath and satisfy his just judgment. For this reason, he must also grapple hand to hand with the armies of hell and the dread of everlasting death.'[10] By taking on the burden of humanity's sin, Jesus Christ becomes a substitute for all of humanity and endures the punishment that was meant for humanity. It is this bearing the sins of the world and dying the death of a sinner, the result of the wrath of God, that is amplified in the confession that Jesus Christ descended into hell.

Calvin recognizes that he is applying something that comes after Jesus Christ's burial to the event that precedes his burial, namely, the crucifixion, yet he does not consider this problematic, as some of his opponents do. He defends himself in the following:

> The point is that the Creed sets forth what Christ suffered in the sight of men, and then appositely speaks of that invisible and incomprehensible judgment which he underwent in the sight of God in order that we might know not only that Christ's body was given as the price of our redemption, but that he paid a greater and more excellent price in suffering in his soul the terrible torments of a condemned and forsaken man.[11]

The confession of his burial describes an external and visible experience of Christ; the confession of the descent into hell describes an interior and invisible experience.

Calvin views the descent into hell as an interpretation of the cry of dereliction. He interprets Jesus Christ's cry of abandonment, 'My God, my God, why hast thou forsaken me?' as genuinely coming from Jesus Christ's own anguish. The cry of dereliction indicates his subjective experience on the cross.[12] Calvin concisely states, 'He bore the weight of divine severity, since he was "stricken and afflicted" by God's hand, and experienced all the signs of a wrathful and avenging God'.[13] This experience of the 'wrathful and avenging God' is nothing short of an encounter with hell, as Jesus Christ is abandoned and forsaken by God. 'No more terrible abyss can be conceived than to feel yourself forsaken and estranged from God; and when you call upon him, not to be heard.'[14]

Reformed theology and confession follow Calvin's interpretation, insisting that the descent into hell expresses Jesus Christ's suffering and agony, which begins in Gethsemane and continues through his crucifixion and death. In opposition to the prevalent Lutheran affirmation that the descent into hell belongs to the *status*

---

10   Calvin, *Institutes*, II.xvi.10, p. 515.

11   Ibid., p. 516.

12   Although Christ indeed felt abandoned and forsaken by the Father, Calvin insists that God was never 'inimical or angry toward him'. Calvin, *Institutes*, II.xvi.11, p. 517.

13   Ibid.

14   Ibid., p. 516.

exaltationis, Reformed theology and confession insist that the descent into hell belongs to the *status exaninitionis* or *humiliationis* – the state of humiliation. Question 44 of the Heidelberg Catechism states, 'Why is there added, "he descended into hell?"' That in my greatest temptations I may be assured, and wholly comfort myself in this, that my Lord Jesus Christ, by his inexpressible anguish, pains, terrors, and hellish agonies, in which he was plunged during all his sufferings, but especially on the cross, hath delivered me from the anguish and torments of hell.' The Westminster Larger Catechism attributes the descent into hell to Christ's humiliation in questions 46, 49 and 50. Question 49 expresses Calvin's view of Christ's experience of hell on the cross, without mentioning the descent into hell.

> Christ humbled himself in his death, in that having been betrayed by Judas, forsaken by his disciples, scorned and rejected by the world, condemned by Pilate, and tormented by his persecutors; having also conflicted with the terrors of death and the powers of darkness, felt and borne the weight of God's wrath, he laid down his life an offering for sin, enduring the painful, shameful, and cursed death of the cross.

The catechism then treats the descent into hell in terms of Christ's humiliation after his death in question 50: 'Christ's humiliation after his death consisted in his being buried, and continuing in the state of the dead, and under the power of death till the third day, which hath been otherwise expressed in these words: "He descended into hell." '

As a comparison of the Heidelberg Catechism and the Westminster Larger Catechism indicates, there is a certain amount of ambiguity in terms of whether the descent into hell is an expression of Jesus Christ's agony from the point of his prayer in the garden of Gethsemane through his death on the cross or whether it refers to the suffering of Christ after his death, in his burial. However, there is consensus among Reformed thought that the descent into hell belongs to Jesus Christ's state of humiliation. There is consensus, against both Lutheran and Roman Catholic theology and confession, that the descent into hell does not refer to a localized or spatial journey by the exalted Jesus Christ to engage in battle with the devil and release the captive believers. The descent into hell functions for the Reformers as a gloss on Jesus Christ's suffering in the passion. It is not distinguished from the crucifixion; rather, the descent into hell is an expression of the gravity of Christ's suffering and death. Jesus Christ did not endure mere physical suffering and death; he endured eternal suffering and death – suffering and death that arises from God's wrath against sin and sinners.

The significance of Jesus Christ's death as grounded in the doctrine of God

We now move our exploration of Barth's treatment of the death of Christ to his first extended reflection on the doctrine of the atonement in the *Church Dogmatics*, in his treatment of the doctrine of divine perfections in volume II part 1. By grounding the doctrine of the atonement in the doctrine of God, Barth avoids significant problems that typically plague an understanding of Christ's death as enduring the wrath of God and as involving Jesus Christ alone falling under the judgment of God, both on our behalf and in our place. There are two prominent liabilities of this view of the salvation achieved by the death of Jesus Christ.

The first involves the issue of a change in God's disposition toward humanity, as a *quid pro quo* entailed in Jesus Christ's death. Proposing that God's posture towards humanity is somehow changed from anger and wrath to love on the basis of Christ's death causes great difficulty in interpreting such passages as Romans 5:8: 'God shows his love for us in that while we were yet sinners Christ died for us.' If God is changed from wrath to love by the death of Christ, as some versions of an Anselmian interpretation of the death of Christ imply, then exactly how does Christ's death show God's love for humanity?

The second liability includes the risk of viewing the work of Christ solely as a human act. This leads to the problematic conclusion that God's disposition towards humanity is not only changed; it is also somehow determined by a human, creaturely act. This liability is emphasized in Gustav Aulén's influential critique of, in his words, the Anselmian, or Latin, theory. In his attempt to demonstrate the superiority of the 'classical' or *Christus Victor* view, as he describes it, over the Latin view, Aulén points to the importance of the connection between incarnation and atonement. This view stresses that Christ's work is a continuous activity of God. According to Aulén, the 'classical' view upholds the significance of the tight relationship between incarnation and atonement and, in turn, considers soteriology as a continuous activity of God. The Latin view, however, fails to affirm the interconnection between incarnation and atonement, and therefore considers soteriology as a discontinuous work of both God and humanity. Aulén concludes:

> It is, indeed, true that Anselm and his successors treat the Atonement as in a sense God's work; God is the author of the plan, and He has sent His Son and ordered it so that the required satisfaction shall be made. Nevertheless, it is not in the full sense God's work of redemption. If the patristic idea of Incarnation and Redemption may be represented by a continuous line, leading obliquely downwards, the doctrine of Anselm will require a broken line; or, the line that leads downwards may be shown as crossed by a line leading from below upwards, to represent the satisfaction made to God by Christ as man. Then, too, the double-sidedness characteristic of the classic idea has disappeared. God is no longer regarded as *at once* the agent and the object of the reconciliation, but as *partly* the agent, as being the author of the plan, and *partly* the object, when the plan comes to be carried out.[15]

---

15   Gustaf Aulén, *Christus Victor: An Historical Study of the Three Main Types of the Idea of Atonement*, trans. A. G. Herbert (New York: Macmillan Paperbacks, 1969; Collier Books, 1986), p. 88.

I contend that Barth is in the line of Anselm, yet he avoids both perceived dangers of a view of Jesus Christ's death that emphasizes Christ's vicarious bearing of the judgment of God against sin and sinful humanity. In Barth's modified Anselmianism, the reconciliation wrought by God in the passion of Jesus Christ is an essential element of Jesus' mission. The passion is the goal of the incarnation. The passion is also a continuous divine act in which God is both the subject and object of Jesus Christ's reconciling work. This being the case, there is no movement from wrath to love on God's part as a response to the suffering and death of Jesus Christ; rather, God's love is the source of the reconciling significance of Christ's death.

With these introductory statements in place, we are able to begin our discussion of relationship between the perfections of God and the doctrine of atonement.[16] In paragraph 30, 'The Perfections of the Divine Loving', Barth explicates the notion of divine love with the aid of three couplets. After defining God as the 'One who loves in freedom', Barth proceeds to reflect upon all that is involved in divine love, and it is here that he determines three couplets: grace and holiness, mercy and righteousness, patience and wisdom (*CD* II/1, p. 322). For the purpose of this study, and for the sake of concision, I will restrict my treatment to the first two couplets, with close attention being paid to mercy and righteousness. These couplets fall under divine love and are not to be considered on a par with divine love. God is not love and holiness, for example; rather, God is love and this love is holy love. Further, God is not love and righteousness; rather, God is love and this love is righteous love. The being of God as revealed in Jesus Christ is love, and every attribute or perfection of God falls under the divine love and enables us to understand more fully the richness of divine love.

Barth defines grace as God's unprovoked and completely free turning toward the creation. God freely decides to enter into a covenantal relationship with his creatures. God is not provoked by something in humanity to enter into fellowship with humanity, and God is not dependent upon the purity of humanity. Humanity is not worthy and need not be worthy on its own in order to create the possibility of fellowship. God's covenantal turning towards humanity is utterly free – sheer grace. 'Grace is the distinctive mode of God's being in so far as it seeks and creates fellowship by its own free inclination and favour, unconditioned by any

---

16 Here I must acknowledge my deep indebtedness to Bruce McCormack's treatment of Barth's doctrine of atonement in relationship to the Reformed tradition. McCormack points to Barth as providing the solution to the defects found in the soteriologies of both John Calvin and seventeenth-century Reformed Theology. McCormack insists that a proper exposition of atonement doctrine is possible only if it is grounded upon the doctrine of God. He writes, 'It is only when we see the atoning work of Christ against the background of a carefully thought through doctrine of God that the unity of mercy and righteousness can be seen and allowed to come to expression in our formulation of the doctrine of atonement.' Bruce L. McCormack, 'For Us and For Our Salvation: Incarnation and Atonement in the Reformed Tradition', *Studies in Reformed Theology and History* Volume 1 Number 2 (Spring 1993), p. 28.

merit or claim in the beloved, but also unhindered by any unworthiness or opposition in the latter – able, on the contrary, to overcome all unworthiness and opposition' (*CD* II/1, p. 353).

God's holiness, coupled with God's grace, constitutes God's love as divine love. God's holiness means that God will not allow human disobedience, turning away or refusal of his love to separate him from the creatures. God will do all that is possible to ensure the integrity of the covenant, even if punishment and condemnation are necessary for the covenantal relationship to be retained. In fact, God's holiness leads to the destruction of sin and sinner.

Barth insists on maintaining the unity of grace and holiness. It is appropriate to draw a distinction between the two, but separation is impossible. Grace describes God's 'favourable inclination towards the creature [that] does not allow itself to be soured and frustrated by the resistance of the latter' (*CD* II/1, p. 360). Holiness must be coupled with grace, because God responds in a particular way to the resistance of the creature to his gracious turning towards humanity. Holiness describes God's activity in which God's 'favourable inclination overcomes and destroys [creaturely] resistance' (*CD* II/1, p. 360).

Barth's account of God's grace and holiness is significant for our exploration of his view of the death of Jesus Christ as involving God's judgment upon humanity and Christ's death at the hands of the wrath of God. As we have seen, Christ does not suffer solely under the wrath of God (wrath abstracted from God's love) and in this suffering move God's disposition towards humanity from wrath to love. Rather, God's wrath is a function of God's love. Therefore, divine love is the source for what took place on the cross, and this love is never jeopardized by the resistance and disobedience of sinful humanity. God's holy love works itself out in the destruction of sin and of human persons as sinners, and this destruction takes place in the outpouring of God's wrath upon Jesus Christ. Salvation does not follow sequentially after this instance of judgment and grace; rather, salvation occurs in the particularity of this event of judgment and wrath, for wrath and judgment destroy sin and put an end to the sinner. As a result, salvation is accomplished – humanity is both justified and sanctified. The forgiveness of sin takes place precisely in the death of Jesus Christ at the hands of the wrath of God, and as a manifestation of God's judgment of sin and sinful humanity. Grace does not follow upon judgment and wrath; rather, grace and holiness are intertwined.

The second couplet employed by Barth to describe the depth of divine love is mercy and righteousness. God's mercy is God's free decision to sympathize with the pitiful state of the human condition. God's mercy, according to Barth, 'lies in His readiness to share in sympathy the distress of another, a readiness which springs from His inmost nature and stamps all His being and doing' (*CD* II/1, p. 369). It must be noted that God's mercy extends beyond mere sharing in sympathy with the distress of another. God does not simply identify with the distress of humanity; rather, God, in sympathy, acts to eradicate the distress and misery of humanity. God's mercy also includes God's genuine involvement in the misery of the human condition. God does not attempt to address the problem of human distress in such a way that he is removed from this situation. God does not work towards the transformation of the distressful human situation from a remote location; rather, he becomes intimately involved with the dreadful state of the human condition. Barth summarizes: 'For the fact that God participates in it [the distress of another] by sympathy implies that He is really present in its midst, and this means again that He wills that it should not be, that He wills therefore to remove it' (*CD* II/1, p. 369).

God's righteousness means that in acting mercifully God is consistent with himself. God acts only in accordance with what is appropriate for him, as God himself determines. And God's love is righteous in that 'when God wills and creates the possibility of fellowship with man He does that which is worthy of Himself, and therefore in this fellowship He asserts His worth in spite of all contradiction and resistance, and therefore in this fellowship He causes only His own worth to prevail and rule' (*CD* II/1, pp. 376–7). Barth makes it very clear that in speaking of God's righteousness we are not speaking of some abstract, freestanding concept of righteousness (or justice, law, etc.) that stands over and against God, and to which God is obligated. Divine righteousness is determined by God alone. In short, God must act in a way that corresponds with the way he has decided to be. In the case of God's reconciling activity, God's righteous wrath works itself out in the punishment of the sinner. God's righteousness leads to an understanding of the atoning death of Jesus Christ in which God is both the subject, in that the incarnate Son of God is the subject of the human person Jesus Christ, and the object, in that the death of Christ pays a penalty and fulfils the punishment God has determined for humanity.[17]

This discussion of the righteousness of God – the righteousness of divine love – brings us to the specific focus of this chapter, that is, the way in which Christ's death is an event of divine judgment upon sin and sinful humanity, which involves Jesus Christ's enduring the wrath of God and experiencing the isolating forsakenness and abandonment of hell. In describing God's love as involving righteous mercy and merciful righteousness, Barth concludes that we are forced to view God's love as both pardoning and judging, both rewarding and punishing. Again, we must recognize that God's mercy and righteousness must be held together; they cannot be seen as competing with one another or as existing in tension with one another. It is not as if God desires to be merciful and pardon humanity, but God's righteousness holds him in check and thwarts his merciful will. At the same time, it is inaccurate to picture God as desiring to destroy sinful humanity with the

---

17   This addresses Aulén's complaint against Latin or satisfaction theories. Aulén complains that the satisfaction theory demands a discontinuous divine activity, in that an offering is made purely from the side of man to satisfy something in God. Barth, by demonstrating how God is both subject and object, is able to propose a 'penal substitution' view which sees God as a genuine object of Christ's work, but which understands Christ's work as a continuous divine act.

punishment that humanity deserves, while his mercy stages an eleventh-hour appeal and restrains him from executing his judgment upon humanity. The interrelation between mercy and righteousness is manifest, for Barth, in the revelation of God in Jesus Christ. In this light, Barth concludes that 'the condemning and punishing righteousness of God is in itself and as such the depth and power and might of His mercy' (*CD* II/1, p. 393). God's mercy and righteousness do not stand side by side; rather, they interpenetrate one another. A distinction may be drawn between the two, but no separation is allowed.

According to Barth, the gospel demands that we recognize and affirm that in the act of God's love, God demonstrates anger, God condemns sinful humanity and God delivers punishment. This view of God is present in the biblical witness and falls under the category of the righteousness of God's love.

> We can only be overlooking or misunderstanding the biblical message if for one reason or another we try to be spared having to take quite seriously the fact that God is the God who for the sake of His righteousness is wrathful and condemns and punishes. He is not only this, but He is also this . . . If we truly love Him, we must love Him also in His anger, condemnation and punishments, or rather we must see, feel and appreciate His love to us even in His anger, condemnation and punishment. For we cannot avoid the conclusion that it is where the divine love and therefore the divine grace and mercy are attested with the supreme clarity in which they are necessarily known as the meaning and intention of Scripture as a whole, where that love and grace and mercy are embodied in a unique event, i.e., in Jesus Christ, that according to the unmistakable witness of the New Testament itself they encounter us as a divine act of wrath, judgment and punishment. (*CD* II/1, p. 394)

Here we see that love is not in tension with wrath; grace is not opposed to judgment; and mercy is not contradictory to punishment. The love of God, when faced with resistance by sinful humanity, takes the form of wrath in order to deal effectively with this resistance, which results in the removal of humanity from its miserable condition. Through the revelation of God in Jesus Christ, from which Barth consistently begins his reflection on the being and activity of God, we see that God's love, grace and mercy take the form of, or encounter us, as wrath, condemnation and punishment. Here we may conclude that wrath serves divine love. Wrath is the form that divine love takes in the face of resistance and opposition.

From this treatment of the interrelationship between love and wrath, mercy and righteousness, we move to an explicit treatment of the shape and significance of the passion of Jesus Christ. For Barth, a proper interpretation of the events of Good Friday cannot be separated from the history of God's dealings with Israel. Both the actual punishments meted out by God upon Israel in the face of Israel's breaking of the covenant, and the constant threat of ultimate judgment, which hung over Israel, must be taken into account if we are to understand properly the character of Jesus Christ's crucifixion. The judgment that Jesus Christ endured in his crucifixion may be rendered both as participating in Israel's suffering and as definitively surpassing the suffering of Israel. The judgment of God displayed in the event of the cross is unique. The suffering of Israel foreshadows the suffering that Jesus Christ endures on the cross, and present-day suffering is a mere token of the suffering endured by Jesus Christ. The death of Jesus Christ is a unique event insofar as on Good Friday, 'all the sins of Israel and of all men, our sins collectively and individually, have in fact become the object of the divine wrath and retribution' (*CD* II/1, p. 395). On the cross, Jesus Christ '[bears] the eternal wrath of God' (ibid.).

Jesus Christ's passion is substitutionary. Barth never wavers from this position:

> The meaning of the death of Jesus Christ is that there God's condemning and punishing righteousness broke out, really smiting and piercing human sin, man as sinner, and sinful Israel. It did so in such a way that in what happened there (not to Israel, or to us, but to Jesus Christ) the righteousness of God which we have offended was really revealed and satisfied. Yet it did so in such a way that it did not happen to Israel or to us, but for Israel, for us. What was suffered there on Israel's account and ours, was suffered for Israel and for us. The wrath of God which we have merited, by which we must have been annihilated and would long since have been annihilated, was now in our place borne and suffered as though it had smitten us and yet in such a way that it did not smite us and can no more smite us. (*CD* II/1, pp. 396–7)

Here we are able to see the contours of Barth's vision of the significance of the death of Jesus Christ. First, it is clear that Jesus Christ suffers the punishment and endures the judgment rightly meant for Israel and all humanity. Second, in the event of Jesus Christ's crucifixion, the righteousness of God is both revealed and satisfied. It is revealed insofar as it is unknowable apart from God's revelation in Jesus Christ.[18] There is no abstract notion of righteousness that can be known by humanity and then applied to God; God's righteousness is determined by God and is known by humanity only through God's revelation. God's righteousness, as determined and revealed by God, is also satisfied in the cross. Later, in his discussion of the doctrine of reconciliation proper in *Church Dogmatics* IV/1, Barth is more precise and in fact more theologically satisfying as he clearly states that it is not the wrath or righteousness of God that is satisfied by the death of Christ; rather, it is the love of God that satisfies itself in the death of Christ (*CD* IV/1, p. 254). This is no minor detail, and we will treat this significant alteration on Barth's part below. At this point, however, in his initial treatment of the significance of Christ's death in *Church Dogmatics* II/1, Barth risks separating

---

18   In revealing the character of divine righteousness, the cross also reveals the magnitude of God's wrath and the gravity of human sin. The accuracy of the revelation of these things hinges on the identity of the one who suffers, namely, Jesus Christ the incarnate Son of God. See *CD* II/1, p. 398.

wrath from love, righteousness from mercy, and holiness from grace.[19] This risk is perilous. McCormack concludes:

> In spite of his best efforts to affirm the unity of grace and holiness, mercy and righteousness as perfections of the divine loving, Barth's treatment of the atonement in *Kirchliche Dogmatik* II/1 suffered from a potentially disastrous weakness. At the crucial point, he repeated the error of the sixteenth- and seventeenth-century Reformed theologians and made the death of Christ a satisfaction offered to the divine righteousness. This way of speaking still tended to abstract righteousness from love as mercy.[20]

A third component of the passage cited above points to the identity of Jesus Christ and the significance of this identity for the effectiveness of his death. Barth asserts that no mere human, no matter how pure and innocent, could endure the wrath of God and bear Israel's and the world's sin, for this mere human would be annihilated by this wrath. Only God can endure God's wrath without being destroyed. God's dealing with human sin involves the complete destruction of sin and the utter destruction of the sinner. In order for this to include the salvation and reconciliation of humanity, the object of God's anger, condemnation and punishment must be no other than the Son of God incarnate, for it is only the Son of God who is capable of enduring the wrath of God without being completely destroyed. For Barth, 'Only God Himself could bear the wrath of God. Only God's mercy was capable of bearing the pain to which the creature existing in opposition to Him is subject. Only God's mercy could so feel this pain as to take it into the very heart of His being. And only God's mercy was strong enough not to be annihilated by this pain' (*CD* II/1, p. 400).

Barth's assertion that God alone is capable of enduring the wrath of God – only Jesus Christ as the Son of God incarnate can bear Israel's and the world's sin and, as a result, suffer under the annihilating terror of the wrath of God – indicates his departure from previous mechanistic theories of the atonement as penal substitution. Although Barth adopts the traditional language of condemnation and punishment, his use of these terms avoids mythological pictures of God as bloodthirsty, vengeful, selfishly concerned with preserving his own honour, obligated to an external standard of justice or committed to a reconciled balance sheet. Barth eschews punishment language insofar as he strongly denies viewing the cross as a

---

19 Soon after this passage Barth repeats his assertion that the death of Christ satisfies the righteousness of God and, in the process, sounds very Anselmian as he speaks of righteousness being satisfied and God's honour not being violated. Barth writes, 'Because it was the Son of God Himself who on Good Friday suffered for us, the destruction which took place there of the suffering and death which resulted from human disobedience to God could justly satisfy and indeed fulfill the righteousness of God. As a fulfillment of the righteousness of God is necessarily meant that in the conflict between God's faithfulness and man's unfaithfulness, the faithfulness of God Himself was maintained, and therefore His honour was not violated.' *CD* II/1, p. 400.

20 McCormack, 'For Us and For Our Salvation', p. 30.

transaction between humanity and God in which a pure, innocent human being volunteers to take the place of all humanity in accepting the punishment in the place of those deserving it. Jesus Christ does not die the death of a perfect and innocent human being; rather, Jesus Christ bears the world's sin and in turn endures the punishment that follows from this sin.

> [Jesus Christ] became the object of divine wrath and judgment and the bearer of our guilt and punishment. Thus we do not have here – as in the travesty in which this supreme insight and truth of the Christian faith is so often distorted – a raging indignation of God, which is ridiculous or irritating in its senselessness, against an innocent man whose patient suffering changes the temper of God, inducing in Him an indulgent sparing of all other men, so that all other men can rather shamefacedly take refuge behind his suffering, happily saved but quite unchanged in themselves. (*CD* II/1, p. 402)

This passage hints at Barth's developed soteriology in *Church Dogmatics* IV, in which he clearly distances himself from both Anselm and common penal substitution theories of the atonement. Barth clearly states this point in *Church Dogmatics* IV/1:

> But we must not make this [punishment] a main concept as in some of the other presentations of the doctrine of the atonement (especially those which follow Anselm of Canterbury), either in the sense that by His suffering our punishment we are spared from suffering it ourselves, or that in so doing He 'satisfied' or offered satisfaction to the wrath of God. (*CD* IV/1, p. 253)

Through a close reading of the previously cited passage from *Church Dogmatics* II/1, we begin to see the complexity of Barth's position. Although Barth endorses the position that Jesus Christ suffers and dies at the hands of the wrath of God in place of humanity, this 'in place of' does not mean completely apart from humanity. We must resist the temptation, so Barth says, both of seeing the suffering and death of Jesus Christ as something that moves God from wrath to love and as something that takes place completely external to humanity. Jesus Christ does not suffer and die in our place, if this means that we are then free from suffering and dying. Rather, although Jesus Christ indeed takes our place in his death, we participate in this death – we ourselves die in Christ's death. It is our participation in Christ's death that is our reconciliation, and this reconciliation means that we are transformed. Perhaps a more accurate way to say this is that Jesus Christ is our reconciliation and we are reconciled to God in Christ through our participation in and with Christ. As a result of this participation, we do not hide unchanged behind Jesus Christ's suffering and death; rather, it is in the particularity of Jesus Christ's suffering and death that we are changed. Christ's death accomplishes our transformation. His death does not simply cover our sins; it destroys our sins and our existence as sinful people.

The fullness of Jesus Christ's suffering does not diminish the reality both of

Israel's suffering and the suffering of the Church today. Jesus Christ's suffering alters the character of Israel's suffering to that of foreshadowing of his own suffering. Jesus Christ's suffering also establishes the contemporary suffering of the Church and individual Christians as signs or tokens of his own suffering. All three instances of suffering are interconnected, with Israel's and the Church's suffering being determined by Jesus Christ's suffering. In short, for Barth, there is both distance and participation between the suffering of Jesus Christ and our suffering. Yes, Jesus Christ experiences alone the full weight of God's wrath and judgment, but we participate in this suffering by being taken up into the body of Christ with Christ as our head. We do not repeat Jesus Christ's suffering in our suffering, nor do we complete his suffering. Instead, we bear witness to his suffering in our suffering and we participate in Christ's own suffering through incorporation into Christ's own body.

We may conclude our discussion of Barth's treatment of the death of Jesus Christ within his doctrine of God's perfections with a passage that highlights the essential elements of Barth's position.

> Because it was the Son of God, i.e., God Himself who took our place on Good Friday, the substitution could be effectual and procure our reconciliation with the righteous God, and therefore the victory of God's righteousness, and therefore our own righteousness in His sight. Only God, our Lord and Creator, could stand surety for us, could take our place, could suffer eternal death in our stead as the consequence of our sin in such a way that it was finally suffered and overcome and therefore did not need to be suffered any more by us. No creature, no other man could do that. But God's own Son could do it. (*CD* II/1, p. 403)

Here we see the importance of the identity of the one who suffers and dies on the cross, namely, Jesus Christ the Son of God incarnate. We also see the importance of Jesus Christ's activity as being done on the behalf of and in the place of all humanity. Next, we see the gravity of this substitutionary activity. Jesus Christ experiences the extremity of suffering; he suffers to the bitter end of eternal death. And, finally, we see the completed character of Jesus Christ's death. In Christ's death, all was accomplished that was necessary. Nothing needs to be added to this suffering and death.

We will now turn from *Church Dogmatics* II/1 to *Church Dogmatics* III/2 and an analysis of Barth's description of Jesus Christ's work as suffering *eternal death* in our stead, which stresses the uniqueness of Christ's death with the consequence that Jesus Christ's death puts an end to eternal death.

Jesus Christ dies the second death

At this point we take up the discussion of Barth's understanding of the uniqueness of Jesus Christ's death against the background of his understanding of the general character of human death. Here we will examine closely Barth's description of Jesus Christ's death as 'judgment', which involves the 'second death' or 'eternal death'. This explication and analysis will allow us to see how Barth understands Jesus Christ's death as the experience of hell. Consequently, we will be able to determine the role, both implicit and explicit, played by the Church's confession of the descent into hell in Barth's understanding of Jesus Christ's reconciling death.

For the sake of clarity and precision, and to provide concrete textual grounding, the focus of this section will be Barth's treatment of death in *Church Dogmatics* III/2 – *The Doctrine of Creation*. Paragraph 47, 'Man in His Time', concludes with a section titled 'Ending Time'. Here Barth treats the issue and problem of human death. Following the formal pattern in his treatment of other doctrines, Barth addresses the question of human death in light of God's revelation in Jesus Christ. It is only by way of an exploration into the unique character of Christ's death that the problem of human death may properly be addressed.

Fundamentally, death as it encounters us is the *sign* of *God's* judgment on us. About this Barth warns, 'We cannot say less than this, but of course we must not try to say more either' (*CD* III/2, p. 596). First, human death is a *sign* of God's judgment. Notice here that Barth deliberately qualifies the statement of death as judgment with the assertion that our death is seen most accurately as a *sign* of God's judgment. This qualification distinguishes the death of every individual human being from the death of Jesus Christ. Jesus Christ's death, according to Barth, is indeed the judgment of God. Jesus Christ bears the full reality of God's judgment, and the death that faces individual human beings functions as a sign of God's judgment as revealed in the particular and unique death of Jesus Christ.

Second, Barth defines human death as a sign of *God's* judgment. We may conclude from this emphasis that death as judgment is determined solely by God. Death as judgment is not built into the physical process; it is not mere physical death, nor is it the natural outworking of human sin, as if God is not always in control. To say that human death is a sign of God's judgment is to recognize that the quality of human death, as judgment of sin, is determined and ordained by God. Death as judgment 'is an evil ordained by God as a sign of His judgment, and not a fate but an ordinance which proceeds and is to be accepted from God' (*CD* III/2, p. 597). Death, viewed as God's judgment, is not something that is 'intrinsic to our human nature' (ibid.); rather, God rightfully determines death as the proper response to human sin. It is proper insofar as it is appropriate to the situation; it is not arbitrary. As a result, sinful human beings cannot complain or question the validity of this divine decision.

The quality of human death as a sign of God's judgment is revealed and determined by the unique character of Jesus Christ's death. 'By undergoing death in His person', Barth writes, 'Jesus provided a total and conclusive revelation of its character' (*CD* III/2, p. 600). Whereas human beings face death, which is imminent, as a *sign* of God's judgment, Jesus Christ indeed suffered death as the actual and full judgment of God. Barth insists that we move from the particular character of Jesus Christ's death as a unique event of God's judgment to a discussion of the general quality of human death, rather than applying a generally conceived notion of death to the specific death of Jesus Christ. Jesus Christ's death is revelatory and decisive because of the identity of Jesus Christ and because of the substitutionary character of this death. Jesus Christ as the incarnate Son of God chooses to be present in the judgment of humanity as both judge and the one judged. Jesus Christ both determines the material content of the proper judgment for sinful humanity and freely chooses to suffer the consequences of this decision, which is 'death as consuming force, eternal torment and utter darkness' (*CD* III/2, p. 600). As a result of this decision by Jesus Christ to enter into the situation of sinful humanity and undeservingly take on the judgment determined for sinful humanity, the quality of human death as a *sign* of God's judgment is established. Jesus Christ alone dies the death of God's judgment, and this unique death causes human death to be a sign of God's judgment, not the reality of this judgment.

> [Jesus Christ] caused this judgment [death as consuming force, eternal torment and utter darkness] to fall on Himself in place of the many guilty sinners, so that it availed for them all, and the judgment suffered by Him was fulfilled on them in Him, and their dying no longer has to be this dying, the suffering of punishment which they have deserved, but only its sign. (*CD* III/2, p. 600)

We must note that Barth is not suggesting that Jesus Christ's unique death spares sinful humanity from judgment. Barth insists that Jesus Christ dies 'in place of' sinful humanity in such a way that the judgment determined by God is fulfilled in the death of Jesus Christ. Sinful humanity is judged in the death of Jesus Christ, and humanity is taken up into the specific death of Jesus Christ.

The precise quality of God's judgment is eternal corruption, as is seen in the cross of Jesus Christ. 'Death to which we all move implies the threat of eternal corruption' (*CD* III/2, p. 602). What hangs over all humanity as a terrifying threat, namely, eternal corruption, in actuality fell upon Jesus Christ in his death. It is in this sense that his death is unique. Jesus Christ's death is more than common human death. His death is the death of the sin-bearer, the one who takes on the world's sin and as a result dies as the one who was made a curse for humanity (Galatians 3:13).

Jesus Christ suffers *eternal* corruption in his death. In other words, Jesus Christ enters hell in his death. It is at this point that the New Testament portrayal of human death, based on the death of Jesus Christ, differs from that of the Old Testament. Hell is introduced in the New Testament, and this advances beyond the Old Testament picture of the destination of human beings in death as Sheol. While the Old Testament presents the picture of dead souls dwelling in the wasteland of Sheol, the New Testament presents the vivid picture of flames, outer darkness, unquenchable fire, and torment that leads to great weeping and gnashing of teeth. Hell, according to the New Testament, involves the positive punishment of sinful humanity by God.

Barth explains the difference between the New Testament and the subsequent tradition on the one hand, and the prophets and the psalmist on the other, by pointing to the centrality of the cross to the New Testament witness. The concept of hell, we must emphasize, is not introduced because of a pessimistic anthropology; rather, hell is an actual threat because this is the only way of explaining the torment that Jesus Christ endured in the face of his imminent death. Death as eternal corruption is the cup from which Jesus Christ requested to be relieved and which he emptied in pure obedience to the Father. Death as eternal corruption is the baptism to which he submitted himself. The death that Jesus Christ faced, the prospect of which caused him great anguish, was not mere physical death as fate or chance. The death that Jesus Christ faced and which he indeed endured was the full weight of the judgment of God (*CD* III/2, p. 603). Jesus Christ joins those who died before him, by entering Sheol, but he moves further and encounters hell itself. The 'loud cry' of Mark 15:37 that marks the futility, from a purely human point of view, of Jesus Christ's death also designates the uniqueness of his death and the transition from Sheol to hell.

The uniqueness of Jesus Christ's death is constituted by the vicarious nature of his death and by the actuality of God's judgment in this death, which otherwise is only a threat that faces individuals as they approach death. Barth stresses the uniqueness of Jesus Christ's death as being done 'in our place' – 'the representative character proper to this death, His vicarious bearing of the sin of all Israel and indeed the whole world, points beyond the comfortless but tolerable situation of the righteous man of the Old Testament as alienated from God in *Sheol*' (*CD* III/2, p. 603). In Jesus Christ, the threat of which the Old Testament speaks becomes a reality. Jesus Christ indeed falls into the hands of the living God and experiences the full horror of God's pure judgment.

Significantly, in his description of the judgment that Jesus Christ endures in his death, Barth alludes to his treatment of the death of Christ in *Church Dogmatics* II/1. God displays his mercy in the judgment carried out in the cross. God demonstrates that he is for humanity by being entirely against Jesus the sin-bearer. The particular death of Jesus Christ demonstrates how God 'must deal with him [humanity] now in His mercy, which is "righteous" to the extent that in it He wills to establish His own right and that of man. Here He treats man as a transgressor with whom He can only deal in His wrath' (*CD* III/2, p. 603). Here divine wrath is a function of God's righteous mercy, which, in turn, is a function of God's love. God demonstrates the righteousness of his mercy by judging humanity completely in unloading his wrath on Jesus Christ.[21]

---

21   God manifests that he is unreservedly for humanity in his being against humanity, in the judgment suffered by Jesus Christ. God's love for humanity necessitates the outpouring of his wrath on Jesus Christ as the one who is capable of and indeed does bear the world's sin. Wrath serves the ends of divine love. Barth confidently states, 'Indeed, it is just as the One who is so palpably against us that He is so much more mightily for us. If the fire of His wrath scorches us, it is because it is the fire of His

Barth affirms at least four interrelated essential elements of an adequate rendering of the salvific significance of Jesus Christ's passion, which are based upon his reflection on the general character of human death as a *sign* of God's judgment. First, the death of Jesus Christ is unnatural and is not an intrinsic part of creaturely existence. Second, the death of Jesus Christ involves the full reality of God's judgment on sin and on sinful humanity. In this respect, death is depicted in the graphic terms of the New Testament as eternal death, the second death, annihilation, as, in short, the complete reality of hell. Third, the death of Jesus Christ as the judgment of God upon sin and sinful humanity is possible and reconciling only because of the identity of Jesus Christ as the incarnate Son of God. And fourth, the death of Jesus Christ is properly understood as 'substitutionary', as something done 'on our behalf', and further, 'in our place'.

Barth address all four of these elements in the following passage:

> Here, namely, in this One whom He has destined and appointed the Head of all who are descended from Abraham and indeed from Adam, the realm of the dead loses the last traces of creaturely naturalness which still cling to the Old Testament perspective. Here it becomes 'hell.' Here the alienation from God becomes an annihilatingly painful existence in opposition to Him. Here being in death becomes punishment, torment, outer darkness, the worm, the flame – all eternal as God Himself, as God Himself in this antithesis, and all positively painful because the antithesis in which God here acts cannot be a natural confrontation, but must inevitably consist in the fact that infinite suffering is imposed upon the creature which God created and destined for Himself, when God reacted against this creature as it deserves. It is, of course, true that this man is the Son of God. In Him God Himself suffers what guilty man had to suffer by way of eternal punishment. This alone gives the suffering of this man its representative power. This is what makes it the power by which the world is reconciled to God. 'God was in Christ reconciling the world unto himself' (2 Cor 5[19]). But this is the Son of God, this man, who in His death as the Representative of all men, as the revelation of what was due to them, endured this suffering, and bore this punishment. And it is this character, this quality of human death as eternal punishment, which the Church of Jesus Christ contemplates in His crucifixion. This is why the New Testament thinks and speaks so much more harshly of man's being in death than does the Old. (*CD* III/2, pp. 603–4)[22]

---

wrathful love and not His wrathful hate. Man has always stood up to the hatred of the gods. But God is not one of these gods of hatred. Man cannot stand up to His wrath because it is the wrath of His love. The reason why His curse falls so hard upon us is that it is surrounded by the rainbow of His covenant. It is the dark side of the blessing with which He has blessed us and wills to bless us.' *CD* III/2, p. 609.

22 It is worth pointing out again that Barth continuously reminds his reader of the necessity of moving from the particular death of Jesus Christ to reflection on the appropriateness of this death and the salvific power of this death. Barth insists that we cannot move from an abstract understanding of the human situation and a humanly constructed solution to this situation and then apply this to the death of Jesus Christ. Rather, the particulars of the death itself are revelatory of the gravity of the human situation as well as the lengths to which God must go in order to remedy this situation.

The death of Jesus Christ is unnatural and is determined by God as the proper way of dealing with sinful humanity. By being unnatural, Jesus Christ's death consists of the fullness of God's judgment and wrath. Barth does not veil the New Testament's shocking depiction of death at the hands of the wrath of God. Jesus Christ's death is best described as eternal punishment and this consists of torment, outer darkness, the worm, the flame, or, to be precise, hell. The unnatural character of death as the full judgment of God, further, demonstrates the pure obedience of Jesus Christ. Jesus Christ, as the sin-bearer, wilfully accepts the burden of death as God's judgment. This death is described by Barth as no other than atonement. In answering the question of what took place in Jesus Christ's death on the cross, Barth affirms that 'Jesus suffered the end of His life in death as an atonement, not for His own sin and guilt but for that of others' (*CD* III/2, p. 628).

Barth continues by affirming that this death as eternal punishment is salvific only because of the identity of the one who died, i.e. Jesus Christ as the incarnate Son of God. This death is salvific, further, because it is a death of representation or substitution (*Stellvertretung*). By affirming the representative and substitutionary quality of Christ's death, which is a necessary condition for it being salvific, Barth emphasizes both the particularity of Jesus Christ's death and the inclusive consequences of this death. By enduring death as the full weight of God's judgment – death as the 'second death' – Jesus Christ spares humanity from the necessity of having to suffer the 'second death'. God's act of judgment in the death of Jesus Christ is God's act of salvation of humanity. Death as the 'second death', 'eternal corruption' and 'eternal punishment' has been relegated to the past through the death of Jesus Christ. Jesus Christ's death, consisting of the quality of 'eternal death', reveals both the quality of human death that would await all human beings if they were to depend solely upon themselves and the actuality of the reconciliation of the world with God through this death. This reconciliation includes the freedom of humanity from needing to endure the gravity of death as God's judgment, as 'eternal corruption', which they deserve.

For the purposes of our exploration of Barth's theology in terms of his view or use of the Church's confession that Jesus Christ 'descended into hell', the previous discussion further demonstrates Barth's affinity with Calvin and Reformed theology. Barth points to such New Testament concepts as eternal punishment, eternal corruption, outer darkness and eternal torment as a way of properly describing the death of Jesus Christ. He does not employ these concepts as a way of treating the state of Jesus Christ in his burial and in the time between the crucifixion and the resurrection; rather, he maintains that the depiction of human death as eternal punishment – as hell – is that which the Church 'contemplates in [Jesus Christ's] crucifixion'. Jesus Christ's encounter with or experience of hell is an apt way of describing the inner experience of Jesus Christ on the cross. It enables us to recognize the gravity of Jesus Christ's suffering in the event of the crucifixion; it does not, however, include a positive reflection on Holy Saturday and the 'descent into hell' which takes place after Jesus Christ's death and burial.

The death of Jesus Christ as the experience of hell in Barth's 'Doctrine of Reconciliation' – *Church Dogmatics* IV

We now turn to the centrepiece of Barth's *Church Dogmatics*, volume IV, 'The Doctrine of Reconciliation'.[23] As in the previous sections, we will focus primarily on Barth's understanding of the death of Jesus Christ as involving the endurance of God's judgment and wrath. This includes his endurance of the full weight of God-abandonment and God-forsakenness. Furthermore, this can only be described as Jesus Christ's experience of 'eternal' corruption or death, the 'second' death, the 'ordeal' or, to be precise, a descent into hell.

For Barth, the death of Jesus Christ includes the death of sinful humanity and the relegation of human persons as sinners completely to the past – humans as sinners have no future. Both the destruction of sin and the termination of human persons as sinners are accomplished in the passion of Jesus Christ. This is the case because Jesus Christ takes the place of sinful humanity and suffers the judgment, punishment or penalty that is imposed by God. Jesus Christ, we must emphasize, does not take the place of sinful humanity as a pure and innocent human; rather, he takes the place of sinful humanity by taking on sin itself – by bearing the world's sin and bearing it away. In the following passage we see how Barth describes the substitutionary activity of Jesus Christ:

> Jesus Christ has taken his [humanity's] place as a malefactor. In his place Jesus Christ has suffered the death of a malefactor. The sentence on him as a sinner has been carried out. It cannot be reversed. It does not need to be repeated. It has fallen instead on Jesus Christ. In and with the man who was taken down dead on Golgotha man the covenant-breaker is buried and destroyed. He has ceased to be. The wrath of God which is the fire of His love has taken him away and all his transgressions and offences and errors and follies and lies and faults and crimes against God and his fellowmen and himself, just as a whole burnt offering is consumed on the altar with the flesh and skin and bones and

---

23   Volume IV is the 'centrepiece' of Barth's *Church Dogmatics* because of its subject matter. This is not to say that it is the apex of Barth's dogmatic structure, as if there were one question or issue that controls Barth's theological reflection. One could make the case that his doctrine of election in II/2 is primary, or perhaps his doctrine of revelation in I/1 and I/2. I intend only to point out that for Barth, the event of atonement/reconciliation lies at the centre of the Christian message. In the opening paragraph of IV/1 Barth indicates that we have arrived at the heart of the matter, as he writes, 'We enter that sphere of Christian knowledge in which we have to do with the heart of the message received by and laid upon the Christian community and therefore with the heart of the Church's dogmatics: that is to say, with the heart of its subject-matter, origin and content. It has a circumference, the doctrine of creation and the doctrine of the last things, the redemption and consummation. But the covenant fulfilled in the atonement is its centre. From this point we can and must see a circumference. But we can see it only from this point. A mistaken or deficient perception here would mean error or deficiency everywhere: the weakening or obscuring of the message, the confession and dogmatics as such. From this point either everything is clear and true and helpful, or it is not so anywhere. This involves a high responsibility in the task which now confronts us.' *CD* IV/1, p. 3.

hoofs and horns, rising up as fire to heaven and disappearing. That is how God
has dealt with man who broke covenant with Himself. (*CD* IV/1, pp. 93–4)

God reconciles humanity to himself in the particular death of Jesus Christ, for in
this death God annihilates humanity as sinner. It is precisely the death of Jesus
Christ, the sin-bearer, that proves to be salvific, for in this particular death sin is
defeated and death itself is put to death and removed.

As we saw in our treatment of *Church Dogmatics* II/1, we must stress that the
love of God is the basis for the salvation wrought in the death of Jesus Christ. In
the death of Christ, the love of God takes the form of wrath. Barth presses the
point that in God love and wrath are not in tension or competition with one
another, nor is the wrath of God somehow satisfied or appeased in the brutal death
of Jesus Christ – as execution or sacrifice. Rather, the wrath of God is intrinsic to
the love of God – God's wrath is 'the fire of His love', and it is the love of God
that works itself out in the form of wrath in order to reconcile humanity to God
and to establish humanity as utterly new creatures.

As we saw in Barth's lectures on the Apostles' Creed, the passion of Jesus
Christ is not only an event of judgment, punishment and sacrifice – an event in
which sin and the sinner are dealt with effectively by being put to death and
annihilated – the passion also involves the establishment of sinful human persons
as new creatures. The passion involves the positive decree that not only has the
human person as sinner become pure past in the death of Jesus Christ, the human
person as righteous has also been established and Jesus Christ becomes the
exclusive future of humanity.

Furthermore, the particularity of Jesus Christ's life and death proves to be
universal in scope. In Jesus Christ, humanity as sinner is destroyed and humanity
as new creation is established. There is both distance and closeness between the
unique and particular person Jesus Christ and all human persons, in whose place
Jesus Christ suffered and died. There is distance insofar as Jesus Christ alone dies
the death at the hands of the wrath of God. Jesus Christ alone accomplishes
salvation. Salvation is not something that encompasses both Jesus Christ and all of
humanity, as if salvation were a gradual process that matures and is complete in
the lives of individual human persons, or were dependent upon on an appropriate
reaction on the part of the individual.[24] Barth unequivocally affirms that salvation
is accomplished once and for all in the death of Jesus Christ.

At the same time, there is participation of all human beings in the particular
person of Jesus Christ, and this participation leads to the actual transformation of
the lives of individual human persons. Barth insists that it is proper to speak of
human persons as being declared righteous by God due to the life and death of

---

24 Barth insists that reconciliation is not something that takes place both in Jesus Christ and,
subsequently, in humanity; rather, reconciliation takes place in Jesus Christ alone and humanity is
reconciled to God precisely in what took place in Jesus Christ. See *CD* IV/1, pp. 229–30.

Jesus Christ, and this declaration is real. It does not involve a masquerade. That human persons are declared righteous by God involves more than a new perspective from which to view humanity, a perspective from which humans appear to be righteous, or are viewed 'as if' they are righteous. Barth asserts, 'Certainly we have to do with a declaring righteous, but it is a declaration about man which is fulfilled and therefore effective in this event, which corresponds to actuality because it creates and therefore reveals the actuality. It is a declaring righteous which without any reserve can be called a making righteous' (*CD* IV/1, p. 95). Barth insists that the particular person Jesus Christ is our righteousness (see 1 Corinthians 1:30, 'Christ Jesus, whom God made our wisdom, our righteousness and sanctification and redemption') and as a result there is a distance between human persons (those in need of a saviour) and Jesus Christ (the Saviour). At the same time, Barth insists that human persons are actually righteous insofar as they are declared righteous and participate, through a fellowship with Christ of union and communion, in the righteousness that is theirs in Jesus Christ.

We now proceed to the segment of *Church Dogmatics* IV/1 that will gain most of our attention, namely, §59.2 'The Judge Judged in Our Place'. In this section Barth most clearly spells out the contents of the divine judgment or condemnation that Jesus Christ endures 'in place of' deserving sinful humanity. Barth begins this section by offering an initial response to the question *Cur Deus homo?* His response describes how God has revealed himself as *Deus pro nobis*. *Deus pro nobis* contains at least two essential elements. First, God is for us insofar as God has not deserted humanity. God has truly entered into humanity's predicament (*CD* IV/1, p. 215). God shares in the human predicament by being present with human persons in their sinful situation – in Jesus Christ as the incarnate Son of God, who assumed human nature and flesh. In this case, Jesus Christ exists with humanity as humanity's brother, and given his identity as the incarnate Son of God, Jesus Christ experiences humanity's situation in a more acute manner than any other human.

Jesus Christ not only participates in the human situation in a form of solidarity, he also participates in the fallen state of human beings as sinners and as enemies of God. Though Jesus Christ did not commit sin, he takes humanity's place as a sinner. This is the second essential element of how God has demonstrated himself as *Deus pro nobis*. God has not only not deserted humanity and humanity's predicament; God in Jesus Christ has indeed 'taken our place when we become sinners, when we become His enemies, when we stand as such under His accusation and curse, and bring upon ourselves our own destruction'(*CD* IV/1, p. 216).

Barth's claim that Jesus Christ has 'taken our place' requires that we account for the uniqueness of the way in which Jesus Christ is not only 'with us', but is in a very real sense 'for us' by being 'in our place'. It is the uniqueness of Jesus Christ's life and passion that enables this life and passion to be the 'redemptive happening which embraces us in [Jesus Christ's] existence, which takes us up into itself' (*CD* IV/1, p. 229). The focal point and culmination of the unique life history of Jesus Christ is the passion, in which Jesus Christ suffered, was crucified, and died. It is the passion to which the gospel narratives point and upon which the rest of the New Testament comments.

Barth accounts for the uniqueness of the passion of Jesus Christ in at least three ways. First, the passion of Jesus Christ is unique because it is an event that is inextricably tied to a particular time and place, and the particular history of a particular person. The passion of Jesus Christ is not the actualization of an abstract and predetermined notion of what is necessary for redemption to take place, which would imply that Jesus Christ were simply an instance of a general class of dying and rising gods. Barth insists that the passion of Jesus Christ is unique insofar as it is unsubstitutable and unrepeatable. Reconciliation is necessarily linked to the particular passion of Jesus Christ and is not something that could have taken place at a different time and place and to a different person. The concepts involved in describing God's reconciling activity are determined by the particular person Jesus Christ and by the unsubstitutable events of his history. In short, the passion of Jesus Christ, according to the biblical witness, is 'a unique occurrence for which there is no precedent and which cannot be repeated' (*CD* IV/1, p. 245).

The next two elements that determine the uniqueness of the passion of Jesus Christ are interrelated, that is, the 'person' and the 'mission' of this particular individual who was executed at the hands of the Romans in Jerusalem in the first third of the first century. The person and the mission of Jesus Christ indicate that we are not simply dealing with a virtuous and innocent individual who was wrongly executed, a mere creature who suffered at the hands of his fellow creatures. When we speak of the person of Jesus Christ we are speaking of no other than the eternal Son of God incarnate who takes upon himself this particular human passion. The mission of Jesus Christ culminates in his being judged and enduring the judgment of God in the place of sinful humanity. By using judicial concepts and language, Barth describes the mission of Jesus Christ as 'the Judge who in this passion takes the place of those who ought to be judged, who in this passion allows Himself to be judged in their place' (*CD* IV/1, p. 246).

It is the uniqueness of the passion of Jesus Christ as determined by his person, mission and particular history that leads to a discussion of the character and quality of his death as the defining event of divine condemnation or judgment. The passion of Jesus Christ both reveals the content of God's condemnation upon sin and sinful humanity, and is the particular event in which this divine condemnation is carried out. The passion of Jesus Christ is not a mere instance of a generally accessible understanding of the content and weight of God's judgment. Rather, the passion of Jesus Christ constitutes and reveals the exact content of this judgment and condemnation.

The passion of Jesus Christ – the suffering, crucifixion and death – stands out from as well as encompasses all instances of human suffering. Jesus' passion is unique and he endures it alone. This passion takes an extreme form that is unknown to all human suffering. In commenting on the unique character of Jesus Christ's passion, Barth writes:

We are not dealing merely with any suffering, but with the suffering of God and this man in face of the destruction which threatens all creation and every individual, thus compromising God as the Creator. We are dealing with the painful confrontation of God and this man not merely with any evil, not merely with death, but with eternal death, with the power of that which is not. Therefore we are not dealing with any sin, or with many sins, which might wound God again and again, and only especially perhaps at this point, and the consequences of which this man had only to suffer in part and freely willed to do so. We are dealing with sin itself and as such: the preoccupation, the orientation, the determination of man as he has left his place as a creature and broken his covenant with God; the corruption which God has made His own, for which He willed to take responsibility in this one man. Here in the passion in which as Judge He lets Himself be judged God has fulfilled this responsibility. In the place of all men He has Himself wrestled with that which separates them from Him. He has Himself borne the consequences of this separation to bear it away. (*CD* IV/1, p. 247)

Although the suffering and passion endured by Jesus Christ is indeed a genuine human suffering and human passion, it is unlike the suffering and passion confronted by any other individual. Jesus Christ is taken to the limit of all human suffering. He faces the death of a human being, but the death he faces and dies goes beyond even the terror of common human death, for the death he dies is 'eternal death'. Death, coupled with the qualifier 'eternal', moves beyond mere physical death to death as utter annihilation, death as governed by the 'power of that which is not'. The suffering and passion of Jesus Christ also includes the presence of the full gravity of the nakedness of sin itself. Jesus Christ does not merely face the massive quantity of human sin as he bears the world's sin. He faces the full gravity of sin itself, everything that is in opposition to God and which leads to the only possible result – complete separation from God. Jesus Christ takes on the full quality of sin and the serious consequence of sin, and in doing so he effectively bears this sin and bears it away; he eliminates sin and relegates it to the status of unreality.[25]

That Jesus Christ's death was a death unlike any human death is demonstrated by the terror that overcame Jesus in the face of his imminent death. He did not approach mere human death as an innocent martyr, for if this were the case then he could have faced it with a calm resignation, as many awaiting execution have done both before and after him, rather than with the struggle and pleading that we see in Gethsemane. In Gethsemane Jesus requests that he be freed from having to

---

25 This passage is significant insofar as it includes two elements that we will encounter in the following chapter on Balthasar. Balthasar describes Jesus Christ's descent into hell in terms of his enduring the *poena damni* – the penalty of damnation. In explicating what is involved in the *poena damni*, Balthasar speaks of three essential aspects, one of which is the 'second' or 'eternal' death, and another is Jesus' encounter with 'sin itself'. Balthasar's treatment of these aspects of Jesus Christ's passion serves a similar purpose as in Barth, i.e., to account for and describe the unique character of the suffering and passion endured by Jesus Christ, the sin-bearer.

endure the terror involved in draining the cup of God's wrath. As it turns out, Jesus did not overestimate the terror, pain and suffering that he would experience in his crucifixion and his death, for in his death he encounters separation from God and bears the unbearable weight of God-abandonment and God-forsakenness. Jesus tastes the bitterness of death and is taken to hell. The precise way in which Jesus Christ's death differs from every human death is that his death is consumed by darkness, and his death involves God's siding with both God's and Jesus' enemies. The possibility that Jesus envisions in the solitary silence of Gethsemane becomes an actuality in his crucifixion and death. For Barth, 'The coincidence of the divine and the satanic will and the work and word was the problem of this hour, the darkness in which Jesus addressed God in Gethsemane' (*CD* IV/1, p. 268). Although, in his predictions of his passion during his ministry (see Mark 8:31, 9:30–2, 10:33–4 and synoptic parallels), Jesus confidently points to his being raised three days after being killed, in Gethsemane he can only see the darkness of his death and the three days and three nights that he will spend in the heart of the earth (Matthew 12:40). The darkness that has moved over Jesus and the events that await him are the darkness of God's will being accomplished through the activity of sinful humanity and Satan himself. Barth starkly describes the scene in Gethsemane as follows:

> It was not a matter of His suffering and dying in itself and as such, but of the dreadful thing that He saw coming upon Him in and with His suffering and dying. He saw it clearly and correctly. It was the coming of the night 'in which no man can work' (Jn. 9⁴), in which the good will of God will be indistinguishably one with the evil will of men and the world and Satan. It was a matter of the triumph of God being concealed under that of His adversary, of that which is not, of that which supremely is not. It was a matter of God Himself obviously making a tryst with death and about to keep it. It was a matter of the divine judgment being taken out of the hands of Jesus and placed in those of His supremely unrighteous judges and executed by them upon Him ... That was what came upon Him in His suffering and dying, as God's answer to His appeal. Jesus saw this cup. He tasted its bitterness. He had not made any mistake. He had not been needlessly afraid. There was every reason to ask that it might pass from Him. (*CD* IV/1, p. 271)

In the garden of Gethsemane, therefore, the elements of Jesus Christ's death that will make it a unique and salvific death are established and the dynamics of his death as a substitutionary death are set into motion. In Gethsemane, the sin of the world is placed upon Jesus, and Jesus becomes the Representative (*Vertreter*) of sinful humanity and alone endures the judgment of God. This is the outcome determined by God's will to which Jesus grants full and perfect obedience.

Fundamentally, sin is the force that drives Jesus Christ to his suffering and death, and sin is the enemy that he faces on the cross. Ultimately, it is sin that is defeated and the consequence of sin, namely death, is put to death and destroyed in the death of Jesus Christ. Sin is what makes the atonement necessary. For Barth, the sole concern of the atonement as accomplished on the cross is to destroy both sin itself and humanity as sinners. Barth describes what is effected in the atonement and how this atonement takes place as follows:

> The very heart of the atonement is the overcoming of sin: sin in its character as the rebellion of man against God, and in its character as the ground of man's hopeless destiny in death. It was to fulfil this judgment on sin that the Son of God as man took our place as sinners. He fulfils it – as man in our place – by completing our work in the omnipotence of the divine Son, by treading the way of sinners to its bitter end in death, in destruction, in the limitless anguish of separation from God, by delivering up sinful man and sin in His own person to the non-being which is properly theirs, the non-being, the nothingness to which man has fallen victim as a sinner and towards which he relentlessly hastens. We can say indeed that He fulfils this judgment by suffering the punishment which we have all brought on ourselves. (*CD* IV/1, p. 253)

By determining the content of this judgment and by bearing this judgment in the place of sinful humanity, Jesus Christ fulfils the judgment upon sin and sinners. He takes on human sin and wrestles with the naked power of sin itself in such a way that he follows the course determined by God for sin and humanity as sinners. Walking the way of the sinner to its ultimate and extreme destination, to the 'limitless anguish of separation from God', Jesus Christ enters hell, the judgment determined by God for sin and sinners, and in doing so he fulfils God's judgment on sin and sinners. As a result, both sin itself and human persons as sinners are destroyed, annihilated. Although all human beings are, as a result of their sin, on the way that leads only to hell, Jesus Christ takes their place and completes this journey alone. Jesus alone encounters the non-being, the nothingness, which rightfully awaits all humans as sinners. It is in this journey to hell that God in Jesus Christ deals effectively with sin, reconciles humanity with himself, redeems humanity and establishes them as new creatures, and forever removes the obstacles that have driven a wedge between God and creation. Barth summarizes this journey that Jesus Christ takes to the utter depths of hell with the familiar language that Jesus Christ suffers, voluntarily and undeservingly, the 'punishment' that humans deserve. It is this punishment that effects the destruction of sin and the sinner in the person of Jesus Christ, and it is this punishment that Jesus Christ suffers alone, yet in which all humanity participates.

Barth does not naively nor uncritically use the language of 'punishment'. It is the specific meaning and use of 'punishment' that demonstrates the innovation of Barth's soteriology, distances him from Anselm's 'satisfaction' theory and subsequent 'penal substitution' theories, and answers critics of a view of Jesus Christ's passion that emphasizes Jesus' bearing God's judgment, enduring God's wrath, and suffering from God-abandonment and forsakenness. Barth recognizes the importance of Isaiah 53 for the introduction and use of the concept 'punishment' in interpreting the cross, yet he challenges common understandings of 'punishment'.

Barth rejects two components of 'punishment', while endorsing two significant elements (*CD* IV/1, p. 253).

Barth rejects the notion that since Jesus Christ suffered the punishment that humanity deserves, humanity is consequently spared from suffering it themselves – a strong version of substitution. This view emphasizes the distance that separates Jesus Christ from the rest of humanity at the expense of humanity's participation in Jesus Christ. It is accurate to state that Jesus Christ's suffering is unique and that he endures the judgment of God alone, but as we saw earlier in this chapter, all of humanity participates in the suffering of Jesus Christ and their status as sinners is annihilated in the unique suffering of Jesus Christ.

The second common component of 'punishment' that Barth rejects is the notion that by enduring the punishment meant for sinful humanity, Jesus Christ 'satisfies' or offers satisfaction to the wrath of God. Barth insists that we refrain from viewing the death of Jesus Christ as an event that moves God's disposition towards humanity from wrath to love, through appeasing God's anger or wrath. Though Barth will accept viewing Jesus Christ's death as providing 'satisfaction', it is not God's wrath that is satisfied; rather, it is God's holy love that is satisfied.

Barth does not reject punishment language altogether. He proposes that punishment is employed properly in two interrelated ways. First, the term punishment is appropriate insofar as it describes the gravity of Jesus Christ's suffering and death. Punishment accurately describes the depth to which Jesus Christ was taken in the work that he accomplished 'for us' and 'in our place'. This punishment refers to Jesus Christ's encounter with hell. Barth concludes, 'If Jesus Christ has followed our way as sinners to the end to which it leads, in outer darkness, then we can say with that passage from the Old Testament [Isaiah 53] that He has suffered this punishment of ours' (*CD* IV/1, p. 253). So, 'punishment' is appropriate insofar as it names the gravity of Jesus Christ's suffering, which includes his journey to hell.

The second aspect of a proper understanding and use of the term 'punishment' has to do with what is accomplished in the 'punishment' endured by Jesus Christ as he travels to hell. At this point, we see the complexity of Barth's acceptance and rejection of the notion that due to the suffering of Jesus Christ humanity is 'spared' from the punishment that they have brought upon themselves. Our discussion of the first component of 'punishment' that Barth rejects must be clarified. Barth acknowledges that in this instance, Jesus Christ suffers what we ought to have suffered in order that we do not have to suffer it, but he insists that this is only derivative from the primary consequence of his unique suffering, which he endures 'in our place'. What is of primary importance is that in the suffering and death of Jesus Christ, sin and humans as sinners are annihilated and exist no more. The suffering that we deserve because of our sin is not merely thwarted or deflected. It is effectively dealt with and is removed by being destroyed. Our sentence is not merely commuted; it is served in its entirety by Jesus Christ and is removed completely as a result. It no longer applies to us. Barth concisely concludes:

In the suffering and death of Jesus Christ it has come to pass that in His own person He has made an end of us as sinners and therefore of sin itself by going to death as the One who took our place as sinners. In His person He has delivered up us sinners and sin itself to destruction. He has removed us sinners and sin, negated us, cancelled us out: ourselves, our sin, and the accusation, condemnation and perdition which had overtaken us. (*CD* IV/1, pp. 253–4)

We may conclude that if one wants to view Barth's interpretation of the passion of Jesus Christ as a form of 'penal substitution', then one must account for his specific use of the term 'punishment'. Perhaps the most significant aspect of his qualified use of 'punishment' is the exact way in which the meaning of 'punishment' is affected by a proper understanding of the relationship between love and wrath in God.

As was pointed out above, Barth insists that the death of Jesus Christ does not in any way satisfy or offer satisfaction to God's wrath. God is not turned from wrath to love as a result of the sacrifice of Jesus Christ or the punishment carried out in the death of Jesus Christ. Here we come to the development in Barth's thought from his initial treatment of the doctrine of the atonement in the *Church Dogmatics*, within the Doctrine of God in II/1. As we noticed earlier in this chapter, in *Church Dogmatics* II/1, Barth states that the meaning of the death of Jesus Christ is that in that event the righteousness of God is satisfied. Although he does not intend to imply that God's disposition is altered from wrath to love through the death of Jesus Christ, by speaking specifically of God's *righteousness* being satisfied in the death of Jesus Christ, Barth risks separating God's mercy from God's righteousness, God's grace from God's holiness, and, most significantly, God's love from God's wrath.

Throughout *Church Dogmatics* IV/1, Barth is careful and precise as he consistently describes the wrath of God as an element of God's holy love. He often speaks of the wrath of God as the 'fire of God's love' (*CD* IV/1, p. 93). Barth also describes God's wrath as the form that God's love takes in the face of resistance and rejection by creatures. God will not allow human rejection of God's love to have the last word. God will pursue humanity by overcoming humanity's resistance through the refining fire of God's wrath. Barth describes the relationship between God and sinful humanity as taking the following form: 'My turning from God is followed by God's annihilating turning from me. When it is resisted His love works itself out as death-dealing wrath' (*CD* IV/1, p. 253). The clearest statement regarding the relationship between divine love and divine wrath, which displays Barth's insistence that God's love is primary and God's wrath serves God's love – God's No is a form of God's Yes – is found in the following passage, which may act as an abstract of Barth's entire doctrine of reconciliation:

For the sake of the best, the worst had to happen to sinful man: not out of any desire for vengeance and retribution on the part of God, but because of the radical nature of the divine love, which could 'satisfy' itself only in the outworking of its wrath against the man of sin, only by killing him, extinguishing him, removing him. Here is the place for the doubtful concept that in the passion of Jesus Christ, in the giving up of His Son to death, God has done that which is 'satisfactory' or sufficient in the victorious fighting of sin to make this victory radical and total. He has done that which is sufficient to take away sin, to restore order between Himself as the Creator and His creation, to bring in the new man reconciled and therefore at peace with Him, to redeem man from death. God has done this in the passion of Jesus Christ. For this reason the divine judgment in which the Judge was judged, and therefore the passion of Jesus Christ, is as such the divine action of atonement which has taken place for us. (*CD* IV/1, p. 254)

Barth's ability to hold God's love and wrath together – by subsuming God's wrath under God's love, and by viewing wrath as a function of love, rather than viewing love and wrath in tension with one another – enables him to dispense with mythological pictures of a bloodthirsty and vengeful God. God does not punish Jesus Christ out of some irrational obsession with punitive justice or retribution. Also, God does not accept the sacrifice of Jesus Christ as a pure and innocent human being in order to appease his anger and wrath and to satisfy his penchant for blood. The passion of Jesus Christ, according to Barth, is from first to last a divine action, and as a divine action it is motivated and carried out by God's love alone.

The goal and the actual consequence of the passion is the single outcome of the reconciliation and redemption of humanity. In the passion, humanity is brought into a proper covenantal relationship with God; humans as sinners are destroyed and, as a result, established as new creatures. Human beings as sinners are purified by the fire of God's love and are recreated by being put to death and resurrected as new creatures. The passion, which Barth describes as the worst event imaginable, is funded by God's love, and God's love is unlike any love known in the creaturely realm. God's love is pure holy love and it is radical. This holy and radical love takes the initiative in effectively removing the obstacle that separates humanity from God. Sin is the obstacle and can be dealt with only through its radical eradication, which leads to its annihilation. God's love takes the initiative in that humans do not offer a sacrifice, no matter how pure, in hopes of satisfying God's wrath, nor do humans benefit from the punishment of a representative human being, and are in turn freed from the punishment that awaits them.[26] Rather, God's radical and holy love *satisfies itself*; God's love takes the form of wrath and God's love is satisfied through its own activity as a result of the outpouring of God's wrath. God's wrath works itself out in such a way that the individual sinner is killed, extinguished and removed. From the rubble of this destruction, the individual is resurrected and recreated, and is established in a right covenantal relation with God as new creature.

---

26   This is not to dismiss the importance of sacrificial language and concepts in exploring the salvific significance of the cross. Rather, it is to highlight the primary role taken by God in the atonement. Humans do not and cannot offer a purely human sacrifice as a way of appeasing an angry God.

Although I have been stressing the quality of Jesus Christ's passion as a divine action, we must not ignore the genuine human element of Jesus Christ's death as sacrifice or punishment. J. B. Torrance concisely captures the significance of holding the divine and the human aspects of Jesus Christ's passion together in an essay treating the priesthood of Jesus, which builds upon Barth's teaching regarding the relationship between Christology and soteriology. Specifically, Torrance highlights the significance of the classical Christological interrelated categories *anhypostasia* and *enhypostasia*, which Barth employs in his constructive Christology, for a full understanding of the substitutionary aspect of Jesus Christ's passion. Torrance writes:

> The doctrine of *anhypostasia* safeguards the fact that the Priesthood and Sacrifice of Jesus are the work of God Himself. God is the Subject of the atoning sacrifice, and not man. It is God who provides the Lamb and makes propitiation for our sins in Christ and who Himself bears our sins by taking the judgment of our sins to Himself . . . The doctrine of *anhypostasia* rules out any Pelagian thought of Jesus as Representative Man propitiating God from the side of man by a meritorious act of human sacrifice . . . It safeguards the teaching of the New Testament that Jesus as our Representative is also our Substitute . . . On the other hand, the doctrine of *enhypostasia* safeguards the fact that in the *assumptio carnis* the priesthood and sacrifice of Jesus are truly human, that within the hypostatic union the sacrifice of Christ is not only God's own act of sacrifice, but is a sacrifice offered to God on behalf of men by Jesus as man . . . If Jesus were not very man He would not be able to 'have compassion on the ignorant and on them that are out of the way' (Hebrews 5:2). He would not be our elder brother. But as very man He was judged in our flesh and as man He has once and for all offered to God a human obedience, a human response, a human witness, and as man He is our surety at the right hand of God . . . Together [*anhypostasia* and *enhypostasia*] teach the substitutionary character of Christ's atonement. *Anhypostasia* emphasizes that God substitutes Himself for us. *Enhypostasia* emphasizes that the man Jesus is substituted for us. This is the doctrine of 'the wondrous exchange' (*mirifica commutatio*) taught by the Reformers. 'He hath made Him to be sin for us, who knew no sin; that we might be made the righteousness of God in Him' (2 Corinthians 5:21).[27]

For Barth, Jesus' suffering and his descent into hell do not represent conflict within God, between the Father and the Son. Christ's suffering and descent into hell is human suffering of God. It is genuine human suffering, death and presence in hell taken up into the very life of God, and as such God triumphs over and destroys suffering, death and hell.

Since it has been established that God himself takes the initiative in effectively dealing with the human predicament (which is due to sin) and that the event or action of the crucifixion and death of Jesus Christ is from first to last a divine

---

27   J. B. Torrance, 'The Priesthood of Jesus', in *Essays in Christology for Karl Barth*, ed. T. H. L. Parker (London: Lutterworth Press, 1956), pp. 168–9.

event, we must recognize that everything that took place in the passion of Jesus Christ is fitting or appropriate given God's self-determined nature. The radical nature of God's love determines and dictates exactly what is appropriate, necessary and satisfactory. God is not bound to an abstract notion of justice and, therefore, is not dependent upon an external set of conditions that must be met or satisfied in order for salvation to be achieved. God determines the content of justice, and God determines and effects what must take place in order for salvation to be achieved and sin and evil to be eliminated. Only in this sense (i.e. God acting in a way that is consistent with the radical nature of his love) can we speak of the passion as being 'satisfactory' or 'necessary'. The passion is 'necessary' only insofar as it is sufficient and accomplishes God's loving intention, the complete victory over sin and evil. That Jesus Christ's passion is satisfactory and sufficient is manifested by the reconciliation and redemption of humanity, which is accomplished by the complete destruction of sin and humanity as sinner. All this takes place and is most clearly understood as the execution of divine judgment. This divine judgment is accomplished as the Judge allows himself – in the person of the eternal Son – to be judged in place of sinful humanity. Barth concludes, 'The divine judgment in which the Judge was judged, and therefore the passion of Jesus Christ, is as such the divine action of atonement which has taken place for us' (*CD* IV/1, p. 254).

At the completion of our perusal of sections in the *Church Dogmatics* relevant to our topic, we are now in a position to draw some conclusions regarding Barth's understanding of the character of the passion of Jesus Christ and its consisting of 'divine condemnation' or 'divine judgment', and in turn to ascertain the significance of the 'descent into hell' for Barth's treatment of the passion of Jesus Christ.

It is clear that the passion of Jesus Christ is a unique event. The suffering that Jesus Christ endures, though pure and genuine human suffering, goes beyond the suffering that any human individual has endured or will encounter. The uniqueness of Jesus Christ's suffering and death may be accounted for by at least two interrelated factors.

First, the identity of Jesus Christ as the eternal Son of God incarnate enables his experience of separation from God to be genuinely salvific. Through the hypostatic union and the communication of attributes, the human experience of abandonment and separation is taken into God's own life, and is therefore overcome. Here we must emphasize that the passion of death of Jesus Christ cannot be considered apart from the divine/human unity of Christ. This passion is not an event between God and God. It is a human event in the very life of God.

Second, the identity of Jesus Christ as the eternal Son of God incarnate ensures the efficacy of his mission to take the place of humanity, bear the world's sin, and serve the sentence determined by God for sinful humanity by enduring God's judgment and condemnation. Jesus' ability to carry out this mission unto death in obedience rests upon his pure dependence upon the empowering agency of the Holy Spirit. Jesus' mission is unique in that the judgment that is carried out in his passion is the full weight of God's judgment on sin and on humanity as sinners.

What confronts sinful humanity as a mere threat or possibility falls upon Jesus Christ with the full weight of actuality. Humans as sinners are on the road that leads to hell; Jesus Christ takes up and completes this journey by travelling to the depths of hell. Humans face the dreadful prospect of the second death or eternal corruption; Jesus Christ's death moves beyond mere human death to encompass the unique quality of the 'second death', which includes torment, annihilating pain, and outer darkness.

Barth avoids the problems that have plagued treatments of the atonement that are considered to be Anselmian, either in the form of 'satisfaction' or the later developed 'penal substitution' theories. As was pointed out, Barth has a careful and nuanced understanding of how Christ's death may be properly understood as involving 'punishment'. Furthermore, though Barth describes the death of Christ using the language of punishment and sacrifice, he also insists that the cross is the locus of God's victory over God's enemies – sin, death, and the devil. Here one could argue that in terms of the common typology, which was developed by Aulén, Barth's soteriology contains aspects of both the Latin motif and the 'classical' or '*Christus Victor*' motif. It is clear that Barth answers Aulén's basic objection to the Latin or Anselmian understanding of the atonement by demonstrating how the passion of Jesus Christ is a divine event from beginning to end. This involves the assertion that the passion of Jesus Christ is initiated and carried out solely by the power and demands of God's holy love. Barth's overcoming of Aulén's objection is crucial for two reasons. First, God's love is primary and, as a result, God is not moved from wrath to love by the death of Jesus Christ. Second, and closely related, since the passion of Jesus Christ is a divine action from first to last, God is both the object and the subject of the event of the passion. God is in no way dependent upon the activity of a mere human being; God is not conditioned in any way by a creature.

As we have seen, Barth follows the Reformed teaching on the descent into hell. Barth understands the descent into hell as referring to the gravity of Jesus Christ's suffering on the cross and the *ordeal* that he encounters in his death. For Barth, the descent into hell is understood properly as a way of interpreting the experience of Jesus Christ on the cross. It is on the cross that Jesus Christ faces eternal death, and it is the cross that marks the bitter end of the journey taken up by Jesus in the place of sinners. It is on the cross that Jesus Christ most profoundly bears the weight of divine wrath and judgment as the climax of his existing under the wrath of God that includes his entire life.

Barth does move beyond typical Reformed teaching regarding the descent into hell by insisting that not only does the descent into hell refer to the extreme suffering and the ordeal experienced by Jesus Christ; the descent into hell must be considered as a victory as well. The descent into hell marks a divine victory over sin because in the descent into hell sin is destroyed, the human person as sinner is annihilated and relegated to pure past, and the human person is established as a new and righteous creature. Human reconciliation with God is accomplished in the

death of Christ, which has the descent into hell as its climax, and human redemption
is accomplished in the destruction of sin and the sinner and the formation of
humanity as new creatures. In this respect, though the descent into hell belongs
most properly to the *status humiliationis*, as is emphasized by Calvin and Reformed
theology, Barth insists that the descent into hell is also a victorious event and,
therefore, belongs to the *status exaltationis*. Here Barth is simply being consistent
with his proposal that the 'states' of Christ be considered not as successive but as
simultaneous.

What is lacking in Barth is an understanding of the descent into hell in terms of
an event that is distinct from the cross, as we have in the work of Balthasar. Barth
does not view the descent into hell as referring to a suffering that takes place after
the suffering of the crucifixion, i.e. on Holy Saturday, the time between the cross
of Good Friday and the resurrection of Easter morning. For Barth, the descent into
hell is understood as a way of emphasizing the gravity of the full weight of God's
wrath that falls upon Jesus Christ on the cross as the bearer of the world's sin. It is
a way of vividly describing all that is involved in Jesus Christ's death as the full
reality of God-abandonment and God-forsakenness. The descent into hell is a way
of describing the death that Jesus Christ dies on the cross as the 'eternal' or
'second' death.

As has been demonstrated through a close reading of a variety of passages in
the *Church Dogmatics* that treat the quality of the death of Jesus Christ in terms of
its involving divine judgment and condemnation, Barth describes the death of Jesus
Christ in terms of Christ's experience of hell. Jesus Christ dies a death that can be
understood properly as the 'second death'. He experiences the full power of God's
wrath and judgment, and the isolating terror of utter separation from God. This
journey in which Jesus treads the way of the sinner has its destination in the depths
of hell, and Jesus indeed arrives at this destination. At the climax of his journey he
both encounters and triumphs over hell.

In the end, however, Barth's view of the descent into hell is not a theology of
Holy Saturday, as the descent into hell acts as an interpretative key that unlocks
the meaning of the crucifixion. The descent into hell does not describe the
experience and suffering that Jesus Christ faces as a consequence of his death on
the cross, and from which he is snatched through God's action in the resurrection.[28]

---

28   In *CD* IV/2, Barth answers the question of where Jesus came from in the resurrection. Here Barth
insists that Jesus came from death itself, from the place where all sinful humans reside in death. But
Barth does not pursue this question and answer as a way of reflecting on the question of the descent
into hell. Barth writes, 'He came not only from dying but from death. He came from death in the most
stringent sense of the term, in which dying means for man the reward for sin, destruction and perdition.
And His specific death on the cross was in every sense the death of a judged and condemned criminal
– an execution. As the Son of God took it on Himself to become man, the Judge to become the judged
in our place, the man Jesus of Nazareth who was identical with Him had to die this death. And then, in
unequivocal assertion and confirmation of what had happened, He was buried . . . He had gone to the
place where all men must go and will finally be carried, but from which none can ever return. And it

Rather, the descent into hell is a powerful lens that sharpens the focus on the quality of Jesus Christ's death as determined by the fullness of the divine judgment and condemnation.

In the following chapter we will treat the work of a theologian whose view of Jesus Christ's passion shares many things with Barth's, but who presents an interpretation of the descent into hell that emphasizes the descent into hell as an event distinct from the cross. Here we have a presentation of a theology of Holy Saturday, properly named, which encompasses many of Barth's concerns and moves beyond Barth by treating the descent into hell as an event in its own right. It is to the complex and innovative theology of Hans Urs von Balthasar that we now turn.

---

was from this place that He did in fact return. He was brought back from death, from the grave, we might almost say from the earth, for it was in the earth that He had been put. He came from this. He now had behind Him that which can only be in front of all other men. This is what the Easter witness of the New Testament says and describes in the accounts of His appearances – assuming we let it say what it does.' *CD* IV/2, p. 151.

CHAPTER TWO

Hans Urs von Balthasar and a theology of Holy Saturday

> What you suffer is a shapeless fear. It is a sea without shores, fear-in-itself. The fear which is the core of sin. The fear of God and his inescapable judgment. The fear of hell. The fear of never again seeing the face of the Father for all eternity. The fear that love itself and every creature with it have dropped you irretrievably into the abyss. You fall into the bottomless; you are lost. Not the faintest shimmer of hope delimits this fear.[1]

These words describe Jesus Christ as he faces the prospect of bearing the weight of humanity's sin and enduring God's judgment of this sin through abandonment and forsakenness. Jesus Christ is about to suffer at the hands of a living and wrathful God; he is about to enter into hell. This description marks the beginning of Hans Urs von Balthasar's consistent and recurring articulation of a theology of Holy Saturday. Balthasar, in exploring the theological significance of Jesus Christ's substitutionary life and passion, locates the apex of this vicarious work in the depths of hell.

Heart of the World, published in 1945 and from which the opening quotation is taken, is Balthasar's first sustained piece of constructive theological writing. He was previously occupied with philosophy, literature and historical studies. *Heart of the World* demonstrates his theological locale and position at the time, i.e. Basle and the company of Karl Barth, and his role as the spiritual director for Adrienne von Speyr. The association with Barth influenced Balthasar's view of soteriology, especially that of substitutionary atonement ('*Stellvertretung*'). His relationship with the mystic Speyr led to Balthasar's preoccupation with the neglected clause of the Church's confession – 'He descended into hell'.

Balthasar acted as Speyr's spiritual director and facilitated her conversion to Roman Catholicism, culminating in her reception into the Church through baptism in November 1940. Speyr's fantastic mystical experiences of solidarity with the dead Christ as he descended into hell were the impetus for Balthasar's theological reflection regarding the shape of Christ's passion, the Trinitarian character of the death of Christ and the primacy of Holy Saturday. In *Heart of the World*, Balthasar articulates Speyr's theological vision and, in turn, adumbrates the specifics of his own theological vision, which are further developed in occasional pieces, sermons

---

1 Hans Urs von Balthasar, *Heart of the World*, trans. Erasmo S. Leiva (San Francisco: Ignatius Press, 1979), p. 109.

and rigorous dogmatic theology.[2] Although the debt owed by Balthasar to Speyr regarding the primacy of Holy Saturday is obvious, we need not consider Balthasar's theological reflection on the descent into hell as a mere echo of Speyr's mystical experiences, or solely as the verbal expression of these experiences. Mindful of Speyr's influence on Balthasar's theology, I will begin my examination of Balthasar's constructive theology of the descent into hell with a treatment of Speyr's mystical experiences and a brief analysis of the extent of Speyr's influence on Balthasar. The bulk of the chapter will consist of an explication and analysis of the function of the descent into hell in Balthasar's treatment of the atonement and in his theology as a whole.

Adrienne von Speyr's gift and *Heart of the World*

Balthasar witnessed and recorded Speyr's remarkable recurring spiritual experience of abandonment and forsakenness, in which she identified with the agony suffered by Jesus Christ in his death and in the interval between this death and the resurrection, the descent into hell of Holy Saturday. Balthasar designates this annual experience as 'the greatest theological gift [Speyr] received from God and left to the Church'.[3] Balthasar describes Speyr's experience as follows:

> From 1941 on, year after year – in the interior experiences which she has described – she was allowed to share in the suffering of Christ . . . A landscape of pain of undreamt-of variety was disclosed to me, who was permitted to assist her: how many and diverse were the kinds of fear, at the Mount of Olives and at the Cross, how many kinds of shame, outrage and humiliation, how many forms of Godforsakenness, of Christ's relation to the sin of the world, quite apart from the inexhaustible abundance of physical pain. Christ's passion, viewed from within, is of a diversity which the biblical texts and images leave hidden; but numerous mystics through the centuries have been allowed to

---

2 Commenting on *Heart of the World*, the influence of Speyr, and its foreshadowing of what will occupy Balthasar in his entire theological career, Andrew Louth writes, 'It is common for a man's early works to foreshadow in significant (and sometimes – with hindsight – unexpected) ways the works of his maturity. In the case of Hans Urs von Balthasar this seems to be strikingly so . . . But *Heart of the World* also strikes us in another way, for it is not only a remarkable foreshadowing of his later work, in that many of the concerns of that work can already be discerned here, it is also an uncanny crystallisation of the vision of Adrienne von Speyr, as Balthasar later sketched it in his introductory book to Adrienne's writings, *First Glance at Adrienne von Speyr*. A paragraph of *Heart of the World* beginning "The magic of Holy Saturday . . ." evokes immediately the peculiar quality of Adrienne's vision and one of its most central themes; when we read that, we know where we are.' Andrew Louth, 'The Place of *Heart of the World* in the Theology of Hans Urs von Balthasar', in *The Analogy of Beauty*, ed. John Riches (Edinburgh: T. & T. Clark, 1986), p. 148.
3 Hans Urs von Balthasar, *First Glance at Adrienne von Speyr*, trans. Antje Lawry and Sergia Englund, O.C.D. (San Francisco: Ignatius Press, 1981), p. 64.

experience a great deal of it in ever-varying aspects – if only by drops, as it were, compared with the Son of God.[4]

For Balthasar, Speyr's episodes, which must be located within the testimonies of charismatic experiences of the company of Christian mystics and saints through-out the history of the Church, shed light on the darkness of the biblical testimony regarding the inner experience of Jesus Christ in his suffering. Witnessing these repeated experiences, however, does not prompt Balthasar to leave Scripture behind in his theological reflection; rather, it informs his reading of Scripture and his life-long attempt to gain a fuller and deeper understanding of the *pro nobis* character of Christ's suffering and death.

Balthasar provides an initial interpretation of the theological significance of Speyr's own 'descent into hell', which began annually at 3 o'clock on Good Friday afternoon and lasted until early Easter Sunday morning. This interpretation high-lights Jesus Christ's passive obedience in the descent into hell and hints at its salvific significance, which Balthasar himself will later draw out in his own theological reflection and construction.

> It is Christ's final act of obedience towards his Father that he descends 'into hell' (or 'underworld', Hades, Sheol). Because hell is (already in the Old Covenant) the place where God is absent, where there is no longer the light of faith, hope, love, of participation in God's life; hell is what the judging God condemned and cast out of his creation; it is filled with all that is irreconcilable with God, from which he turns away for all eternity. It is filled with the reality of all the world's godlessness, with the sum of the world's sin; therefore, with precisely all of that from which the Crucified has freed the world. In hell he encounters his own work of salvation, not in Easter triumph, but in the uttermost night of obedience, truly the 'obedience of a corpse.' He encounters the horror of sin separated from men. He 'walks' through sin (without leaving a trace, since, in hell and in death, there is neither time nor direction); and, traversing its formlessness, he experiences the second chaos. While bereft of any spiritual light emanating from the Father, in sheer obedience, he must seek the Father where he cannot find him under any circumstances. And yet, this hell is a final mystery of the Father as the creator (who made allowances for the freedom of man). And so, in this darkness, the Incarnate Son learns 'experientially' what until then was 'reserved' for the Father. Hell, seen in this way, is, in its *final* possibility, a Trinitarian event.[5]

Here Balthasar anticipates what he will elaborate in his full treatment of the descent into hell in his most extensive articulation of a theology of Holy Saturday, *Mysterium Paschale*, and in the centrepiece of his dogmatic theology – his soteriology found in *Theo-Drama*, volume IV, *The Action*. First, the descent into hell involves an endurance of the 'second death'; hell is precisely what 'the judging God condemned and cast out of his creation'. Second, the descent into hell includes

---

4   Ibid., pp. 64–5.
5   Ibid., p. 65.

a vision of sin itself, or 'the horror of sin separated from men'. Finally, the descent into hell is intelligible only as a 'Trinitarian event', a drama that includes the Father, Son and Holy Spirit.

In *Heart of the World* Balthasar employs poetic language to spin the story of God's unfathomable love, the heart of God, which in the person and action of Jesus – the Sacred Heart – manifests the human heart of God. The extent to which the love of God will go in order to redeem sinful humanity is seen in the depths to which Jesus Christ descends in his identification with sin and, consequently, his abandonment by the Father. The Father abandons the Son and sides with the Son's human enemies.

> The Father no longer knows you. You have been eaten up by the leprosy of all creation: how should he still recognize your face? The Father has gone over to your enemies. Together they have plotted their war-plan against you. He has loved your murderers so much that he has betrayed you, his Only-begotten. He has given you up like a lost outpost; he has let you go like a lost son.[6]

The death of Jesus Christ, understood with the complement of the descent into hell, is more than mere solidarity with the suffering and physical death of humanity; his death involves the terror of abandonment, forsakenness, isolation and non-existence. Jesus dies at the hands of the wrathful God.

The death of Jesus Christ reached beyond mere physical suffering and transported him in his very soul to the depths of hell, to the extremity of separation from God, from life. This timeless event of the death of the incarnate Son of God is the expression of inexhaustible character of divine love. The dead Christ is taken to hell, not at the whim of divine anger or hate, but as a working out of the depth of divine love, which at this point takes the form of divine wrath.

The death of Jesus Christ and his plunge into the deepest fathoms of the sea of hell is not only the working out of God's wrath upon sin, and therefore, an aspect of Christ's agonizing suffering; the descent into hell also marks the beginning of God's triumph over sin and death. Hell is indeed, to use a contrasting image, a place of barren desolation, but it also houses a fecund wellspring. A wellspring of life arises in the chaos of hell. 'A wellspring in the chaos. It leaps out of pure nothingness, it leaps out of itself ... It is a beginning without parallel, as if Life were arising from Death, ... And is this wellspring in the chaos, this trickling weariness, not the beginning of a new creation?'[7] The descent into hell and Holy Saturday can be separated neither from Good Friday's cross nor from Easter morning's resurrection. The descent into hell is an extension of Jesus Christ's suffering and death, and it also marks the defeat of sin and death and acts as the transition from death to resurrection. The salvific significance of Jesus' death and

---

6   Balthasar, *Heart of the World*, p. 110.
7   Ibid., p. 152.

descent into hell is fully revealed in the dead and descended Son being raised by the Father into new life.

The descent into hell may be considered a wellspring precisely because of the vicarious nature of Jesus Christ's passion. Jesus Christ dies at the hands of the wrath of God by bearing the sin of the world. In this death, sin is annihilated, death is defeated and humanity as a new creation is established. Here in Balthasar's earliest theological work, we see the theological issues that will govern his entire theological corpus, i.e. the substitutionary character of Jesus Christ's life and work, and the centrality and indivisibility of the paschal mystery – from Gethsemane to Easter morning. Jesus Christ, Balthasar insists, lives, dies, goes to hell, and is raised 'for us' and 'in our place'. At the close of *Heart of the World*, Balthasar has Jesus, the Heart of the World, recount the events and significance of his death to Thomas after the disciple plunges his finger into Christ's open side:

> Look, this is my secret, and there is no other in heaven or on earth: My Cross is salvation, my Death is victory, my Darkness is light. At that time, when I hung in torment and dread rushed into my soul because of the forsakenness, rejectedness, and uselessness of my suffering, and all was gloomy, and only the seething rage of that mass of teeth hissed up mockingly at me, while heaven kept silence, shut tight as the mouth of a scoffer (but through the open gates of my hands and feet my blood bubbled out in spurts, and with each throb my Heart became more desolate, strength poured out from me in streams and there remained only faintness, death's fatigue, infinite failure), and at last I neared that mysterious and final spot on the very edge of being, and then – the fall into the void, the capsizing into the bottomless abyss, the vertigo, the finale, the un-becoming: that colossal death which only I have died. Through my death this has been spared you, and no one will ever experience what it really means to die: This was my victory.[8]

Here we recognize the influence of Speyr, as Balthasar describes the agony of Christ's suffering in the images of 'the void' and 'the bottomless abyss', which result from Christ's bearing the sin of the world to the point of being forsaken and abandoned by God. We also see the uniqueness and substitutionary character of Jesus Christ's suffering and death. The suffering that Christ endures and the death that he dies are restricted to him alone. Christ is our representative and our substitute. Through Christ's death, which he alone dies, humanity is spared the terror and horror of the second death – 'no one will ever experience what it really means to die'.

A final element present in *Heart of the World* that will inform Balthasar's entire theological work is the centrality of the doctrine of the Trinity. Balthasar insists that we must ground all theological reflection regarding soteriology and atonement in the triune life of God. Balthasar writes:

---

8   Ibid., p. 175.

For let us not forget: if human limits became capable of receiving God's fullness, this was through a gift of God and not through the creature's own ability to contain it. Only God can expand the finite to infinity without shattering it. And greater still than the miracle that a heart can be extended to God's proportions is the marvel that God was able to shrink to man's proportions; that the Ruler's mind was contained in the mind of the servant; that the Father's eternal vision, without annulling itself, became blinded even to the blindness of a trampled worm; that the perfect Yes to the Father's will could be uttered in the midst of a storm of impulses impelling the death-tormented Lamb to take flight; that the eternal distance of love between Father and Son (eternally enclosing itself by the embrace of both in the Spirit) could gape wide as the distance between heaven and hell, from whose pit the Son groans his 'I thirst,' the Spirit now no longer anything but the huge, separating and impassable chaos; that the Trinity could, in suffering's distorted image, so disfigure itself into the relationship between judge and sinner; that eternal love could don the mask of divine wrath; that the Abyss of Being could so deplete itself into an abyss of nothingness.[9]

For Balthasar, the possibility of redemption through the suffering, death and descent of Christ into hell lies in the Trinitarian life of God.

In *Heart of the World*, Balthasar embarks on a path that he will follow throughout his theological career. This path includes characteristics that we discussed above, i.e., the descent into hell, the vicarious character of Christ's person and work, the passion of Jesus Christ as his bearing the sin of the world and enduring the wrath of God, the possibility of participation by believers – through obedience and discipleship – in Christ and the location of all of this within the Trinitarian relations of the Godhead. The contemplative theology of *Heart of the World* is augmented by Balthasar's voluminous theological writings that follow. In occasional pieces, sermons and in his theological trilogy, Balthasar circles around these themes, drawing them from different angles and different vantage points. He probes the density of these themes through biblical exegesis, exploration into the history of theology and creative theological reflection and construction. These themes are expanded, and others are added, but they are never abandoned.[10]

---

9 Ibid., p. 54.
10 Andrew Louth points to the significance of *Heart of the World* in terms of both form and content, style and material, in concluding his fine study, 'The very language and structure of the work are significant. The relation of God to man, of Christ's redemption and our response, is so close that they cannot be separated – and so the book is in some ways repetitive, though it is the repetition of a spiral, not of a circle. Also the style is appropriate to a mystery that entices us and involves us: it comes as no surprise that when Balthasar eventually writes a dogmatics it is called *Theodramatik*, or (perhaps it is the same thing) when Balthasar focuses his concern with beauty and form on one art form, it is drama. But enough has been said to show how the fundamental perceptions of Balthasar's theology have already crystallised in this early work, so that *Heart of the World* can be seen to contain *in nuce* not only the characteristic themes of his theology, but also the style which is inseparable from the apprehension of these themes.' Louth, 'The Place of *Heart of the World*', p. 163.

The shape of Balthasar's soteriology

Having recognized the importance of the descent into hell for Balthasar from the very beginning of his theological work, we will now discuss the general shape of his soteriology. This overview will enable us to see clearly how the confession of the descent into hell functions in Balthasar's soteriology and in his complete theological vision.

In a sermon, 'Bought at a Great Price', preached during Holy Week with 1 Corinthians 6:20 as its text, Balthasar concisely elucidates his vision of the significance of Jesus Christ's passion:

> 'Bought at a great price.' The first Christians were well aware of this when they put these two little words, *'pro nobis,'* at the heart of the Creed. It was 'for us' that the Son came down from heaven, 'for us' that he was crucified, died and was buried. And this means not only 'for our benefit' but also 'in our place,' taking over what was our due. If this is watered down, the fundamental tenet of the New Testament disappears and it looks as if God is always reconciled, sin is always forgiven and overcome, irrespective of Christ's self-surrender; then the Cross becomes merely a particularly eloquent symbol of God's unchanging kindness, only a symbol, indicating something but not effecting anything. There would no longer be a Lamb of God who takes away the sins of the world. No longer would God 'reconcile the world to himself,' as Paul explicitly says, 'through his Son.' Without noticing it, we have become like the men of the Enlightenment, aware of God's kindly disposition but refusing to countenance his anger over sin, of which Scripture speaks so insistently, because it does not fit in with our enlightened concept of God; in the end we make it all into an anemic, transparent philosophy. Then, as a result, what Grünewald endeavored to portray in his crucifixion seems to us to be a tasteless medieval exaggeration. And the high price becomes a cheap price; costly grace becomes cheap grace.[11]

Clearly, central to Balthasar's understanding of soteriology is the substitutionary character of Jesus Christ's work. Jesus Christ does something for humanity that is impossible for humanity to carry out. This substitutionary work is focused in the passion of Christ. Christ's passion begins in Gethsemane and includes the cross and the descent into hell is the height of Jesus Christ's work for humanity and is not solely exemplary or revelatory; it is not a mere 'eloquent symbol'. Rather, these events actually effect something, namely, the removal of sin and the destruction of death.

The gravity of Jesus Christ's substitutionary work is seen in his bearing the sins of the world and his suffering at the hands of a wrathful God. This gravity is expressed in Jesus Christ's request to be spared from having to drink the 'cup', which contains God's wrath, and in the purity of his obedience in accepting this

---

11   Hans Urs von Balthasar, *You Crown the Year with Your Goodness: Radio Sermons*, trans. Graham Harrison (San Francisco: Ignatius Press, 1989), pp. 78–9.

'cup' if it were the Father's will. In a sermon for Good Friday, 'The Scapegoat and the Trinity', Balthasar describes the horror and emptiness of Christ's being forsaken by the Father in our place and for our salvation:

> The man who cries out knows only that he is forsaken; in this darkness he no longer knows why. He is not permitted to know why, for the idea that the darkness he is undergoing might be on behalf of others would constitute a certain comfort; it would give him a ray of light. No such comfort can be granted him now, for the issue, in absolute seriousness, is that of purifying the relationship between God and the guilty world.[12]

This substitutionary suffering that leads to the isolation of the forsaken Christ is salvific only because of his unique relationship to God, only because he is the incarnate Son of God. No mere human, no matter how pure and innocent, is capable of embracing the world's sin and bearing it away. Balthasar's vision of Jesus Christ's substitutionary death does not involve the punishment of an innocent human victim meant to appease God's anger and prompt God to cancel the sentence that humanity was obligated to serve, a kind of *quid pro quo*. Rather, Christ's substitutionary death is efficacious solely because it goes beyond the death of a mere human, as it is the human death of the eternal Son of God incarnate.

> Jesus, the Crucified, endures our inner darkness and estrangement from God, and he does so in our place. It is all the more painful for him, the less he has merited it . . . it is utterly alien and full of horror. Indeed, he suffers more deeply than an ordinary man is capable of suffering, even were he condemned and rejected by God, because only the incarnate Son knows who the Father really is and what it means to be deprived of him, to have lost him (to all appearances) forever.[13]

Balthasar affirms the centrality of the passion for a proper theological under-standing of the life and significance of Jesus Christ. Consequently, he devotes himself to the exegesis of various biblical passages that are striking because of their particularity, and that affirm universality as a result of this uncompromising particularity. These passages include: 2 Corinthians 5:14 'one has died for all; therefore all have died', 5:19 'in Christ God was reconciling the world to himself', 5:21 'For our sake he made him to be sin who knew no sin, so that in him we might become the righteousness of God', and Galatians 3:13 'Christ redeemed us from the curse of the law, having become a curse for us'.[14]

---

12 Ibid., p. 84.

13 Ibid., p. 85.

14 William Thompson comments on the centrality of these passages for Balthasar, and also for Barth, and the tradition within which this decision places them. 'Balthasar and his theological mentor Karl Barth are two contemporary theologians taking their bearings most extensively from the trajectory of Gal 3:13 and 2 Cor 5:21. They make a strong case for some form of atonement understood as vicarious and/or substitutionary and are in a line running back to John Wesley; to Bérulle, Olier, with the seventeenth-century French School of Spirituality; to Calvin and Luther; to Aquinas and Anselm's *Cur*

We now move to the centre of Balthasar's theological vision and dogmatic work, the *Theo-Drama: Theological Dramatic Theory*.[15] Furthermore, the centre of the *Theo-Drama*, in Balthasar's mind, is the mystery of the atonement, and it is this mystery that informs every other aspect of dogmatic theology. The doctrine of the atonement is no isolated doctrine; rather, it impinges upon all other doctrines within the purview of dogmatic theology. For Balthasar, all doctrines are interconnected, and soteriology and the doctrine of the atonement lie at the centre of this interconnected web.

Balthasar contends that Scripture in its entirety points to the passion of Jesus Christ. Everything in the Old Testament leads to the death of Christ on the cross, and everything in the life of Christ points to this event.[16] The passion narrative marks the climax of the gospel writers' witness to the life of Jesus. Although the passion contains continuity with the life of Jesus, which precedes it, the passion is a unique event, and there is a rupture between the words and deeds of Jesus and the passion of Jesus – the 'hour'. Balthasar insists upon a rupture between the 'life' of Jesus and the 'hour' of his passion, because he denies that the death of Christ is the mere outcome of his vocation, an event that can be fully explained in historical

---

Deus Homo; to Augustine, and even to the Greek fathers. In my view, Luther and Calvin, followed by Barth, bring a new and nearly unmatched emphasis and creativity to their exploration of this rich trajectory. Reformation sensitivities, and a heightened sensitivity to human evil and sin, are likely factors at work here. On the Roman side, Balthasar is analogous.' William M. Thompson, *The Struggle for Theology's Soul: Contesting Scripture in Christology* (New York: The Crossroad Publishing Company, 1996), p. 175.

15   In Edward Oakes' estimation Balthasar's crowning theological accomplishment can be found in his response to a pointed statement by Gregory Nazianzus, which Balthasar uses to begin his study of the mystery of Easter – *Mysterium Paschale*. The words of Gregory are as follows: 'Our task now is to consider that problem, that part of Christian teaching, which is so often passed over in silence but which – for that very reason – I want to study with all the more eagerness. That precious and glorious divine Blood poured out for us: for what reason and to what end has such an extraordinary price been paid?'

'In answering this question', Oakes observes, 'Balthasar has reached the apex of his theological achievement, for I regard the last three volumes of the Theodramatics as the culmination and capstone of his work, where all the themes of his theology converge and are fused into a synthesis of remarkable creativity and originality, an achievement that makes him one of the great theological mind[s] of the twentieth century. Here, more than anywhere, is where his work should be judged. But this is also the most difficult part of his work to summarize, not only because so many themes converge but also because of the way they are then, as it were, dramatically "compacted" by the descent of the dead Jesus into the realm of the dead and "reversed" by the victory of the resurrection. That is, through the density of this event, all of the previous themes of Balthasar's thought are not just intensified but also converted and upended in the "great reversal" that took place between God and the dead man Jesus during the Triduum of Good Friday, Holy Saturday and Easter Sunday'. Edward T. Oakes, *Pattern of Redemption: The Theology of Hans Urs von Balthasar* (New York: Continuum, 1994), p. 230.

16   See Balthasar's introduction to his treatment of the passion in *The Glory of The Lord*, volume VII, his biblical theology of the New Testament. Hans Urs von Balthasar, *The Glory of the Lord: A Theological Aesthetics*, volume VII, *Theology: The New Covenant*, ed. John Riches, trans. Brian McNeil, C.R.V. (San Francisco: Ignatius Press, 1989), p. 202.

terms alone. There is a rupture because there is a movement from Jesus being active to his engaging in complete passive obedience, and God then becoming the primary actor. Balthasar also insists on the novelty of the passion, because the passion or the 'hour' is not something that Jesus brings about due to his own activity; rather it is something for which he awaits and which ultimately overtakes him. 'Jesus refuses to anticipate either the time or the content of the hour, yet he sees them both, time and content, as something that God has immutably appointed (*dei*) and that he, the Son has unconditionally to go through' (*TD* IV, p. 234).

Balthasar summarizes his view of the relationship between the life of Jesus and the hour towards which this life moves as follows:

> There is perfect unity between the (active) life of Jesus and his 'hour', but it would be wrong, for the sake of preserving continuity ('solidarity with sinners,' and so forth), to gloss over the deep incision this hour represents. His life leads up to the hour. (When Mark 3:6 says that his enemies had already decided to 'destroy him' as soon as he began his ministry, we cannot assume that he was unaware of this.) However, his life remains the result of his own initiative, whereas, in the hour, it is his 'being given up' that dominates. He is given up by men, by Christians, Jews and Gentiles, and finally by the Father too. This is a seemingly passive letting-things-happen, but once Jesus, in Gethsemane, has wrestled and won through to it, it clearly becomes a 'super-action' in which he is at one with a demand that goes beyond all limits, a demand that could only be made of *him*. (*TD* IV, p. 237)

The transition from the active life of Jesus to the hour of his passion is determined by the obedience of Jesus. Jesus awaits the hour, which was appointed for him by God, and he accepts the entire content of this hour in obedience, by allowing the will of God to prevail. Through obedience, Jesus ensures that he is not a mere victim who suffers at the hands of an arbitrary and angry God. Rather, Jesus willingly accepts the suffering that results from his bearing the sin of the world. Jesus does not determine the time or the content of the hour; he does not commit suicide in a heroic attempt to save the world. At the same time, Jesus is not a passive victim, used as a pawn in God's vicious act of retribution. For Balthasar, it is the obedience of Jesus to the will of God, and further of the Son to the Father in the intra-Trinitarian life of God, that defines the shape of the 'hour' of Jesus' passion.

As we have emphasized, the central element of Balthasar's interpretation of the passion is the substitutionary character of Jesus Christ's life and passion. Balthasar is not merely concerned with an emphasis on Jesus Christ's passion; he is concerned specifically with the interpretation of the passion as something done on our behalf and in our place. It is this *pro nobis* character of Christ's death that Balthasar explicates in his constructive treatment of the atonement. As Balthasar affirms:

> The *pro nobis* is the central theme of the purification of the covenant and the creation of a New Covenant. Here the apparently irreconcilable postulates come together: on the one hand, there is a judgment, and there must be

atonement; on the other there is the triumph of grace, in and through judgment, so that the covenant may be definitely reestablished in a totally new way. (*TD* IV, p. 239)

This *pro nobis* is not only the interpretative key for reading Jesus Christ's passion; it also determines our view of God and of the Church. Since the passion is the centre of the gospel narratives and in turn the centre of Scripture, the atonement becomes the centre of theology and the doctrine that determines the shape of all other doctrines. Since Balthasar insists that the *pro nobis* is the central interpretation of the 'hour', then he must further conclude that 'It [the *pro nobis*] unlocks not only all Christology but the entire Trinitarian doctrine of God that flows from it, as well as the doctrine of the Church. At the heart of the Nicene Creed stands the *crucifixus etiam pro nobis*; it already contains the words *propter nostram salutem descendit de caelis*' (*TD* IV, p. 239).

In order to establish a template for his own constructive view of atonement, Balthasar determines five essential elements of atonement in the New Testament. These five elements must be incorporated into any contemporary interpretation of the redemptive significance of Christ's passion, if this interpretation is to be biblical, ecclesial, and therefore theologically acceptable.

The first feature of atonement in the New Testament is the affirmation that the redemptive significance of Jesus Christ's passion depends upon God's active involvement. The passion is not the suffering and death of a mere exemplary individual as the result of a violent response to his message and actions. Rather, the passion involves God's handing over God's 'only Son' for the salvation of the world. Jesus is the one whom God has 'given up'. We cannot stop here, though, for Jesus is not given up by God as a passive victim; rather, Jesus surrenders himself and allows himself to be given up by God. Jesus lays down his own life (John 10:17). Following the logic of the Epistle to the Hebrews, Balthasar recognizes that by emphasizing Jesus' being given up by God as well as his actively consenting to be given up, we may view Jesus as both the sacrificial Lamb and Priest.

The second feature of atonement in the New Testament is a result of the first. In giving himself up for humanity, Jesus changes places with humanity. Here the emphasis is on a real transaction between God and humanity in the person and work of Jesus. The redemptive activity of God in Christ does not take place outside of humanity; rather, humanity is intimately involved in a genuine exchange of places – the 'wondrous exchange' – the *admirabile commercium*. This exchange of places effects genuine reconciliation, and this reconciliation precedes any active consent or acceptance on the part of humanity. The exchange of places means that 'we are ontologically "transferred" (Col 1:13) and expropriated (1 Cor 6:19; 2 Cor 5:15; Rom 14:7), insofar as, in the Paschal event, we have died with Christ and are risen with him (Rom 6:3ff; Col 3:3; Eph 2:5)' (*TD* IV, p. 242). The exchange of places reveals that Jesus, as the 'Lamb of God who takes away the sins of the world' (John 1:29), genuinely takes on the sins of the world and bears them away. Jesus actually 'becomes sin' so that humanity may 'become the righteousness of God' (2 Corinthians 5:21). Further, the exchange of places, which involves Jesus Christ's bearing humanity's sin so that humanity may become righteous, requires an intimate relationship between Jesus, as the Lamb, and God. No mere human, no matter how virtuous and innocent, has the capacity to bear the sin of the world to the effect that sin is destroyed and humanity is made righteous. Only the incarnate Son of God can fill this role. The sacrificial Lamb must be more than an innocent victim. 'It must be really the Lamb of "God", *God's* Lamb, who occupies the place of sin, otherwise he could not so occupy it' (*TD* IV, p. 241).

The fruit of God's handing over the Son and the Son's giving up of himself to the point of an exchange of places may be considered, first of all, as liberation. This is the third essential element of atonement in the New Testament. Redemption involves being liberated *from* various burdens. God's redemptive activity in the passion of Christ includes liberation from: 'slavery to sin (Rom 7; Jn 8:34), from the devil (Jn 8:44; 1 Jn 3:8), from the "world powers" (Gal 4:3; Col 2:20), from the power of darkness (Col 1:13), from the law (Rom 7:1) and from the "law of sin and death" (Rom 8:2) and, finally, from the "wrath to come" (1 Th 1:10)' (*TD* IV, 242). Viewed as a liberating activity, Christ's passion may be interpreted as ransom (Mark 10:45), propitiation (Romans 3:25) and as an expiation, which involves blood and without which there is no forgiveness (Hebrews 9:22).

The fruit of God's redemptive activity in Christ is indeed liberation, but it is also more than liberation. Humanity is redeemed *from* something through the passion of Christ, but humanity is also redeemed *for* something through this work. We are not only liberated from various forms of oppression; through this liberation, we are freed for a new form of existence in which 'we are *drawn into the divine, trinitarian life*' (*TD* IV, p. 242). For Balthasar, 'The "redemption through his blood, the forgiveness of sins" is only one element within the all-embracing divine purpose. God's purpose is to enable us, by grace, to share in Christ's sonship (Eph 1:5ff) by becoming "members of his body" (1 Cor 12; Eph 4, and so forth)' (*TD* IV, pp. 242–3).

The fifth and final element essential to atonement in the New Testament treats the question of initiative. Jesus Christ's passion does not arise from the anger of God. God's anger does not need to be appeased in order for God to be reconciled to humanity. God is not an enemy of humanity; rather, humans are enemies of God. Humanity must therefore be reconciled to God, and must be transformed from foe to friend. This reconciliation is possible only through God's merciful and forgiving love. Love is primary in God's redemptive activity in the passion of Christ, and this divine love uses wrath as a way of accomplishing reconciliation. There is no tension between divine love and divine wrath, and Balthasar insists that we must not think that God's wrath needs to be satisfied in order for God's love to be in effect. Balthasar insists again and again that 'the entire reconciliation process is attributed to God's merciful *love*. On the basis of the love of the Father

(Rom 8:39) and of Christ (Rom 8:35), the Son was given up "for us all" (Rom 8:32) by the Father. It is God's immense love for the world that has caused him to give up his only Son (John 3:16) and thereby to reconcile the world to himself (2 Cor 5:19; Col 1:20)' (*TD* IV, p. 243).

Balthasar insists that a truly ecclesial soteriology must incorporate all five New Testament elements. These elements must be held together, yet they must be granted a certain amount of autonomy. One cannot be absorbed by another. The demands of holding these five elements together inhibits, in Balthasar's mind, the systematizing of Christ's redemptive passion and the construction of a single theory of atonement. The task of developing a genuinely biblical and ecclesial soteriology, one that holds together these five elements, faces three primary dangers. First, one must refrain from emphasizing one element at the neglect of the others. Second, one must employ the biblical concepts and terminology and must not engage in a strong translation, which intends to make the biblical language understandable to the contemporary person. In Balthasar's words, 'The full content of the central assertion (which is the goal of all five aspects) may not be replaced by some alleged equivalent that is more "intelligible" to the spirit of a different epoch but in fact lacks the center of gravity of the biblical assertion' (*TD* IV, p. 243). Third, one must not overlook the tension between any two of these elements. One must not attempt to resolve or dissolve the tension; rather, the tension must 'be *endured*' (*TD* IV, p. 243).

After laying out what he considers to be the five essential elements of atonement in the New Testament, which need to be accounted for equally, Balthasar presents an extended treatment of various interpretations of atonement in the history of theology. The thread that runs through Balthasar's review of the interpretation of atonement in the history of theology is his emphasis on the true identification of Jesus Christ with sinful humanity – a realistic understanding of Jesus' taking on the world's sin. He faults the Fathers for not going far enough in their explication of the 'wondrous exchange'. He departs from Anselm at the specific point of the meaning of Jesus Christ's death. It is not Jesus' death as an innocent and pure man that is meritorious or redemptive, as Balthasar reads Anselm; rather, it is Christ's taking on the sin of the world and enduring the consequences of sin that is redemptive.[17] Thomas, though an improvement on Anselm, also has a shallow reading of the passion. Thomas stops short of affirming true contact between Christ and the sinners for whom he suffered and died.[18] Though Balthasar's overall

---

17   For Balthasar's interpretation of Anselm see *TD* IV, pp. 260–1.

18   Thomas does view the passion as more than an exemplary symbol, which expresses God's constant and antecedent desire to be reconciled with the world. The passion, for Thomas, is indeed the very event that accomplishes the redemption of humanity by satisfying God's wrath and turning away God's anger from the sinner. Balthasar sees this as an improvement on Anselm, but he is troubled by Thomas' explication of the passion. According to Balthasar, Thomas fails to recognize the central importance of Christ's actual experience of abandonment by the Father, which is illustrated most clearly in Thomas' affirmation that Christ is never without the beatific vision. Balthasar rejects this. The gravity of Christ's

critique of Karl Rahner is extensive and unrelenting, in this instance the criticism centres on the salvific character of Christ's passion.[19] According to Balthasar, Rahner's view of the cross lacks the dramatic element that is central to an adequate soteriology – Christ's passion actually effects something; it is not a mere illustration or eloquent symbol. For Rahner, according to Balthasar's critique, the death of Jesus does not involve his bearing the sin of the world and effecting the destruction of sin, the defeat of death, and the inauguration of a new creation. Rather, the death of Jesus is an unsurpassed example of complete self-surrender to God. This death is an example to be emulated rather than a unique event that is salvific in and of itself.

Balthasar's dramatic soteriology

With Balthasar's treatment of soteriology in the history of theology, and his evaluation of New Testament soteriology as the backdrop, we can now address his own constructive proposal regarding atonement and his own interpretation of Christ's passion. Balthasar's stated objective in reflecting on the significance of Christ's passion hinges on the attempt to hold all five New Testament elements together. In order to accomplish this goal, Balthasar will 'try to see all the biblical data together, along with all the valid and fruitful motifs that arise during the history of theology' (*TD* IV, p. 319). This is an ambitious and complicated objective, and it precludes any systematizing, a tendency in modern theology that Balthasar rigorously challenges.

For our purposes, namely, to explicate and analyse the function of the descent into hell in Balthasar's soteriology and interpretation of the passion, I will restrict my comments on Balthasar's dramatic soteriology to two elements. The first element is the importance of the Trinity for a proper interpretation of the cross. The second is Balthasar's understanding of 'representation', which includes Jesus Christ's bearing the sin of the world and enduring the wrath of God.

For Balthasar, the Trinity makes the passion of Jesus Christ intelligible. Here

---

suffering is overlooked by Thomas, and he falls short of affirming a true exchange of places, in which Christ bears the sin of the world so that humans might be made righteous.

19   For a fine treatment of the extent of Balthasar's critique of Rahner see: Rowan Williams, 'Balthasar and Rahner', in *The Analogy of Beauty*, ed. John Riches (Edinburgh: T & T Clark, 1986), pp. 11–34.

Balthasar grounds his critique of Rahner's view of Christ's passion in Rahner's theological method – this is the source that leads to the specific doctrinal problem in the area of atonement and soteriology. For Balthasar, it is Rahner's unyielding drive towards systematizing and his apologetic goal of translating aspects of Christian faith, confession, and doctrine into concepts and terminology that will be intelligible to the modern world that leads to his inadequate understanding of the salvific nature of Christ's passion. Rahner, according to Balthasar, 'seeks to put theology's fundamental structure into a tightly ordered system – together with the philosophy that is inseparable from it. As a result, many elements or the organism of Christian faith that have been handed down to us must either drop out or be entirely reinterpreted.' Balthasar, *TD* IV, pp. 273–4.

we see the importance of elements one and five of the New Testament elements of atonement. The passion of Christ takes place only from the initiative of God's love, and the passion involves the Father's 'giving up' the Son and the Son's self-surrender. Further, the passion is efficacious solely because of the hypostatic union; Jesus as mere man is incapable of bearing the sins of the world in such a way that sin is destroyed and humanity is reconciled with God.

Balthasar retains the significant distinction between the immanent Trinity and the economic Trinity, and desists from completely following Rahner's maxim 'The economic Trinity *is* the immanent Trinity, and vice versa', in order to avoid collapsing the immanent into the economic. In Balthasar's estimation, this close identification leads to an improper accent on the economic activity of God at the expense of affirming the completeness of the life of God apart from the created world. The identification of the immanent Trinity and the economic Trinity, Balthasar warns, leads to a mythological picture of God in which God is caught up in and determined by the world. Balthasar denies that the immanent Trinity is constituted by the economic Trinity. His primary objective in affirming the distinction, without separation, between the immanent Trinity and the economic Trinity is to avoid two extremes. On the one hand, Balthasar wants to avoid any strain of process theology, which leads to subjecting God to the world process. This leads to a tragic and mythological view of God. On the other hand, he wants to affirm that Christ's passion does not leave God unaffected. Balthasar rejects any view of God that sees God as static, abstract or self-enclosed. He insists that there are dynamic relations internal to the Godhead, which provide the possibility for God's relationship with the world. God's relationship with the world does not introduce dynamic movement into an otherwise static divine existence.[20] God does not hover above the suffering of Jesus Christ. God is somehow involved in this suffering.

Although Balthasar does not allow a view of the Trinity in which the immanent Trinity is somehow constituted by the economic Trinity, he does not ignore the economic activity of God as present in history and narrated in Scripture. Balthasar does not engage in idealist speculation in his treatment of the Trinitarian life of God. Rather, he engages in an extrapolation from the actuality of the cross to an affirmation of God's Trinitarian life. The order of being moves from the eternal procession of the Son by the Father to creation, then to establishment of the covenant, and culminates in the incarnation, which is inseparable from the cross.

---

20   Balthasar is clear in his denial of any dependence of God on the world for divine self-actualization. 'It is pointless to call this primal drama [the begetting of the Son by the Father], which is above all time, "static", "abstract", 'self-enclosed". Those who do so imagine that the divine drama only acquires its dynamism and its many hues by going through a created, temporal world and only acquires its seriousness and depth by going through sin, the Cross and hell. This view betrays a hubris, an exaggerated self-importance, on the part of creaturely freedom; it has succumbed to the illusion that man's ability to say No to God actually limits the divine omnipotence. It imagines that, by saying No to God, it is *man* who has drawn God into a momentous drama and made him consider how he (God) may extract himself from a trap he himself has set.' *TD* IV, pp. 326–7.

The order of knowing begins with the cross and moves back through incarnation, covenant and creation, to the ineffable mystery of the Trinity. Balthasar works back from the actuality of Christ's passion to the mystery of the divine life.

> There is only one way to approach the Trinitarian life in God: on the basis of what is manifest in God's kenosis in the theology of the covenant – and thence in the theology of the Cross – *we must feel our way back into the mystery of the absolute*, employing a negative theology that excludes from God all intramundane experience and suffering, while at the same time presupposing that the possibility of such experience and suffering – up to and including its christological and Trinitarian implications – is grounded in God. To think in such a way is to walk on a knife edge: it avoids all the fashionable talk of 'the pain of God' and yet is bound to say that something happens in God that not only justifies the possibility and actual occurrence of all suffering in the world but also justifies God's sharing in the latter, in which he goes to the length of vicariously taking on man's God-lessness. The very thing that negative ('philosophical') theology prohibits seems to be demanded by the *oikonomia* in Christ: faith, which is beyond both yet feels its way forward from both, has an intuition of the mystery of all mysteries, which we must posit as the unfathomable precondition and source of the world's salvation history [my emphasis].
> (*TD* IV, p. 324)

Balthasar considers the immanent Trinity as the 'unfathomable precondition and source of the world's salvation history' in light of what he speaks of as the 'primal kenosis'.[21] The eternal generation of the Son by the Father is the primal kenosis, which makes the kenosis of creation and covenant, and, in turn, the kenosis of the incarnation possible. In this 'primal kenosis', the Father 'gives' his divinity away to the Son in such a way that the Father does not 'lose' any quantity of his divinity, and in a way that the Son 'possesses' this divinity in a fashion equal to the Father. Balthasar describes divine self-giving and its consequent 'separation' between the persons of the Trinity as he states:

---

21 A proper interpretation of Balthasar on this point depends upon a clear understanding of the relationship between the immanent Trinity and the economic Trinity. Gerard O'Hanlon demonstrates the importance of recognizing the proper relationship between the immanent Trinity and the economic Trinity as he writes, 'On the Cross (with the descent into hell of Christ) the full distance between the Father and Son is visible as never before. The Holy Spirit who continues to unite them does so in a way which appears precisely as this distance. In this we are given an insight into the full seriousness of the inner-divine drama. This drama of the immanent Trinity, revealed in the economic, can be appreciated properly only if one avoids an incorrect notion of the relationship between the immanent and economic Trinity. It will not do, like Rahner, to identify too closely the two, emphasising the economic Trinity excessively and formalising the immanent. Nor may one, like Moltmann, propose a Hegelian-type identification in which the cross is seen as the fulfilment of the Trinity in a Process Theology-like way which has no difficulty in directly ascribing change and suffering to God, and which ends up with a mythological, tragic image of God.' Gerard F. O'Hanlon, S.J., *The Immutability of God In the Theology of Hans Urs von Balthasar* (Cambridge: Cambridge University Press, 1990), p. 37.

> God the Father can give his divinity away in such a manner that it is not merely 'lent' to the Son: the Son's possession of it is 'equally substantial'. This implies such an incomprehensible and unique 'separation' of God from himself that it *includes* and grounds every other separation – be it never so dark and bitter. (*TD* IV, p. 325)

God exists in this manner of self-giving and in no other. This self-giving is not dependent upon God's entering into the process of the created world; the world is not necessary for God's self-actualization. This self-giving takes place eternally, and it is only in this self-giving that God is God. Balthasar summarizes:

> The Father, in uttering and surrendering himself without reserve, does not lose himself. He does not extinguish himself by self-giving, just as he does not keep back anything of himself either. For, in this self-surrender, he *is* the whole divine essence. Here we see both God's infinite power and his powerlessness; he cannot be God in any other way but in this 'kenosis' within Godhead itself. (*TD* IV, p. 325)

Although we must insist that creation is not necessary for God's self-actualization, we must affirm the profound fittingness of creation. Since God is most accurately understood as self-giving, the self-giving that takes place within the eternal triune life of God is not restricted to God alone; God does not hoard, so to speak, the divine self-giving that stems from absolute love. Rather, God as absolute love desires to share the loving self-giving of the eternal Trinity with something outside of himself, i.e. creatures and creation. Hence, creation is neither necessary nor is it utterly arbitrary. It is fitting given the identity of God as absolute love.

The procession of the Son from the Father grounds both the creation of the world and the incarnation of the Son of God – the 'mission'[22] of Jesus Christ, which includes his acceptance of the 'hour' – the bearing of the sin of the world, death by crucifixion and the descent into hell. The world is created within the generation of the Son, his procession; therefore, the world can be redeemed only through the activity of the Son, which is his 'mission'. The significance of locating the world within the generation of Son by the Father is the affirmation that God does not need the world in order to be fully realized. There is genuine dynamic activity within the triune life of God and the creation of the world, which includes God's involvement in the world through incarnation, is an utterly gracious act on God's part and takes place without any trace of necessity. Though Balthasar indeed emphasizes God's independence from the world, at the same time he affirms God's real involvement with the world. This involvement is possible only because of the dynamic character of the divine life. God is not aloof, yet God is not dependent

---

22 Balthasar employs the concept of mission as the central concept that guides his Christology. Balthasar, like Barth, rejects any separation of Christ's person from Christ's work, and is confident that using mission as the central concept to guide his Christology will prevent any separation. See *TD* III, pp. 149–50.

upon the world. Again, Balthasar wants to walk the perilous path between talk of a 'suffering God' and talk of an isolated, thoroughly immutable God.[23] A proper view of God's relationship with the world must be approached from two sides, 'from that of negative theology, which excludes as 'mythology' any notion that God *has to* be involved in the world process; and from the point of the view of the world drama, the possibilities of which must be grounded in God' (*TD* IV, p. 327). Balthasar honours the traditional view of God's immutability, and God's independence from creation, yet he insists that we must consider the concrete events of history, especially the passion of Jesus Christ, as genuinely revelatory. If we take the events of history seriously, then we must make room for the possibility of suffering in God.[24]

From the primal kenosis of the Son's being eternally begotten from the Father, we move to the kenosis of creation and covenant. God's activity in creation involves a certain amount of 'self-limitation' as God grants freedom to creatures. God engages in risk by endowing with freedom creatures who might exercise this freedom through rejection of and resistance to divine love. In the 'kenosis' of God's covenant with the people of Israel, God pledges himself to an indissoluble

---

23 Fergus Kerr notes the following about Balthasar's view of God: 'Balthasar insists that we must avoid reducing God to one more suffering being in the world. But he is even more sensitive to the traditional temptation to attach so much importance to the immutability of God that we remove him from solidarity with the tragic predicament of humankind. Far from being static, as people are inclined to think, the inner mystery of the divine life is endlessly dynamic and dramatic. The drama consists primarily in the circle of the eternal self-emptying of the three divine persons. The Father wills to be Father only with the Son, and so from all eternity gives his being away to the Son. The Son, in turn, gives his being back to the Father, again from all eternity. This self-emptying of the Son to the Father is such that the Son is willing to undertake in obedience to the Father the mission to save humanity. The self-emptying of the Incarnation is simply the historical form of the self-emptying by which the Son is always who he is in relationship to the Father.' Fergus Kerr, 'The Doctrine of the Atonement: Recent Roman Catholic Theology', *Epworth Review* 22 (1995), p. 22.

24 Balthasar affirms the genuine fear experienced by Jesus in the face of the hour that is about to overtake him. This hour is an essential part of his mission, which he willingly accepts, and it is in the hour that Jesus hands over the control of his mission and responds in pure obedience. At this point, Balthasar insists that we must address the possibility of suffering in God. Commenting on John 12:27, 'Now is my soul troubled. And what shall I say? "Father, save me from this hour"? No, for this purpose I have come to this hour', Balthasar writes, 'At this point, where the subject undergoing the "hour" is the Son speaking with the Father, the controversial "Theopaschist formula" has its proper place: "One of the Trinity has suffered." The strict Antiochenes did not like this; for them, only the humanity of Christ could suffer, not God. But the formula can already be found in Gregory Nazianzen: "We needed a God who took flesh and was put to death", a "crucified God", and the twelfth of Cyril's condemnations put it in an almost provocative way: "If any one does not confess that the Word of God suffered in the flesh and was crucified in the flesh and in the flesh tasted death and became the first-born from among the dead . . . *anathema sit*." . . . If it is possible for one Person in God to accept suffering, to the extent of Godforsakenness, and to deem it his own, then evidently it is not something foreign to God, something that does not affect him. It must be something profoundly appropriate to his divine Person, for – to say it once again – his being sent (*missio*) by the Father is a modality of his proceeding (*processio*) from the Father.' *TD* III, p. 226.

covenant, on God's side, with a people who possess the freedom to reject God and break this covenant. Finally, there is the kenosis of the incarnation of the Son of God, which is the fulfilment of the kenosis of the covenant. The reality of creation, covenant and incarnation is dependent upon the Trinitarian life of God and the primal kenosis of the eternal generation of the Son by the Father.

The location of soteriology within the Trinitarian life of God determines how we are to understand his emphasis on the descent into hell. The Trinity establishes the ground for the incarnate Son's bearing the world's sin to the extreme of being abandoned and forsaken by the Father. The 'distance' between the Father and the Son provides the space for the radical separation experienced by the Son, who has taken on the condition of sin, from the Father. The eternal self-giving of the Father is the ontological condition for the possibility for the extravagance of the self-giving of the Son in willingly taking on the world's sin and enduring the abandonment that this sin necessitates. In speaking of the possibility and actuality of the incarnation, Balthasar writes, 'The exteriorisation of God (in the Incarnation) has its ontic condition of possibility in the eternal exteriorisation of God – that is, in his tripersonal self-gift' (*MP*, p. 28). The eternal 'exteriorisation' of God not only provides the ontological condition for the possibility of Christ's incarnation and his redemptive death; it is also mysteriously more profound than any manifestation of this exteriorization in the created world, in the economy of salvation.

> Everything that can be thought and imagined where God is concerned is, in advance, included and transcended in this self-destitution which constitutes the person of the Father, and, at the same time, those of the Son and the Spirit. God as the 'gulf' of absolute Love contains in advance, eternally, all the modalities of love, of compassion, and even of a 'separation' motivated by love and founded on the infinite distinction between hypostases – modalities which may manifest themselves in the course of a history of salvation involving sinful humankind. (*MP*, p. viii)

In the final analysis, the depth of Jesus Christ's suffering and his abandonment by the Father, which takes place in the cross and the descent into hell, points to the more profound separation and distance that exists within the Trinitarian relations motivated by absolute love.[25] This separation and distance, which is the result of the Father's complete self-giving, encompasses and surpasses all creaturely separation and distance, including the death of Jesus Christ and his being plunged into the depths of hell.

Although Balthasar is circumspect in his use of language of 'primal kenosis', 'separation' and 'distance', this potentially speculative language risks undermining Balthasar's conviction regarding the unity of God and the eternally perichoretic relationship among the members of the Trinity. Even given Balthasar's insistence

---

25 Balthasar insists that 'God is not, in the first place, "absolute power", but "absolute love" and his sovereignty manifests itself not in holding on to what is its own but in its abandonment.' *MP*, p. 28.

on the analogical and metaphorical function of theological language, one is justified in challenging his use of 'primal kenosis', 'separation' and 'distance'. For Balthasar, 'separation' and 'distance' are positive attributes in God, even though they are negative for humanity. Even granting these qualifications, a challenge to Balthasar is appropriate. A challenge is needed in order to clarify the precise character of 'separation' that Jesus experiences in his being abandoned by the Father and descending into hell. This experience, as Barth correctly emphasizes, is a human experience – the human suffering of God. The separation and distance that Jesus experiences in the descent into hell is the end of the presence of the Father in the power of the Holy Spirit to the human consciousness of Jesus. It does not mean an ontological rupture in the relationship between the Father and the Son. Balthasar indeed wants to uphold the unbroken unity of the Trinity, but his speculative depiction of the eternal life of God risks undermining this desire. At this point, Balthasar's creative and imaginative theological vision needs to be held in check by Barth.

Next we move to the discussion of the reality of sin and God's dealing with sin in Jesus Christ as the 'representative', and as the one who drains the chalice of God's wrath. Here, in the second element of his dramatic soteriology, Balthasar explicates the notion of the 'wondrous exchange' – the *admirabile commercium*. This is the second element of a biblical and ecclesial soteriology. The 'exchange' must also be interpreted in such a way as to strike a middle position between an isolated and unaffected God and a God who, of necessity, becomes entangled in the world process.

'Representation' involves the identification of Jesus with humanity to the extreme of taking on the sin of the world. Jesus and humanity exchange places, and Jesus becomes sin to the end that humans might become righteous.[26] Jesus is both willing and able to bear the sin of the world, to be made sin by God so that humanity in him may become the righteousness of God (2 Corinthians 5:21). Jesus Christ's willingness is important because Balthasar recognizes the complexity of describing what took place on the cross as God's punishment of Jesus. Balthasar insists that Jesus is not a victim who endures the wrath of God as a punishment, which takes him by surprise and which is completely external to him. Christ's willingness is a part of his 'mission', which is grounded in the Son's procession from the Father and which reaches its culmination in the 'hour' towards which his entire life points. Although the 'hour' of Christ's passion is indeed something that Jesus Christ endures and is carried out by the Father – Christ does not bring about his suffering through his own heroic activity – it is also something that he accepts in obedience as a part of his mission. Jesus actively obeys the Father, and willingly accepts the time and content of the 'hour' as determined by the Father. Balthasar stresses Christ's obedience in approaching the 'hour' of his passion and in

---

26   In *TD* III, Balthasar determines four aspects of 'representation' illustrated by Paul and compatible with the Epistle to the Hebrews and the first Epistle of Peter. See *TD* III, p. 113.

accepting the content of the 'hour'. Christ accepts the 'hour' as the 'hour of darkness' (Luke 22:53) and identifies fully with sinful humanity, and this radical identification leads to his passivity and willing impotence. For Balthasar, Christ's willingness is a part of his acceptance of the mission designed for him by the Father, and the salvific consequence of his bearing the sin of the world is due to the hypostatic union – Jesus Christ is the incarnate Son of God. What Christ willingly accepts in fulfilling his mission in obedience to the Father is the furthest alienation from God that stems from sinful humanity's rejection of God's love.

> [The 'hour'] calls for an *inner* appropriation of what is ungodly and hostile to God, an identification with that darkness of alienation from God into which the sinner falls as a result of his No. Consequently, in accepting the 'hour', the Son – essentially bound to the Father in loving obedience – can only be totally overwhelmed by it. All he can do, in trembling weakness of mortal fear, is to pray for it to pass him by and then, 'strengthened' (even in weakness) by the angel, to affirm it as his Father's will, not his own. Indeed, it cannot be the Son's will to appear before the Father bearing the No of the whole world; his will is only to carry out the Father's will – his mission – into ultimate darkness. (*TD* IV, pp. 334–5)

Jesus Christ, in fully identifying with the sin of humanity, experiences alienation from God and takes on humanity's Godlessness. Jesus Christ enters into hell for the sake and in the place of humanity. And this entrance of Christ into the hell of separation and alienation from God is the product of God's self-giving love. 'Representation', according to Balthasar, reaches its height in the depths of the deepest abyss of hell. The drama of Christ's passion reaches its climax in the following:

> Perverse finite freedom casts all its guilt onto God, making him the sole accused, the scapegoat, while God allows himself to be thoroughly affected by this, not only in the humanity of Christ but also in Christ's Trinitarian mission. The omnipotent powerlessness of God's love shines forth in the mystery of darkness and alienation between God and the sin-bearing Son; this is where Christ 'represents' us, takes our place. (*TD* IV, p. 336)

Balthasar insists that Jesus Christ's death involves dying the death that is the consequence of sin. Jesus Christ, by taking on humanity's sin, experiences the wages of this sin, i.e. death. Here Balthasar departs from both Anselm and Rahner. It is not the supererogation of Jesus' death as a perfect and innocent human, nor is it his exemplary death of self-surrender to God that is meritorious or salvific. Jesus Christ's death is salvific because in this death he bears the sin of the world and dies at the hands of God's wrath. Though Christ does indeed participate in the darkness of sin, he does not become a God-hating sinner. Balthasar does not want to go as far as Luther in his view of the identification of Jesus with sinful humanity and his use of the concept of 'substitution'. Christ's experience of alienation and forsakenness is similar to that of a God-hating sinner, but it is also something much more profound. Christ does experience the 'sinful state', but he does not become a sinner who is hateful of God. In this sense, there is no 'identification of the Crucified with the actual No of sin itself' (*TD* IV, p. 336). Jesus Christ's experience of the darkness of alienation and forsakenness is more profound than any human experience because of the hypostatic union. Jesus, as the incarnate Son of God, knows the intimacy of the intra-Trinitarian relations first-hand, something that is beyond the scope of creaturely knowledge; therefore, his experience of forsakenness is deeper and darker than any other human experience.

'Representation' exceeds the notion of 'solidarity', which is common in contemporary interpretations of Christ's work. Balthasar insists that Jesus Christ genuinely takes on the sin of the world, and dies a death at the hands of a wrathful God. This death effects the elimination of sin and the reconciliation of the world with God. 'Solidarity', as exemplified in Rahner for example, neglects this dramatic element and risks viewing the cross as a symbol that reveals the reality of God's reconciling will. For Balthasar, Christ's passion is not a mere exemplary instance of 'being-unto-death'. Rather, Christ's passion actually effects the reconciliation of the world with God, and is perfect and complete, in need of nothing to bring it to fulfilment. In a brief essay on 'vicarious representation' Balthasar writes:

> The real essence of Jesus is illumined from this soteriological exchange of places, and in its light the true image of God comes into view. The suffering of Jesus Christ is more than a mere symbol by which one can discern God's reconciling will that had always been there but was only just now [in this symbol] clearly emerging into view; rather, it is the act of reconciliation itself: 'God has reconciled the world to himself *in* Christ (2 Cor 5:9).'[27]

I must raise a final issue regarding whether Balthasar's soteriology is a form of 'penal substitution'. Balthasar neither endorses nor dismisses 'punishment' language outright. He acknowledges the prevalence of the concept of 'vicarious punishment' in the history of theology, beginning with the Fathers, moving through the Middle Ages, and present in both Evangelical and Catholic theology. He insists that we must employ 'punishment' language in order to move beyond the idea of 'solidarity'. Balthasar clarifies his own position on 'punishment' language by distinguishing between the *sensus poenae* and the *vis poenae*. Balthasar affirms that in the crucifixion Jesus 'subjectively' experiences God's dealing with him as 'punishment', even though 'objectively' this is impossible given his identity as the incarnate Son of God. This does not mean that Christ's suffering is somehow less than the suffering of sinful humanity; rather, it means that Christ's suffering is more profound. 'The sufferings of Christ on man's behalf are far above all possible sufferings entailed by sin' (*TD* IV, p. 338). We can conclude that for Balthasar 'punishment' language must be employed judiciously, as there clearly are invalid

---

27   Hans Urs von Balthasar, 'On Vicarious Representation', in *Explorations in Theology*, volume IV, *Spirit and Institution*, trans. Edward T. Oakes, S.J. (San Francisco: Ignatius Press, 1995), p. 415.

notions of 'punishment' (for example, 'an innocent man as such cannot be "punished," even if he is atoning for the guilty', *TD* IV, p. 337). But we cannot eschew punishment language altogether, because it is demanded by the gospel narratives and the interpretative writings of the New Testament. Punishment language must be used in our interpretation of Christ's identification with sinful humanity in obedience to the Father, through the acceptance of his mission. The crucifixion is not the story of an innocent, righteous man being punished so that guilty humanity is free from this punishment; rather, it is the story of the incarnate Son of God willingly identifying with humanity to the point of bearing the weight of human sin and enduring the punishment proper to this sin, as the working out of the extravagance of God's love.

Although there is ambiguity regarding the propriety of employing 'punishment' language to describe what took place in Christ's passion, Balthasar affirms emphatically the outpouring of God's wrath at the crucifixion upon Christ, who has taken the world's sin upon himself. The 'cup', which in Gethsemane Christ requests be removed from him, is none other than the cup of God's wrath. This cup of wrath, mentioned throughout the Old Testament, contains God's anger and penetrates the one who drinks it. Balthasar does not mute the many biblical references to God's anger – God's anger with sin and sinners. He stands firm against the theological trend that strives to eliminate all mention of God's 'emotions'. For Balthasar, wrath or anger, as attributed to God, is not in tension with or opposition to divine love; rather, wrath is a function of God's love. God's wrath is the form divine love takes in the face of creaturely resistance. Wrath is not an arbitrary emotion, which must be held in check; rather, divine wrath constitutes the extravagance of God's love and is always controlled by the primacy of divine love. According to Balthasar, 'The love in God's heart is laid bare in all its radicality, showing its absolute opposition to anything that would injure it. And it is precisely the Trinitarian form of this revelation of love in Jesus Christ that allows us to discern the necessary unity of love and anger' (*TD* IV, p. 341). Divine love and divine wrath are unified. Divine wrath is used to raze the barriers of creaturely resistance.

Balthasar cites Barth extensively in his contention that divine wrath cannot be overlooked, insisting that we must affirm that 'God unloaded his wrath upon the Man who wrestled with his destiny on the Mount of Olives and was subsequently crucified' (*TD* IV, p. 345). Jesus' role as mediator demands that he bear the weight of the world's sin and the burden of the punishment brought about by this sin. He must bear it, and he alone is fully capable of bearing it. Balthasar here refers to Barth's discussion of divine perfections in *Church Dogmatics* II/1.

> What was suffered there on Israel's account and ours was suffered for Israel and for us. [Namely,] The wrath of God that we had merited ... The reason why the No spoken on Good Friday is so terrible, but why there is already concealed in it the Eastertide Yes of God's righteousness, is that he who on the Cross took upon himself and suffered the wrath of God was none other than

God's own Son, and therefore the eternal God himself in the unity with human nature that he freely accepted in his transcendent mercy. (*CD* II/1, p. 396)

Jesus is capable of suffering under the wrath of God because he is the incarnate Son of God, and his being the incarnate Son of God makes this suffering redemptive.

Balthasar's accent on the descent into hell of Holy Saturday is a direct working out of his emphasis on the vicarious nature of Christ's suffering and death, and his draining the chalice of the God's wrath as a result of his complete identification with humanity to the point of bearing the world's sin. For Balthasar, if we are to interpret Christ's sacrificial and substitutionary death with the radical seriousness that Scripture demands, then we must say a word about the gravity of his abandonment by the Father and the extreme distance of his separation from God. This word, therefore, must include the stark reality of Jesus Christ's death, which is followed by his descent into hell. His identification with humanity, in order to be complete, must include his descent into hell, for 'if Jesus has suffered on the cross the sin of the world to the very last truth of this sin-godforsakenness – then he must experience, in solidarity with the sinners who have gone to the underworld, their – ultimate hopeless – separation from God'.[28]

The descent into hell

In exploring the question of the function of the descent into hell in Balthasar's soteriology, the basic question that must be answered can be stated as follows: How does the descent into hell contribute to our interpretation of the salvific significance of Jesus Christ's passion?

The doctrine of the descent into hell is important, according to Balthasar, first of all because it signifies the reality of Christ's death. Jesus truly dies and partakes completely in all that befalls humanity in death. Here the emphasis is on the solidarity of Jesus with humanity. One indication of Jesus' solidarity with humanity, which includes the actuality of his death, is Scripture's silence regarding the time between Jesus' burial and the empty tomb. This silence is in stark contrast to the gospels' detailed narrative of the crucifixion and burial. 'The more eloquently the Gospels describe the passion of the living Jesus, his death and burial, the more striking is their entirely understandable silence when it comes to the time inbetween his placing in the grace and the event of the Resurrection' (*MP*, p. 148). This silence on the part of Scripture is appropriate because Jesus is in solidarity with the dead and is therefore isolated and completely inactive. Not only do the four

---

28 Hans Urs von Balthasar, 'The Descent into Hell', in *Explorations in Theology*, volume IV, *Spirit and Institution*, trans. Edward T. Oakes, S.J. (San Francisco: Ignatius Press, 1995), p. 408.

Gospels refrain from offering descriptions of a variety of events that took place between Jesus' burial and the resurrection; Jesus himself, 'as the Risen One, will not provide any report about what he has seen or done there [among the dead]'.[29]

The reality of Jesus' death and the incommunicable character of death itself, as illustrated in the silence of Scripture regarding the interval between the burial and the resurrection, preclude any notion of Christ descending into hell fully alive, capable of carrying out a variety of activities. Balthasar rejects the strain of Patristic interpretation of the descent into hell as the harrowing of hell by insisting that in his death Jesus becomes completely passive and incapable of any activities, whether they consist of proclamation or liberation. In contrast, Balthasar asserts that Jesus 'did not use the so-called "brief" time of his death for all manner of "activities" in the world beyond' (*MP*, p. 149). Jesus is completely passive in death, and this passivity confirms his solidarity with humanity. 'In that same way that, upon earth he was in solidarity with the living, so, in the tomb, he is in solidarity with the dead' (*MP*, p. 149). This solidarity consists of complete passivity and total isolation.

We must offer two clarifications to the question of the destination of Jesus in his descent into hell. First, Balthasar is dissatisfied with the language of 'descent', as it indicates an activity on the part of the dead Jesus. The use of the word 'descend' gives the impression that Christ, by his own initiative and through his own power, travels to the realm of the dead. Balthasar prefers to speak of Jesus 'going to the dead', as this avoids giving the confession of Jesus' descent into hell the 'unintended and unexamined meaning of an action such as, at root, only a living man, not a dead one, can perform' (*MP*, p. 149). For Balthasar, Jesus does not actively 'descend' to the dead; rather, he is taken to the dead, as he is truly a dead man. 'We have here no active descent – far less, a triumphant descent to take possession, or even only a descent that is struggle in battle; we have only, in this "sinking down" into the abyss of death, a passive "being removed." '[30]

Second, the initial destination of Jesus' descent is Sheol of the Old Testament. For Balthasar, this is the only possibility. Sheol is the realm of the dead and contains both righteous and wicked. Here Balthasar endorses Augustine's conclusion that there are distinguishable 'sections' of Sheol or Hades, i.e., a lower *infernum* and a higher. The 'rich man' dwells in the lower *infernum*, while Lazarus resides in the higher. Though these two places are separated by a great chasm, they both belong properly to Sheol or Hades. Jesus descended to the lower *infernum* in order to redeem sinners. The condition of Sheol may be described as darkness, silence, and dust. There are no activities in Sheol. No one returns from Sheol; there is no praise of God in Sheol, and there is no communication between those in Sheol and those living on earth. Those in Sheol are stripped of all power, and all called *refa'im*. These 'powerless ones' 'dwell in the country of forgetfulness'

---

29   Balthasar, 'The Descent into Hell', p. 408.
30   Balthasar, *Glory of the Lord* VII, p. 229.

according to Psalm 88. It is to Sheol that the dead Christ descends. He becomes one of the *refa'im*.

Balthasar rejects the blueprint of the underworld as drawn by medieval theology, which affirmed four distinct areas in the underworld – pre-hell or Limbo of the Patriarchs, Purgatory, hell of unbaptized infants, and hell properly understood as the depository for the damned. With this bluepring in hand, medieval theology determined the exact destination of Jesus' descent and the manner in which he descended, either in personal presence or in effect only. Balthasar dismisses this blueprint and the questions that accompany it. For Balthasar, before Christ (logically) there is neither hell nor Purgatory. We know nothing concerning a hell for unbaptized infants. What is left is simply Hades or Sheol. The most we can do is divide Hades into upper and lower parts, and then affirm that it is from this Hades or Sheol that Christ delivered humanity through his solidarity in going to the dead.[31]

Balthasar insists that the hell of the New Testament is Christologically determined. It is brought into existence only as a result of Jesus' experience in death. To say that the hell of the New Testament is Christologically determined is to emphasize the uniqueness of Jesus' experience in death. Jesus not only demonstrates his solidarity with humanity by entering into the condition of all humans after death (i.e. Sheol); he dies the death of the sin-bearer – the one who takes on the sin of the world. Jesus' descent into hell is not a mere intermission during which he simply awaits the commencement of a new scene, i.e. his resurrection. Rather, his death and descent is the end in all its finality.

Jesus is indeed in solidarity with all who have died – he experiences everything that they experience – but he moves beyond the experience of death common to all humans, to experience the full reality of death. For Balthasar:

> This rupture is [not] simply the quasi-natural one of the dying man of the Old Testament, who descends into the grave, returning to the dust from which he was made. This is the plunging down of the 'Accursed One' (Gal 3:13) far from God, of the One who is 'sin' (2 Cor 5:21) personified, who, falling where he is 'thrown' (Rev 20:14), 'consumes' his own substance. (*MP*, p. 50)

Here we move from Jesus' solidarity with humanity to the uniqueness of his vicarious work. Jesus not only experiences that which is common to all human physical deaths; he experiences the 'second death', which is God's ultimate judgment of sin. For Balthasar, what Jesus experiences in his death is

> More profound than what an ordinary human death can bring about in the world . . . the real object of a theology of Holy Saturday does not consist in the completed state which follows on the last act in self-surrender of the incarnate

---

31 See *MP*, pp. 176–7.

Son to his Father – something which the structure of every human death, more
or less ratified by the individual person, would entail. Rather does that object
consist in something unique, expressed in the 'realization' of all Godlessness,
of all the sins of the world, now experienced as agony and a sinking down into
the 'second death' or 'second chaos', outside of the world ordained from the
beginning by God. (*MP*, pp. 51–2)

Balthasar repeatedly insists on the uniqueness of Christ's passion. Though he
locates the experience of Christ's abandonment by God within the tradition of
God's forsaking the people of Israel and individuals as representatives of the
people due to their faithlessness and violation of the covenant, Jesus' experience
takes the instances of judgment in the Old Testament to the extreme and surpasses
them.

For Balthasar, the Old Testament events of judgment of Israel for failure to
follow God's commandments and for breaking the covenant (Leviticus 26:14–39,
Deuteronomy 28:15–68, and the instances of God's abandonment of individuals –
Moses, Jeremiah, Ezekiel, Job and the Suffering Servant of Second Isaiah), though
genuine, serve as no more than mere pointers to the abandonment of Jesus by the
Father in the passion. Balthasar asserts that 'the decisive breakthrough by way of
the "wrath of God" into the uttermost abyss came about only on the Cross' (*MP*,
p. 73). Jesus fulfils completely the judgment that was hinted at in the Old
Testament. Jesus alone experiences the gravity of the *poena damni*. What hung
over Israel, and all humanity, as a threat – the punishment of damnation – actually
falls onto Jesus as the sin-bearer. For Balthasar, the reality of the *poena damni*,
which is characterized by a loss of the vision of God, and further, the extremity of
being completely forsaken and abandoned by God, exists only as a threat prior to
Christ, but is fully actualized in Christ's abandonment upon the cross and in the
depth of his descent into hell on Holy Saturday.

Although, as we have seen, it is correct to view the doctrine of Christ's descent
into hell as an affirmation of Jesus' solidarity with humanity, even to the point of
being isolated, powerless, passive and silent in death, the concept of solidarity does
not take us far enough. Jesus indeed demonstrates solidarity with humanity, but
due to the particularity of his person – he is the incarnate Son of God – and his
mission – he vicariously bears the sin of the world – Jesus' condition in death is
utterly unique. As we saw in our discussion of the shape of Balthasar's dramatic
soteriology, an essential aspect of Balthasar's position is the substitutionary
character of Christ's work. The work of Jesus Christ carries the distinctive
characteristic of being something done on our behalf and, further, in our place.
This emphasis is also crucial for Balthasar's reflection on Holy Saturday and the
descent into hell. Jesus not only died in our place; he descended to hell in our
place and tasted death fully, in the form of the *poena damni*. Balthasar summarizes:

Given that the Redeemer, in his solidarity with the dead, has spared them the
integral experience of death (as the *poena damni*), so that a heavenly shimmer

of light, of faith, love, hope, has ever illuminated the 'abyss' – then he took, by substitution [*Stellvertretend*], that whole experience upon himself. The Redeemer showed himself therefore as the only one who, going beyond the general experience of death, was able to measure the depths of that abyss ... for the death of Christ to be inclusive, it must be simultaneously exclusive and unique in its expiatory value. (*MP*, p. 168)

Here we see two essential themes of Balthasar's soteriology and his interpretation of the descent into hell. First, as we have pointed out repeatedly, Christ's work as Redeemer is something done in our place (*Stellvertretend*). Second, included in this affirmation is Balthasar's recurrent insistence on the particularity and uniqueness of Jesus Christ's person and work. Jesus' peculiar identity as the incarnate Son of God enables his particular, unique and exclusive work to be universally significant for salvation.

The substitutionary experience of the fullness of death, as the *poena damni*, includes three elements. First, the experience of death as the *poena damni* includes the experience of the 'second death', which involves the New Testament concept of hell. Second, this death involves the vision of 'sin as such'. This, for Balthasar, leads to viewing the descent into hell as triumph. And third, this substitutionary death may be properly understood only as a Trinitarian event. This follows from Balthasar's conviction that the Trinity alone makes the events of Christ's passion intelligible (*MP*, p. 168).

Interpreting the descent into hell as an experience of the 'second death' acts for Balthasar as an assurance that there is a distinction between Good Friday and Holy Saturday. There is a distinction but not a separation. Here Balthasar departs from Calvin and Reformed theology. By rendering the descent into hell as an expression of the suffering endured by Jesus on the cross, Calvin affirms the 'continuity and homogeneity between the God-abandonment before death and that same abandonment after death' (*MP*, p. 170). Balthasar focuses on the distinction between the cross and the descent into hell in his discussion of Jesus' 'going to the dead' and his theology of Holy Saturday. We must stress that Balthasar does not suggest that the sacrificial death on Good Friday is somehow inadequate and incomplete, and is therefore in need of the descent into hell in order to be salvific. Rather, Good Friday and Holy Saturday are two distinct but inseparable elements of Jesus Christ's passion. Christ's death on Good Friday is marked by his activity of willingly facing death by execution and enduring the torture of the cross. In Gethsemane he actively accepts the imposition of the world's sin upon himself and the consequence of this acceptance, the cup of God's wrath. On the cross he drains this cup in free and active obedience to the Father. On Holy Saturday Christ is emptied of all activity, becomes completely passive, as is in complete solidarity with the dead. This solidarity includes isolation, loneliness and utter passivity. The descent into hell demonstrates Christ's passive obedience (Balthasar here employs the descriptive notion of 'cadaver obedience'), an obedience that expresses the extremity of his self-giving and the unbroken character of his obedience.[32]

This passive obedience, which involves solidarity with the dead, includes a suffering that is distinct from the suffering on the cross. Here Balthasar closely follows Nicholas of Cusa, who insists on a 'passion of Holy Saturday' (*Karsamstagsleiden*). Nicholas writes:

> The vision, *visio*, of death by the mode of immediate experience, *via cognoscentiae*, is the most complete punishment possible. And since the death of Christ was complete, since through his own experience he saw the death which he had freely chosen to undergo, the soul of Christ went down into the underworld, *ad inferna*, where the vision of death is . . . Christ's suffering, the greatest one could conceive, was like that of the damned who cannot be damned any more. That is, his suffering went to the length of infernal punishment (*usque ad poenam infernalem*) . . . He alone through such a death entered into glory. He wanted to experience the *poena sensus* like the damned in Hell for the glorifying of his Father, and so as to show that one should obey the Father even to the utmost torture (*quod ei obediendum sit usque ad extremum supplicium*).[33]

Jesus Christ's experience of the second death, suffering 'like that of the damned who cannot be damned any more', is the consequence of his complete solidarity with humanity coupled with his taking on the world's sin and dying the death of the 'Accursed One' (Galatians 3:13), of the one who has 'become sin' (2 Corinthians 5:21).[34] In the descent into hell, Christ experiences the gravity of complete abandonment by the Father. This abandonment, which is the core of damnation – the 'second death' – is endured by him alone, for he is the only person capable of experiencing the depth of the loss of communion with God.[35] Jesus Christ alone experiences the eschatological No – the complete judgment of God – depicted in the Revelation to John (2:11; 20:6, 14; 21:8) as the lake of fire and as life separated from God. This death is not mere physical death; rather, it is

---

32   See Balthasar, 'The Descent into Hell', p. 422. 'But there is, on Holy Saturday, the descent of the dead Jesus into hell: that is (speaking very simplistically), his solidarity in nontime with those who have been lost to God . . . Into this definitiveness (of death) the Son descends; but now he is no longer *acting* in any way but from the Cross is instead robbing every power and initiative by being the Purely Available One, the Obedient One, but in an obedience that has been humiliated to the point of being pure matter, the absolutely cadaver-like obedience that is incapable of any active gesture of solidarity, let alone of "preaching" to the dead. He is dead with the dead (but out of final love).'

33   Nicholas of Cusa, *Excitationes* 10 (Basle 1565), p. 659. As quoted in *MP*, pp. 170–1.

34   See Balthasar, *MP*, pp. 50–1.

35   Balthasar addresses the unique suffering of Jesus that results from the uniqueness of his identity by insisting that 'the vicarious experience of being dead (in the biblical sense) had to be suffered, indeed could only be suffered, more deeply by the Son of God than by any other human being, because he possessed a unique experience of being connected with God the Father and *therefore* he had a much deeper access to the experience of being dead and forsaken (again, in the biblical sense) than was available to a creature'. Balthasar, 'The Descent into Hell', p. 408.

the death about which Jesus warns in Matthew 10:28: 'And do not fear those who kill the body but cannot kill the soul; rather fear him who can destroy both soul and body in hell.' As we have indicated, what hangs over Israel and all of humanity as a threat actually falls, in its entirety, on Jesus – the substitutionary sin-bearer.

Although Balthasar interprets the suffering of Christ and his being plunged into the abyss of Godforsakenness – damnation – with great seriousness and realism, he also proceeds with caution. Following Nicholas of Cusa, Balthasar asserts that Jesus Christ has a 'vision' of death, including the 'second death' of damnation, but he is not actually damned. Balthasar insists:

> We cannot say that Jesus, instead of the sinner, is 'punished' by God. Nor can we say that he feels 'damned' by God and placed in 'hell'. For we associate the state of 'hell' with a hatred of God. It would be meaningless to ascribe to the Crucified the slightest resentment toward God. But it is quite possible to speak of the Son of God suffering what the sinner deserved, i.e., separation from God, perhaps even complete and final separation.[36]

Here Balthasar walks along a perilous precipice. On the one hand, he wants to affirm that Christ's work in our place is not 'something removed from the darkness of sin', and that Christ 'does not bear the burden as something external: he in no way distances himself from those who by rights should have to bear it' (*TD* IV, pp. 336–7). On the other hand, he denies that there is an 'identification of the Crucified with the actual No of sin itself' (*TD* IV, p. 336), which would lead to an actual rift between the Father and the Son. Balthasar asserts that there is a distinction between Jesus' experience of utter abandonment as our representative and the reality of the relationship between the Father and the Son. Subjectively, Jesus experiences the full depth of abandonment by God, through his taking on the world's sin, though, objectively, there is no actual severing of the communion between the Father and the Son.

Jesus Christ's experience of the 'second death' provides the basis for the transition from Sheol of the Old Testament, which is the destination of every human, righteous or wicked, to the hell of the New Testament. Hell is a function of Christology and is logically dependent upon the redemptive work of Jesus Christ, for hell is the condition prepared for those who reject the love of God poured out in the life and death of Jesus Christ. It is this hell, which is prepared for those who reject him, that Jesus witnesses in his descent into hell and his vision of the 'second death'.

The second trajectory that we may follow in an interpretation of Christ's descent into hell and his enduring the *poena damni* is his 'experience of sin as such'. The description of Christ's 'vision' of sin as such punctuates the passive character of his condition as being dead. Christ does not actively engage in a struggle with the

---

36   Hans Urs von Balthasar, *Does Jesus Know Us? Do We Know Him?*, trans. Graham Harrison (San Francisco: Ignatius Press, 1983), p. 36.

demons in hell, for he has been stripped of all power and capabilities for action. He is thoroughly passive and can only observe. The object of Christ's observation is full reality of sin, detached from any human being. Again, since hell, as Balthasar insists, is Christologically determined, Christ does not descend to a populated hell, Purgatory, or pre-hell – Limbo of the Patriarchs. Rather, Christ's descent into hell involves the vision of the 'pure substantiality of "Hell" which is "sin in itself"' (*MP*, p. 173).

How are we to understand this notion of 'sin itself' – sin separated from any individual human being? Our understanding depends upon Balthasar's interpretation of Jesus Christ's redemptive death. In his death, Jesus Christ bears the world's sin. In Gethsemane at the commencement of the 'hour', the world's sin is separated from humanity and laid upon Christ. In turn, Christ obediently accepts the 'cup' of God's wrath, which he must drain as the sin-bearer. In consuming the 'cup', Christ bears the world's sin and bears it away, confining it to the depths of hell. What we have in Balthasar's depiction of Christ's vision of 'sin itself' – the 'pure substantiality of hell' – is a vision that is in actuality a vision of Christ's triumph. It is a vision of Christ's triumph because it is a vision of the reality of sin separated from human beings, which is the result of Jesus Christ's substitutionary and sacrificial death. Christ's death leads to the removal of sin from humanity and, ultimately, to the destruction of sin. This destruction of sin takes place in the establishment of hell – as the lake of fire – and it is over this hell that the resurrected Christ is granted jurisdiction. Balthasar concludes, 'Hell is a *product* of the Redemption, a product which henceforth must be "contemplated" in its own "for itself" by the Redeemer so as to become, in its state of sheer reprobation that which exists "for him": that over which, in his Resurrection, he receives the power and the keys' (*MP*, p. 174).

Although it is proper to speak of Jesus Christ's passive vision of 'sin itself' as indicative of the triumph of the descent into hell, we must be clear and emphasize that Christ did not subjectively recognize this vision as triumphant. The victory over sin wrought by his sacrificial death was kept from Jesus Christ in the descent into hell. The descent into hell is the product of Jesus' pure obedience, obedience that persists even in the face of utter hopelessness and abandonment – in the face of everything that is in opposition to God. The actuality of the vision by the dead Christ, who is thoroughly passive and completely isolated, of sin and of hell precludes his perpetual enjoyment of the beatific vision. No vestige of God remains in sin and hell; therefore, there is no comfort for the dead Christ who passively encounters 'sin as such'. Jesus is taken to the depths of hell as the final consequence of his unbroken obedience to the will of the Father. The ultimate outcome of this obedience is kept from Jesus, and this makes his obedience all the more pure, and his death and descent into hell truly redemptive. It is only by genuinely experiencing the utter hopelessness of the abandonment, forsakenness, and separation from God, which is the consequence of sin, that Jesus can destroy sin and restore hope to humanity.

John Saward critiques Balthasar's treatment of the relationship between Jesus' subjective experience and the objective relationship between the Father and the Son. Saward writes:

> Balthasar's presentation of Christ's dereliction is beautiful but very difficult. First, he seems to me to distinguish insufficiently between the *feeling* of abandonment and its *reality*. As Pope John Paul has said in his catechetical address on the cry of dereliction, 'if Jesus feels abandoned by the Father, he knows however that that is not really so. He himself said: "I and the Father are one" (Jn 10:30).' I think it would be helpful to state more clearly that the Father's abandonment of the Son is not a spurning or rejection, but, as St Thomas says, his non-protection of the Son from his persecutors. A link with the other modes of salvation would also be illuminating. Christ assumes Godforsakenness not for its own sake but in order to make satisfaction for human sin. To quote the Holy Father again, 'if sin is separation from God, Jesus had to experience, in the crisis of his union with the Father, a suffering proportionate to that separation.' The experience of Godforsakenness, according to Balthasar, is all-consuming, enveloping and penetrating the whole of Our Lord's soul, excluding, *at any level*, joy or beatitude. This runs counter to the Scholastic view that from his conception, even during his Passion, Jesus as man was *simul viator et comprehensor*, at once pilgrim and beholder, sufferer and seer, enjoying the beatific vision of his father, and yet feeling a sorrow surpassing all the suffering endured or endurable by men in this present life.[37]

Although Saward is correct to point to Balthasar's departure from the Scholastic teaching regarding Christ's unbroken enjoyment of the beatific vision, his criticism that Balthasar fails to distinguish sufficiently between the '*feeling* of abandonment and its *reality*' is misplaced. Balthasar is fully aware of the significant distinction between the subjective experience of Jesus Christ on the cross and in the descent into hell, and the reality of the unbroken relationship between the Father and the Son. Jesus Christ demonstrates the intimacy between himself and the Father in his full obedience to the Father, even to the point of being abandoned by the Father. The cry of dereliction is in no way a denial of the truth of Christ's affirmation that 'I and the Father are one.' For Balthasar, Christ's experience or feeling of complete abandonment by the Father precludes any 'knowledge' to the contrary. For Jesus Christ's death to be salvific, he must feel completely cut off from the Father, and for this abandonment to be genuine, the redemptive outcome of his suffering death in God-abandonment must be kept from him. In this case, it is Balthasar who actually distinguishes between 'feeling' and 'reality', while Saward, John Paul II and the Scholastics fall short of affirming the profound gap between Christ's subjective experience and the reality of the unbroken relationship between the Father and the Son.

As we saw in our discussion of Balthasar's dramatic soteriology, the work of

---

37   John Saward, *Mysteries of March: Hans Urs von Balthasar on the Incarnation and Easter* (Washington, DC: The Catholic University of America Press, 1990), pp. 55–6.

Jesus is intelligible only as a Trinitarian event. This condition determines a proper interpretation of the specific event of the descent into hell as well. The descent into hell is the final element of Jesus' pure obedience to the Father. It is the end of his 'mission'. For Balthasar, 'The "exploration" of Hell is an event of the (economic) Trinity' (*MP*, p. 175). It is a Trinitarian event because hell belongs to the Father and the Father sends the Son to hell. Hell belongs to the Father insofar as it is the furthest consequence of human freedom.

> If the Father must be considered as the Creator of human freedom – with all its foreseeable consequences – then judgment belongs primordially to him, and thereby Hell also; and when he sends the Son into the world to save it instead of judging it, and, to equip him for this function, gives 'all judgment to the Son' (John 5:22), then he must also introduce the Son *made man* into 'Hell' (as the supreme entailment of human liberty). (*MP*, p. 175)

The Son must be introduced into hell, because as the substitutionary sin-bearer, he must experience the consequences of humanity's rejection of divine love, which is the extremity of creaturely freedom.

In order for the descent into hell to be considered a unique event – an event during which Jesus alone experiences death as the *poena damni* in all its fullness – the descent into hell must be a Trinitarian event. One of the Trinity must experience hell in order for it to be unique, substitutionary and salvific. Jesus' complete vision of hell as the 'second death' and as 'sin as such' is possible only because of his identity as the incarnate Son of God. In the event of the descent into hell, 'it is really God who assumes what is radically contrary to the divine, what is eternally reprobated by God, in the form of the supreme obedience of the Son towards the Father' (*MP*, p. 51).

In summary, Balthasar locates the descent into hell at centre stage in his dramatic soteriology because it logically follows within his vision of the pattern of redemption. It is genuinely 'fitting'.[38] Christ's descent into hell fits specifically within the internal logic of Balthasar's soteriology, and more broadly, within his theological vision as a whole.

Balthasar begins with the actuality of the historical events of redemption. He begins with the actuality of the cross and then moves back to describe the

---

38 Here we must follow Oakes' remarks in his superlative study of Balthasar's entire theology. Commenting on the novelty of Balthasar's treatment of the descent into hell and the tendency of readers to dismiss hastily this central aspect of Balthasar's theology as groundless speculation, Oakes writes, 'I think it should be said at the outset that, at least in my judgment, Balthasar is sticking strictly to the logic of redemption (in the Anselmian sense, of course) and is certainly breaking no more new ground theologically in the 20th century than Peter did in the 1st century, with his sudden and strange talk of Jesus being made "Lord" (!) and "Christ" and receiving from the "Father" the "Spirit," etc. Nothing can top *that* innovation. Balthasar's "innovations," if such they be, are merely the drawing out in a more radical way than has been done in the past of the implications of Peter's sermon on Pentecost Sunday.' Oakes, *Pattern of Redemption*, pp. 241–2.

conditions for the possibility of this actuality. Balthasar insists that we refrain from pursuing speculative questions regarding the options that God might have had in terms of God's desire to reconcile the world to himself. The cross of Christ is the actual avenue chosen by God to enact his reconciling will. We must therefore explore the 'necessity', or better, 'fittingness', of this actuality. What must be avoided are 'all theories which, missing the point of actual redemption, start looking at other "possible" methods for the world's reconciliation: considering whether a simple divine "decree", or the mere Incarnation, or "a single drop" of Christ's blood might have sufficed' (*MP*, p. 137). There is an evident pattern or logic to the redemption wrought in the life and death of Jesus Christ. This is a logic that is not determined by any mere human notion of logic, but which is determined by God and God's logic. Balthasar asserts:

> It is in the measure that Jesus' death is a function of absolute love – 'he died *for* all' – that this death has, first and foremost, the validity and the efficacious power of a principle. There is, of course, no question here of a 'formal logic'; what is involved is a logic whose content is the uniqueness and personality of the eternal Logos become man, a logic created by him and identical with him. And this unique efficaciousness belongs with the 'scandal' and must not be 'watered down' or 'emptied out'. Of any other logic than this, the New Testament knows nothing. (*MP*, p. 54)

For Balthasar, theology must begin with the irreducible fact of Jesus Christ, and must resist the temptation for abstraction and generalization. Jesus Christ is utterly unique and can be understood properly only as unsubstitutable, unique and irreducible. Jesus Christ is not a specific instance or example of a general class. The actuality of the uniqueness of Jesus Christ determines what the theologian may properly say regarding God, salvation, humanity, creation and the Redeemer. And the uniqueness of Jesus Christ's identity and mission leads Balthasar to assert that the descent into hell is essential to a proper and thorough understanding of Jesus Christ's saving life and passion.

CHAPTER THREE

The biblical character of the descent into hell

In the previous two chapters, I engaged in an explication and analysis of the significance of Jesus Christ's descent into hell, or his experience of hell on the cross, for the theological interpretations of the passion offered by Karl Barth and Hans Urs von Balthasar. In the next three chapters, I will take a closer look at three essential aspects of the descent into hell, which contribute to our understanding of the function of this confession in soteriology. The first aspect, which will be addressed here, is the biblical character of the descent into hell. The second is the internal doctrinal coherence of the descent into hell. At this point, I will address the interrelatedness of the descent into hell and the doctrine of the Trinity. The third aspect is the practical significance of the descent into hell. At this point, I will address the issue of the Christian discipleship and the way in which the descent into hell informs Christian love and the New Testament mandate to love and pray for all people, especially one's enemies.

A biblical basis for the descent into hell?

In a 1991 essay, which is conspicuously titled 'He did not Descend into Hell: A Plea for Following Scripture Instead of the Apostles' Creed', Wayne Grudem sets out to 'give reasons why it seems best to consider the troublesome phrase "he descended into hell" a late intruder into the Apostles' Creed that really never belonged there in the first place and that, on historical and Scriptural grounds, deserves to be removed'.[1] After surveying five New Testament passages that have been used to support the idea that Jesus Christ descended into hell (Acts 2:27; Romans 10:6–7; Ephesians 4:8–9; 1 Peter 3:18–20; and 1 Peter 4:6), Grudem reaches a conclusion he considers indisputable: 'The idea of Christ's "descent into hell" is by no means taught clearly or explicitly in any passage of Scripture', and, further, 'this idea is not taught in Scripture at all'.[2] As a result of this apparent lack of biblical warrant, Grudem calls for the elimination of the clause 'He descended into hell' from the Church's confession with the following strong words, '["He descended into hell"] is at best confusing and in most cases misleading for modern

---

1 Wayne Grudem, 'He Did Not Descend into Hell: A Plea for Following Scripture Instead of the Apostles' Creed', *Journal of the Evangelical Theological Society* 34 (1991), p. 103.
2 Ibid., p. 112.

Christians. My own judgment is that there would be all gain and no loss if it were dropped from the Creed once for all.'[3]

Although we will not engage in a direct dialogue with Grudem and other critics of the 'descent into hell', we will devote this chapter to the issue of the biblical character of Jesus Christ's descent into hell. Given the vehemence of Grudem's critique of the descent into hell on biblical grounds, which is shared by others, this task is essential to the viability of a view of the atonement that considers the descent into hell as doctrinally essential. Barth and Balthasar would counter Grudem's sweeping conclusion that nothing is lost and everything gained in excising the clause 'he descended into hell' from the Church's confession of faith, by asserting that in such a removal nothing is gained and everything is lost – especially a theologically proper and satisfactory understanding of God's love and the reconciliation and redemption wrought by God in the passion of Jesus Christ.

In examining the issue of the biblical character of the descent into hell in the soteriological reflection of Barth with the help of Balthasar, it is necessary to begin by exploring how they interpret the handful of passages that have been used traditionally in support of the descent into hell, and, further, how their respective interpretations correspond with and contribute to the understanding of the salvific significance of Jesus Christ's passion, if at all.[4]

Scripture and Barth's interpretation of the descent into hell

As we demonstrated in Chapter One, Barth identifies the Church's confession that Jesus Christ descended into hell with his experience on the cross and does not explicitly locate the descent into hell during the time of Holy Saturday. Given his interpretation, it is not surprising that Barth's exegesis of the New Testament passages often used in defending the descent into hell offer little help in the construction of a theology of Holy Saturday or a doctrine of the descent into hell.

Although in *Credo* Barth accounts for the interpretation of Christ's death as a *victory* by mentioning 1 Peter 3:19, he does so without elaboration.[5] However, in a detailed exegesis of 1 Peter 3:18–22 within his discussion of baptism in *Church Dogmatics* IV/4, Barth denies that this passage supports a teaching of Christ's descent into hell.[6] This passage, according to Barth, refers to the proclamation of

---

3 Ibid., p. 113. See also Randall E. Otto, '*Descendit in inferna*: A Reformed Review of a Creedal Conundrum', *The Westminster Theological Journal* 52 (1990): pp. 143–50.

4 I must emphasize that in this chapter, I am not interested in the exegesis of the fragmentary passages that refer to the descent in the history of biblical interpretation. I am precisely interested in the way in which Barth and Balthasar understand these passages, and how they do or do not make use of them in their constructive soteriologies.

5 See *C*, p. 91.

6 Cf. Karl Barth, 'Die Vorstellung vom Descensus Christi ad Inferos in der kirchlichen Literatur bis Origenes', in *Vorträge und kleinere Arbeiten 1905–1909*, ed. Hans-Anton Drewes and Hinrich

the gospel to those who provoked God's wrath before the Flood and who subsequently perished in the Flood. The proclamation took the form of the command for Noah to build ark, and by entering into the ark a 'few souls' were saved 'through water'. Barth then points to the typological relationship that exists between baptism and the ark, which 'was a witness, a sign, a signal of salvation above the abyss of destruction which engulfed everything and all things' (*CD* IV/4, p. 211). In a concise summary statement of the relationship between Christian baptism and the command for Noah to build an ark Barth writes, 'As an antitype . . . of the preaching of Jesus Christ to the generation of the flood by the building of the ark and deliverance therein through water, baptism saves, protects and keeps Christians, not for their own sake, but for the sake of their ministry of witness in the world' (*CD* IV/4, p. 212). In short, 1 Peter 3:18–22 cannot support the task of demonstrating the biblical character of the descent into hell. Barth states directly, 'The reference [1 Peter 3:19–20] is not to a descent of Jesus into Hades or hell, nor to His preaching to the departed spirits who are kept there, but to His proclamation in that primeval sphere of human transgression and divine patience' (*CD* IV/4, p. 211).

Barth appears to be making at least three points in this enigmatic statement regarding the 'primeval sphere of human transgression and divine patience'. First, he denies that the 'preaching to the spirits' of 1 Peter 3:19 refers to an activity of preaching performed by Jesus Christ during the time between his death on the cross and his resurrection; this passage does not support the confession that Jesus Christ descended into Hades or hell. Second, the spirits in prison, who were disobedient during the time of the Flood (*das Flutgeschlect*), act as a type for all forms of human transgression. The designation of the 'spirits in prison' does not refer to a specific group of people; rather, it refers to all unredeemed persons who lived and died before the historical existence of Jesus Christ. Third, 1 Peter 3:18–19 manifests God's patience. Those who were judged during the time of the great Flood are not without hope; God is patient (2 Peter 3:9), and provides a way for the gospel to be proclaimed even to them.

Barth also finds no support for the teaching of the descent into hell in the 'ascending' and 'descending' motif found in Romans 10:6 and Ephesians 4:8–10.

Stoevesandt (Zurich: TVZ, 1992), pp. 244–312. This essay, written in 1908 when Barth was a student, includes a survey of the exegetical options surrounding the texts in the New Testament that refer to the descent and describes the development of the doctrine of the descent in Patristic theology. Although in this essay, Barth allows as valid an interpretation of this passage from 1 Peter 3, as well as others, that affirms Jesus' going to the *Unterwelt* in his death, he denies the soteriological significance of this descent and insists that the descent is not a distinct doctrinal locus – it belongs to the entire scope of the passion. He does not consider it worthy of separate treatment. I am interested in Barth's interpretation of these specific passages as found in *Credo* and the *Church Dogmatics*, because I am interested in Barth's mature thought and the function of the descent into hell in his understanding of the atonement as found in his construction of a doctrine of reconciliation. His 1908 essay is a work in the history of doctrine and not a work of dogmatic theology.

Barth interprets these passages as emphasizing the exaltation or ascension of the Son of Man that takes place in the humiliation or descending of the Son of God, and, further, as affirming the unity of these states. These passages are significant for Christology – the specific issue of the person of Jesus Christ – and do not directly address soteriology – the issue of the redemptive work of Jesus Christ.[7] Barth uses Ephesians 4:9 as a way of illustrating his assertion of the unity of the state of humiliation and the state of exaltation, which denies the traditional position that these are different and successive states, and as a way of introducing the proper subject matter of *Church Dogmatics* IV/2 §64, 'The Exaltation of the Son of Man'.

> It was God who went into the far country, and it is man who returns home. Both took place in the one Jesus Christ. It is not, therefore, a matter of two different and successive actions, but of a single action in which each of the two elements is related to the other and can be known and understood only in this relationship . . . As we read in Ephesians 4:9 'Now that he ascended, what is it but that he also descended first to the lower parts of the earth. He that descended is the same also that ascended up far above the heavens, that he might fill all things.' It is to this ascension, the coming in, the return home of the Son of Man, as it took place in Him, that we have now to address ourselves. (*CD* IV/2, p. 21)

Barth also does not consider Peter's sermon at Pentecost, recorded in Acts 2, as biblical support for the teaching of the descent into hell.[8] The significance, according to Barth, of Acts 2:22–28 does not lie in the description of Christ's state in his death as the 'pangs (or pain) of death', from which God raised him up; rather, it is found in the clause that immediately follows – 'because it was not possible for him to be held by it [the pangs of death]'. This is significant as it identifies Jesus Christ as 'the One for whom it was impossible that the resurrection from the dead should not take place' (*CD* II/1, p. 606).

Unlike Balthasar, who, as we shall see, considers these passages (1 Peter 3:18–22, 4:6; Romans 10:6; Ephesians 4:8–10; Acts 2:24) as legitimate starting points for theological reflection regarding Christ's descent into hell on Holy Saturday, Barth does not associate these passages with the teaching of the descent into hell. And in the case of the most widely considered support for the teaching of the descent into hell, i.e., 1 Peter 3:18–22, Barth denies explicitly that Christ's preaching 'to the spirits in prison' refers to his descending into Hades or hell after

---

7 See Barth, 'Die Vorstellung vom Descensus Christi ad Inferos', pp. 255–7.

8 Calvin, in his Genevan Catechism of 1545, cites Acts 2:24, along with Christ's cry of dereliction from the cross, as a principal reference to the Church's confession that Christ descended into hell. Calvin writes in question 65, 'That he descended into hell, what does this mean? – That he endured not only common death, which is the separation of the soul from the body; but also the pains of death, as Peter calls them (Acts 2:24). By this word I understand the fearful agonies with which his soul was tormented.' Barth picks up on Calvin's use of the cry of derelicion (Matthew 27:46 and Mark 15:34) and uses these words from the cross and Calvin's interpretation of them in his own interpretation of the descent into hell, but he does not do the same with Peter's sermon in Acts 2.

his death and before his resurrection in order to proclaim the gospel to those who are being held there. We must not conclude, however, that Barth denies the biblical character of the descent into hell; rather, we must look elsewhere in Scripture to find the basis for Barth's particular interpretation of the *descensus ad inferna*. Since Barth considers the descent into hell as a powerful hermeneutical tool for a theological understanding of the weight of God's wrath that is unloaded on Jesus Christ in the event of the cross, we must look to the passion narrative itself for the clearest evidence of how Barth biblically grounds his view of the descent into hell. To be precise, we may concentrate our attention on Barth's interpretation of Jesus' haunting question – 'My God, my God, why hast thou forsaken me?' (Mark 15:34, Matthew 27:46) and the 'loud cry' (Mark 15:37) uttered by Jesus immediately before he died.

In his direct treatment of the Church's confession – 'he descended into hell' – Barth, as we have seen, basically endorses Calvin's position that the descent into hell describes the interior agony of Jesus Christ on the cross, expressed most clearly in his cry of dereliction. For Calvin, the descent into hell refers to Christ's feeling himself forsaken and estranged from God and, further, to God's silence in the face of Christ's calling out to him. According to Calvin, 'We see that Christ was so cast down as to be compelled to cry out in deep anguish, "My God, my God, why hast thou forsaken me?"' and Calvin further explains that Christ's words were reflective of his inner experience as they 'clearly were drawn from anguish deep within his heart'.[9] Barth directly attributes his interpretation of *descendit ad inferos* as describing what happens to Jesus as 'the misery of an *ordeal*' to Calvin's reading of Mark 15:34. Barth supports such a reading of Jesus Christ's death and his cry of abandonment with the theological claim that in Jesus Christ, God becomes intimately involved in the tragic and sinful situation of humanity. An interpretation of Christ's death in terms of the *descendit ad inferos* is possible only because of the claim that 'what is involved in the life and, crowning all, in the death of Jesus of Nazareth is the self-surrender of *God* to the state and fate of man' (*C*, p. 88).[10]

Barth provides detailed exegesis of Jesus' cry from the cross in a number of places in the *Church Dogmatics*.[11] In his discussion of Jesus Christ as the Rejected, within his doctrine of Election in *Church Dogmatics* II/2, we find an exemplary

---

9   Calvin, *Institutes* II.xvi,11, pp. 516–17.

10   See also Barth, *The Faith of the Church*, which is Barth's commentary of the Apostles' Creed based on Calvin's Catechism. Here Barth locates the centre of Calvin's interpretation of the descent into hell in his interpretation of Jesus' cry of abandonment. Barth comments, 'Calvin interpreted the descent into hell in the light of these words of Christ on the cross: My God, my God, why hast thou forsaken me? The descent into hell deals with Jesus Christ cast into despair, into distress of conscience, into that feeling that God is against him. The descent into hell is, so to speak, the inward explanation of what is outwardly happening in his death and tomb.' Barth, *The Faith of the Church*, pp. 94–5.

11   For representative texts that are relevant to the topic of the descent into hell and the atonement, see: *CD* II/1, pp. 421–2; II/2, p. 496; III/2, pp. 602–4; IV/1, pp. 215–16, 306, 458; IV/2, pp. 487–8.

statement regarding what is involved in Jesus Christ's role as the Rejected, which leads to the accomplishment of human salvation – reconciliation to God.

> The meaning and the purpose of the election of Jesus Christ consists, indeed, in His honour and glory as the blameless and spotless lamb, foreordained before the foundation of the world to the shedding of His precious blood (1 Pt 1:19f), to the offering of His life in place of many, to become poor that they might become rich. According to his divine nature, Jesus Christ is the eternal Son who reposed in the bosom of the eternal Father, and who coming thence took our flesh upon Him to be and to offer this sacrifice, for the glory of God and for our salvation, and by taking our place to accomplish our reconciliation to God. But as such and in the accomplishment of this reconciliation He is, necessarily, the Rejected ... He must suffer the sin of many to be laid upon Him (and it is the faith of His Church that it can and should lay all its sin upon Him), in order that He may bear it away: out from the camp into the greatest shame (Heb 13:12f); out into the darkness, the nothingness from which it came and to which alone it belongs; and just as radically away from the many, that it may no longer and never again be to them a burden. For this, in our flesh, according to His human nature, as the Son of David, He must be the Rejected. He must be delivered up by His people to the heathen, *descending into hell, where He can only cry*: 'My God, my God, why hast thou forsaken me?' [my emphasis] (*CD* II/2, p. 365)

This passage is instructive for a number of reasons, not least of which is Barth's placement of Jesus Christ's cry of abandonment in his descent into hell. God accomplishes the reconciliation of humanity to himself precisely in Christ's solidarity with sinful humanity, and, further, in the unloading of the sin of the world onto Jesus Christ. He not only bears the sin of the world; he bears it away and consigns it to nothingness, non-existence and impossibility. His bearing of the world's sin and his enduring God's punishment for sin relieves the world of the burden of sin. Jesus alone is 'delivered up to the heathen' and Jesus alone descends into hell.

The central role that Jesus' cry of dereliction from the cross plays in Barth's discussion of the descent into hell indicates that, in contrast to Balthasar, Barth does not hold that the descent into hell is a distinct event of Jesus Christ's passion. Occasionally, Barth hints at the suffering of the dead Christ. For example, in his commentary on Calvin's catechism, he interprets Jesus' cry of abandonment as indicating that 'as soon as the body is buried, the soul goes to hell, that is, into remoteness from God, into that place where God can only be the Adversary, the enemy'.[12] Yet, he consistently identifies Christ's descent into hell or his experience of hell with the event of the cross. As a result, Barth is subject to the same critique that Balthasar offers of Calvin, as they both insist that Christ experienced the tortures of hell on the cross in the place of sinful humanity, and, therefore, there is

---

12   Barth, *The Faith of the Church*, p. 95.

no need for a similar experience of hell by the dead Christ on Holy Saturday.[13] Although Balthasar certainly agrees with the emphasis by both Calvin and Barth that Christ's experience on the cross is unique and surpasses the suffering and death common to humanity, he questions their assertion of the 'continuity and homogeneity between the God-abandonment before the death and the same abandonment after death' (*MP*, p. 170). Balthasar, as we shall see in greater detail below, affirms a significant distinction between the cross of Good Friday and the descent into hell (or better, the 'being with the dead') of Holy Saturday.

Scripture and Balthasar's interpretation of the descent into hell

At the opening of the chapter in *Mysterium Paschale* that explicitly treats Holy Saturday and the descent into hell, Balthasar acknowledges the necessity of examining 'the biblical data to see in what degree the expression *descendit ad inferna* can be considered as a valid interpretation of the Bible' (*MP*, p. 149). In approaching this task, Balthasar sets out to chart a middle course between two commonly held opinions regarding the relationship between Scripture and the teaching of the descent into hell. On the one hand, he denies the possibility of a direct grounding of the descent into hell on a handful of passages that are viewed as referring explicitly to the descent into hell. This strategy, Balthasar concludes, is 'exegetically unfounded' (*MP*, p. 152). On the other hand, he challenges the view held by some scholars that denies 'each and every dramatic interpretation of the Descent in Scripture' (*MP*, p. 151). Balthasar refrains from attempting to construct a doctrine of the descent into hell on the basis of gathering together 'proof texts', while accepting, as theologically necessary and possible, the task of demonstrating that the descent into hell is indeed a valid interpretation of Scripture.

Balthasar emphasizes the passive solidarity of the dead Christ with all who have died. In this solidarity, Jesus Christ partakes of the condition common to all human beings in death, and as a result of his identity and mission, transcends it. Balthasar directly confronts the view of the descent into hell that has dominated the history of theological reflection, i.e., the view of the triumphant Christ actively descending to hell in order to engage in battle with the devil and his demons and to liberate the inhabitants who are being wrongly held within the prison of hell. It is precisely this view of the descent into hell that Balthasar considers to be biblically unfounded and coloured by mythology to the point of unintelligibility.

Rather than approaching the question of the descent into hell and biblical interpretation from the perspective of the traditionally held picture of the harrowing of hell, Balthasar proposes to view Holy Saturday as referring to Jesus Christ's 'being with the dead'. In Chapter 4 of *Mysterium Paschale* titled 'Going to the

---

13   See *MP*, p. 169.

Dead: Holy Saturday',[14] Balthasar endeavours to draw out the biblical and theological implications of Jesus Christ's solidarity with the dead and, further, the unique condition of the eternal Son of God incarnate in his death. His interpretation of specific texts in chapter 4 of *Mysterium Paschale* will occupy us in this section.[15]

Balthasar begins his reflection on Holy Saturday with a brief yet telling interpretation of the *locus classicus* of the descent into hell – 1 Peter 3:18–21 and 4:6. This interpretation reflects Balthasar's insistence that as a dead human being, Jesus is completely passive, and, therefore, incapable of actively descending to the dead in order to perform a variety of tasks. The significance of Holy Saturday, as the carefully chosen title of the chapter suggests, is Jesus' being with the dead – his 'going to the dead'. Balthasar poses the following rhetorical question in support of this interpretation of the descent into hell:

> Should we not be content . . . to speak of a 'being with the dead'? The title of this chapter, which deliberately avoids the word 'descent' speaks of a 'going to the dead', an expression justified, in our opinion, by I Peter 3, 19: 'he went, *poreutheis*, and preached to the spirits in prison' – preached – that is, the 'good news' as I Peter 4, 6 adds by way of a self-evident clarification. At the end of the passage, this 'going' is placed in unmistakable parallelism with the Resurrection, which is the departure point of the 'going to heaven', *poreutheis eis ouranon* (I Peter 3, 22). It should not be overlooked that both Resurrection and Ascension are first described as a passive event: the active agent is God (the Father). (*MP*, p. 150)

So, for Balthasar, Jesus' 'going to the dead' is most accurately understood as his being taken to the dead by God the Father. Jesus is genuinely dead and does not and cannot engage in any activities. His obedience is no longer active obedience, by which he goes to the cross; rather, it is cadaver obedience – the obedience of a corpse.[16] Balthasar, however, does not ignore the description in 1 Peter of Jesus preaching to the spirits. He interprets this 'action' in such a way that conforms to his assertion of the utter passivity of the dead Jesus. The 'preaching' of which 1 Peter 3 speaks is not an activity that is separate from the death of Jesus Christ on the cross. Rather, 'preaching' refers to the objective announcement or 'publication of the "redemption", actively suffered, and brought about by the Cross of the living Jesus' (*MP*, p. 150). Balthasar summarizes his initial reading of 1 Peter 3:18–22; 4:6 as follows: 'The actively formulated term "preaching" (I Pt 3, 19; in 4, 6 it is passive, *evengelisthe*) should be conceived as the efficacious outworking in the

---

14 Balthasar treats the same material and argument in a condensed form in *The Glory of the Lord* VII, pp. 228–35.

15 Elsewhere Balthasar discusses at length the allusion made by Jesus to Jonah and the three days and three nights he spent in the belly of the fish, which Jesus compares with the time that he will spend in the heart of the earth (Matthew 12:39–41, Luke 11:29–32). See Balthasar, 'The Descent into Hell', pp. 403–11.

16 This designation of the form of obedience of the dead Christ comes from St Francis of Assisi. See *MP*, p. 174.

world beyond of what was accomplished in the temporality of history' (*MP*, pp. 150–1).

Although he will return later in the chapter to a fuller discussion of 1 Peter 3:18–22; 4:6, Balthasar now takes up a discussion of other texts that historically have been crucial to a biblical account of the descent into hell. Both Romans 10:6ff and Ephesians 4:8ff employ the motif of 'ascending' and 'descending'. On their own, these passages do not move beyond the affirmation that Jesus in his own death shared the condition of the dead in Sheol. In Romans 10:7, Paul equates the fact of Christ's being dead to his being in the abyss, which may be interpreted as Sheol. Even though the Ephesians passage is ambiguous, Balthasar resists the interpretation that it refers merely to the event of the incarnation. Even if 'the lower parts of the earth' in Ephesians 4:9 is not intentionally identified with the realm of the dead, its concern is not simply incarnation itself, but 'an Incarnation whose internal logic led Christ to the Cross, where, by dying, he triumphed over the deathly powers' (*MP*, p. 154). These texts may act as a starting point for theological reflection on the Church's confession that Christ descended into hell, but as isolated pericopes they are inconclusive.

In the parable of binding the strong man found in Mark 3:24–27, Matthew 12:29 and Luke 11:21–22, Balthasar is confronted once again by biblical material that has been seen as ascribing a specific and detailed activity to Jesus Christ during the time between his death on the cross and his resurrection. This activity does not consist of proclamation (1 Peter 3:18–22); rather, it involves an active struggle and armed combat between Christ and Satan. Jesus Christ triumphs over Satan, binds him, plunders his goods, and liberates hell. Balthasar's interpretation of this parable reflects two important elements of his understanding of Jesus Christ's passion. First, the tragic nature of the human situation, i.e., death, can be overcome only from within. Applying the language of the parable to this conviction, Balthasar affirms that 'the total depotentiation of the enemy coincides with a forcible entry into the innermost terrain of his power' (*MP*, p. 155). This entry into the depths of death and hell – the fortress of Satan and his demons – effects the incapability of the gates of hell to prevail against the Church (Matthew 16:18) and is alluded to in the pronouncement by the exalted Christ in John's apocalyptic vision: 'I died, and behold, I am alive for evermore, and I have the keys of Death and Hades' (Revelation 1:18).

The second closely related element of Balthasar's understanding of Jesus Christ's passion, as indicated by his interpretation of the parable of the binding of the strong man, is the mode in which Christ accomplishes this infiltration beyond enemy lines and defeats Satan in his own territory. Again, Balthasar interprets the 'activity' of binding the strong man in such a way that it is coherent with his insistence on the complete passivity of the dead Christ. There is power that stems from the death of Jesus Christ on the cross, which continues in his passive state of being dead. The binding of Satan and the related possession of the keys of Death and Hades, according to Balthasar, 'is neither a question of a "struggle" nor of a "descent," but of absolute, plenary power, due to the fact that the Lord was dead (he has experienced death interiorly) and now lives eternally, having vanquished death in itself and for all, making it something "past"' (*MP*, p. 156).

At this point, Balthasar returns to his interpretation of 1 Peter 3:18–22 and 4:6, which he calls a 'controversial text' with a 'turbulent exegetical history' (*MP*, p. 156). Balthasar presents five theses regarding this text. The first four include statements about the inseparable relationship between spiritual and physical death, the realism of the proclamation of the good news in the 'world beyond', the identification of the preaching of the gospel referred to in 1 Peter 4:6 and the preaching to the spirits in prison of 1 Peter 3:19, and the relationship between the Flood and eschatological judgment – the first and the final judgment of the world. In the fifth thesis, Balthasar expands his previous interpretation of this complicated text by analysing further the meaning of Christ's 'proclamation' in the realm of the dead, and it is this thesis that is the most significant.

Balthasar begins with the statement in 4:6 that describes the intent of the proclamation of the gospel in the realm of the dead. The gospel was preached to the dead in order that 'though judged in the flesh like men, they might live in the spirit like God'. This leads Balthasar to claim that the preaching to the spirits in prison in 3:19 is nothing but 'a preaching of salvation to the dead' (*MP*, p. 158). This statement, however, does not stand without further interpretation. Balthasar immediately qualifies this declaration of the 'preaching of salvation' by reiterating the notion that this preaching is not a 'subjective kind of preaching' that will lead to the conversion of the audience; rather, this 'preaching' is an 'objective announcement of a fact' (*MP*, p. 159). This distinction is significant because Balthasar denies that the descent into hell completes something that Jesus Christ's vicarious death on the cross lacked. God is victorious over sin, death and evil in the death of Christ by crucifixion and in the descent into hell the accomplishment of this victory as something that has already taken place is proclaimed. The 'fact' that is proclaimed is 'the reconciliation of God with the world as a whole (II Corinthians 5, 19; Colossians 1, 23), achieved in Christ as a finished (*factum*) event' (*MP*, p. 159).

This proclamation, however, is not simply a statement of fact, like a terse press release by an anonymous spokesperson. The message cannot be separated from the messenger. Further, the way in which this proclamation or announcement takes place is of utmost importance for Balthasar. It takes place precisely in the event of Jesus Christ's going to the dead in prison. This 'going to the dead' involves the complete solidarity of the dead Christ with those who have died, including those who did not believe at the time of the Flood – the time of the first judgment. Secondly, the announcement that the dead Christ brings to the dead is the actuality of the reconciliation of God with the world as a whole (2 Corinthians 5:19; Colossians 1:23), which was accomplished in Jesus Christ and is a finished event (*MP*, p. 159).

The content of the announcement that is proclaimed by the dead Christ in the realm of the dead is brought into sharp focus by contrasting the depiction of

Christ's journey to the dead in 1 Peter with the description of Enoch's trip to the fallen angels of Genesis 6 found in the Ethiopian book of Enoch, which in all probability acted as a model for this section of the Petrine epistle. Whereas Enoch delivers the dreadful message that the fallen angels 'would find no peace and no forgiveness and that God would reject their plea for peace and mercy',[17] in 1 Peter, the dead Christ proclaims that he 'died for sins once for all, the righteous for the unrighteous' (1 Peter 3:18). The salvation that was accomplished on the cross is proclaimed as efficacious even for those who are dead, who have been judged in the flesh, and who are lost and seemingly without hope.

After a detailed treatment of Jesus Christ's solidarity with humanity even in death, and the unique condition of the dead Son of God as an exclusive experience of the *poena damni*, Balthasar concludes this chapter on Christ's 'going to the dead' by returning for a second time to the text with which he began, 1 Peter 3:18–22, 4:6. Here, once again, he treats the question of the 'work' of Christ in his solidarity with the dead. And in so doing, he concisely evaluates the visual depiction of the descent into hell and the resurrection in the iconography of the Eastern Church, as well as dispenses with a variety of minute problems that were debated endlessly from the Patristic period through Protestant Scholasticism.

Drawing upon both the passage in 1 Peter and Peter's sermon in Acts 2, Balthasar acknowledges that two themes have occupied theological reflection on Jesus Christ's work in his descent into hell – proclamation and liberation. As a consequence of his insistence on the passivity and objectivity of Jesus' condition in his solidarity with the dead, Balthasar interprets Jesus Christ's work of 'proclamation' in its 'sheer objectivity' and proposes that it ought to be understood as 'an action which plants within eternal death a manifesto of eternal life' (*MP*, p. 180). The objectivity of the proclamation or announcement of the gospel negates the significance of the vexing questions regarding how the proclamation is made and by whom, and regarding the subjective dispositions of those who receive this announcement. The theme of 'liberation', or the 'salvation offered to the dead, as the content of proclamation' (*MP*, p. 180), must be understood with an equal stress on its objectivity. Since we are unable to describe the subjective aspect of Jesus Christ's condition in death, we are equally unable to describe the subjective effect of his presence among the dead. Though Balthasar affirms the victory and triumph that is present in Christ's death and descent into hell, he denies that this victory and triumph are experienced subjectively by Christ himself or by the dead with whom he is in solidarity in his death. In fact, this lack of subjective experience of the triumph and victory is necessary for Christ's death and descent into hell to be actually triumphant and victorious.

In our close reading of Balthasar's treatment of the few texts that traditionally have been viewed as supporting the Church's confession that Christ descended into

17   J. Jeremias, *Der Opfertod Jesu Christi* (Stuttgart, 1963), p. 8, as quoted in Balthasar, 'The Descent into Hell', p. 402.

hell (or the realm of the dead), we have seen the complexity of his thought and the originality of his exegesis. It ought to be evident that Balthasar views these passages as starting points for theological reflection on Jesus Christ's descent into hell. The restrictive use of these passages indicates negatively that they are incapable, in and of themselves, of supporting a construction of a doctrine of the descent into hell. Yet, their status as starting points demonstrates positively that there is indeed biblical warrant for exploring the issue of Jesus Christ's descent into hell. It is clear that Balthasar brings a great deal to the exegesis of these texts, and the exegetical outcome reflects his primary commitment to the sheer passive solidarity of the dead Christ with those who have died.

Interpretative and theological decisions

In order to account for the similarities and differences between Balthasar and Barth regarding the biblical character of the descent into hell, it is necessary to explore various theological decisions that inform the way in which they approach particular texts and articulate the biblical character of the descent into hell. We will begin with significant similarities between Balthasar and Barth, and then we will turn to factors that might account for the differences between the two in terms of the proper understanding of the descent into hell. Given the salient similarities, we will attempt to answer the question of why and how Balthasar moves beyond Barth's identification of the descent into hell with the cry of dereliction on the cross of Good Friday by affirming Jesus Christ's descent into hell as an event proper to Holy Saturday and distinct from the cross of Good Friday.

One theological decision that shapes the interpretation of Jesus Christ's passion and the descent into hell is the issue of the mode of God's involvement in the human situation in the event of reconciliation. Motivated by the character of divine love, God, in the mode of his eternal Son, freely enters into the predicament of human existence and suffers and dies in order to remedy the sinful state of humanity and reconcile the world to himself. Balthasar's affirmation of the centrality of the death of Jesus Christ in the logic of God's redemptive activity determines the structure of his vast corpus of theological reflection and construction. He concisely formulates the subject that controls the whole of his *Theo-Drama* as follows: 'The central issue in theo-drama is that God has made his own the tragic situation of human existence, right down to its ultimate abysses; thus, without drawing its teeth or imposing an extrinsic solution on it, he overcomes it' (*TD* II, p. 54).[18]

---

18 Edward Oakes provides a more compelling translation of this passage as he writes, 'What is at stake in theodrama is this: that God acts so as to take upon himself and make his own the tragedy of human existence even to the depths of the abyss, and thus conquering it without at the same time

The descent into hell, therefore, follows from the logic present in the reality of God's intimate involvement with the tragic and sinful situation of human existence – in the suffering and death of his Son Jesus Christ.[19] If we approach the reality of the cross with the seriousness with which the gospels portray it, then we must investigate the question of the depth of Christ's suffering amenable to the possibility of endorsing the essential importance of the descent into hell. Balthasar writes:

> If Jesus has suffered on the Cross the sin of the world to the very last truth of this sin – godforsakenness – then he must experience, in solidarity with sinners who have gone to the underworld, their – ultimately hopeless – separation from God, otherwise he would not have known all the phases and conditions of what it means for man to be unredeemed yet awaiting redemption.[20]

In sum, the doctrinal significance of the descent into hell is contained in the theological conviction that in his passion Jesus Christ bore the sin of the world.

Barth places a similar emphasis on the full reality of God's intimate involvement with the human condition that takes place in the solidarity of the Son of God with humanity, and which leads to the limit of human sinfulness and misery. Barth insists, along with Balthasar, that any understanding of the incarnation that does not affirm the full reality of God's solidarity in Jesus Christ with the 'fallen and perishing state of humanity' is docetic, and therefore theologically unacceptable. Barth emphatically states:

> The self-humiliation of God in His Son would not really lead Him to us, the activity in which we see His true deity and the divine Sonship of Jesus Christ would not be genuine and actual, the humble obedience of Jesus Christ would not be rendered or the will of the Father fulfilled, the way into the far country would not be followed, if there were any reservation in respect of His solidarity with us, of His entry into world-history. But the self-humiliation of God in His Son is genuine and actual, and therefore there is no reservation in respect of His solidarity with us. He did become the brother of man, threatened with man, harassed and assaulted with him, with him in the stream which hurries downwards to the abyss, hastening with him to death, to the cessation of being and nothingness . . . *Deus pro nobis* means simply that God has not abandoned the world and man in the unlimited need of his situation, but that He willed to bear this need as His own, that He took it upon Himself, and that He cries with man in this need . . . He did not float over the human situation like a being of

---

robbing it of its sting or going around this tragedy externally, overtaking it by avoiding it.' Oakes, *Pattern of Redemption*, p. 238.

19   It must be noted that Balthasar attributes the reality of the 'tragic existence of human existence' to human sin. The tragedy and suffering that mark human existence are the direct result of humanity's rejection of God, and this tragic predicament can be overcome only by effectively eradicating sin. God alone can accomplish this, by bearing the sin of the world and the tragic consequences of this sin and by bearing it away. Death is both the consequence of human sin and the enemy over which God triumphs.

20   Balthasar, 'The Descent into Hell', p. 408.

a completely different kind. He entered into it as a man with men. [This] means that God in Jesus Christ has taken our place when we become sinners, when we become His enemies, when we stand as such under His accusation and curse, and bring upon ourselves our own destruction. (*CD* IV/1, pp. 215–16)

Both Balthasar and Barth emphasize God's full participation in the tragic and sinful situation of humanity, which takes place in the complete solidarity of Jesus Christ with fallen humanity. Jesus Christ stands in the place of humanity as sinner, and further, as an enemy of God – yet without actually becoming God's enemy. As a consequence, he experiences the destructive wrath of God that emerges as God's response towards those who reject him.

A second theological decision refers to the identity of Jesus Christ and the significance of this identity for the saving work of Jesus Christ in solidarity with humanity. The death of Jesus Christ is efficacious only if Jesus Christ is the eternal Son of God incarnate. Balthasar insists that the full humanity and full divinity of Jesus Christ must be maintained if the cross is to be properly interpreted and if salvation is to be actual. The suffering of Jesus is indeed the human suffering of God. Given the identity of Jesus Christ as the incarnate Son of God, the human experience of suffering, forsakenness and death is taken into the life of God and, because of this, death is overcome and defeated.

All meaning hangs on the fact that, in Jesus, the God who 'cannot suffer' is able to experience death and futility, without ceasing to be himself. Every suggestion that underplays the genuine humanity of Christ (Gnosticism) and his genuine divinity (Arianism), as expressed by the formula of Chalcedon, threatens and actually destroys the full meaning of the '*pro nobis*' upon which all Christian theology depends. God alone can forgive sins, and so only he can 'bear sins'; and the way in which he actually bears them cannot be discovered through speculation but must be presented, for our belief, in the mystery of the Cross – which is a stumbling block to Jews and folly to Gentiles. (*TD* II, p. 120)

For Balthasar, the soteriological implication of the claim that Jesus Christ, who is fully divine and fully human, dies in complete solidarity with sinful humanity by bearing the sin of the world lies in the unique and extreme character of his abandonment and isolation.

Barth also insists that the actuality of reconciliation and redemption depends upon the eternal Word of God being the subject of the life and action of Jesus of Nazareth. If this is not affirmed, then God is a mere distant empathetic observer, and sin and death remain. Human salvation, which the Church proclaims is effected in the death of Jesus Christ, depends upon the identity of Jesus Christ as the eternal Son of God incarnate. The divine–human unity of the person of Jesus Christ must be maintained if his death is to be redemptive. Jesus Christ's humanity enables him to have genuine human experiences, and through the hypostatic union, suffering and death are taken up into the Word of God – into the Godhead. Jesus Christ, because of his divine nature, can experience death as the second death without being annihilated. Finally, Jesus Christ's divinity enables his death to be both representative and substitutionary.[21]

Balthasar also returns, in the passage cited above, to a theme that is prominent in his entire dogmatic theology, and which we can consider as a third theological decision. This theme, which in Balthasar's estimation is the heart of the gospel, is contained in the two modest yet profound words '*pro nobis*' – 'for us'. The concept *Stellvertretend* flows out of the prominence of the '*pro nobis*' motif present in the wide range of New Testament texts. Balthasar draws from a variety of texts in order to shore up his argument for locating God's reconciling and redemptive activity in the unique substitutionary death of Jesus Christ – God's incarnate Son. Balthasar mines Paul's writings and extracts four ways of approaching the interpretation of Jesus Christ's death as representative or substitutionary: cultic, penal law, slavery, and obedience as the Second Adam.[22]

Related to Balthasar's emphasis on the uniqueness of Jesus Christ's suffering on the cross and his condition in death, which is the result of his commitment to a Chalcedonian Christology and to the '*pro nobis*' motif of the New Testament, both of which are indispensable, is the interpretative priority that Balthasar grants to two closely related clusters of biblical passages. First there is the set of Pauline passages that affirms the uniqueness of Jesus Christ's death as the death of the sin-bearer. Balthasar consistently points to the significance of Romans 8:3, 2 Corinthians 5:21, and Galatians 3:13 as hermeneutical keys for unlocking the meaning of the death of Jesus Christ. Jesus Christ's death is not the same as other human beings', who die, are buried, and return to the dust from which they were made. Jesus Christ's death involves the 'plunging down of the "Accursed One" (Galatians 3:13) far from God, of the One who is "sin" (2 Corinthians 5:21) personified, who, falling where he is "thrown" (Revelation 20:14), "consumes" his own substance (Revelation 19:3)' (*MP*, p. 50). This unique quality of Jesus Christ's death as the death of the sin-bearer enables it to be redemptive for all.

This brings us to the closely related second set of passages that informs Balthasar's interpretation of Jesus Christ's passion, i.e. those passages that account for the inclusive character of his life and death by way of the exclusive nature of his singular existence. These passages include: images of Christ's becoming poor so that we might become rich (2 Corinthians 8:9), the juxtaposition of Christ and Adam – sin and death for all humanity come from Adam's (the 'one man's') disobedience, while righteousness and life for all humanity come from the 'one man' Jesus Christ (Romans 5:12–21), and the death and resurrection of all humanity that takes place in the vicarious death and resurrection of Jesus Christ (2 Corinthians 5:14). Balthasar succinctly summarizes the significance of this exclu-

---

21   See *CD* III/2, pp. 603–4.

22   Balthasar insists that we view the traditional and biblical idea of representation from four sides: cultic, penal law, slavery and obedience. See *TD* III, pp. 113–4.

sive/inclusive dialectic for a full understanding of Jesus Christ's passion, which includes as inseparable his death, descent into hell, and resurrection, in his comments on 2 Corinthians 5:14, 'One has died for all; therefore all have died':

> This 'being dead with him' does not at all imply a 'being drawn with him into the abyss', since: he died for all, that those who live might live no longer for themselves but for him who for their sake died and was raised (II Corinthians 5, 15). The descent of One alone into the abyss became the ascent of all from the same depths, and the condition of possibility for this dialectical change-about lies on the one hand in the 'for all' of the descent (and not just in the 'dying', but in becoming a holocaust as the scapegoat outside the camp of God, Hebrews 13, 11ff), and on the other in the prototypical Resurrection with which this passage deals. Without the Resurrection Christ would sink into the abyss, but 'all' would not be raised. He must be, then, the 'first-fruits of those who have fallen asleep' (I Corinthians 15, 20), the 'first-born from the dead' (Colossians 1, 18). (*MP*, p. 53)

To these two closely related sets of passages we may add a third set, which supports Balthasar's conviction that Jesus Christ died for the whole world, for all human beings – for all sinners and not only for the elect. This conviction answers the question regarding the composition of the 'all' or the 'many' found in the various passages that we just discussed. Balthasar demands that we acknowledge Scripture's witness to the affirmation of the universal scope of God's loving will, which is implemented in Jesus Christ's salvific death. Jesus Christ 'gave himself as a ransom for all' (1 Timothy 2:6); the 'grace of God has appeared for the salvation of all' (Titus 2:11); God will have 'mercy on all' (Romans 11:32); God's patience is long and God does not wish 'that any should perish, but that all should reach repentance' (2 Peter 3:9); Jesus, in anticipation of his death by crucifixion, affirms its universal scope when he declares, 'when I am lifted up from the earth, [I] will draw all people to myself' (John 12:32). The fullness of the gospel pronounces that 'God so loved the world that he gave his only Son' (John 3:16). This world, which God loves and for which Jesus Christ was sent and died, is inhabited by sinners who are God's enemies. It is precisely the salvation of these sinners and enemies that was accomplished by God in the death of his Son, Jesus Christ (Romans 5:8, 10). Included in the 'all' for whom Christ died, Balthasar maintains, are not only sinners and enemies of God, but, more pointedly, those who in fact reject God's loving offer of salvation. Jesus Christ dies for those who reject him, and as a result, endures the eschatological 'No' that ought to be imposed upon them. The significance of the descent into hell for Balthasar's understanding of the passion of Christ is seen clearly in his concise conclusion: 'If Christ has suffered, not only for the elect but for all human beings, he has by this very fact assumed their eschatological "No" in regard to the event of salvation which came about in him' (*MP*, p. 172).

Barth, as we have seen, also stresses the '*pro nobis*' element of Christ's saving life and death, and accounts for the distinction between Jesus Christ's death and all other human deaths by affirming the centrality of the same cluster of Pauline passages that play such a prominent hermeneutical role in Balthasar's theology of Holy Saturday, that is, Romans 8:3, 2 Corinthians 5:21, and Galatians 3:13. In his death, Jesus Christ suffered '*eternal* corruption'. This, according to Barth, is 'what distinguishes His death from all others. "He was made a curse for us" (Galatians 3:13). This cannot be said of every one who is hanged or who dies in any other way. But of Him it must be said' (*CD* III/2, p. 602). As we have seen, in *Credo*, Barth insists that only Jesus Christ's death may be described correctly as 'curse, punishment, and ordeal', and he explains that these are proper designations for Christ's death only because of the unique presence of God in Jesus Christ.

> The eternal Word has to be present in our flesh, that, as it is put in Romans viii. 3, 'sin may be condemned in the flesh,' ... The presence of God, and only that, makes the cross the Cross, that is the cursed tree; makes death punishment, that is righteous and irrevocable retribution; makes the inconceivable way that is to be trodden in death the descent into hell ... God makes Him 'Who knew no sin' 'to be sin' (2 Cor. v. 21), that is to be one over whom breaks curse, punishment and ordeal. (*C*, pp. 89–90)

In the same way that these passages function for Balthasar as a hermeneutical lens through which to view the depiction of the passion in the gospels, Barth asserts that a proper interpretation of the cross must be in accord with the strong interpretation presented by the apostle Paul.[23]

This treatment of the theological decisions shared by Barth and Balthasar regarding the material content of Scripture enables us to see the proximity of their interpretations of the atonement, as well as the biblical character of their respective interpretations of Jesus Christ's passion, which they hold in common. Yet, the significant difference that exists between Barth and Balthasar in terms of the descent into hell remains to be elucidated. The question remains of how and why Balthasar moves beyond Barth by proposing an interpretation that considers the descent into hell as an event of the passion that is distinct from the cross of Good Friday and belongs properly to the time of Holy Saturday.

---

23   The centrality of this cluster of passages in Barth's thought can be well documented. See, for example, *CD* II/1, pp. 363–7; IV/1, pp. 70–8, 165; IV/2, pp. 255–8. In this small print excursus, Barth argues for the harmony that exists between the depiction of the passion in the synoptic gospels and the Pauline theology of the cross. In *CD* II/1, pp. 397–8 Barth, in no uncertain terms, stresses both the solidarity of Christ with sinful humanity and the way in which Christ's death is unique insofar as he experiences the full reality of God's wrath in the place of sinful humanity. He does this by unleashing a barrage of biblical passages, including: Jn 3:16, 8:46; Tit 2:14; Gal 2:20; 3:13, 4:4–5; Rom 3:20; 5:6–10; 6:10, 16ff; 8:1, 3, 32; 2 Cor 5:19–21; 8:9; Phil 2:6f, Heb 4:15; Col 1:22; 1 Pt 2:24, 3:18.

Barth and Balthasar on the construction of atonement doctrine

In order to frame a comparison between Balthasar and Barth on the descent into hell, I will use Michael Root's account of the structure of constructive soteriology as elaborated in his essay 'The Narrative Structure of Soteriology'.[24] In this essay, Root describes what is involved in constructing a soteriology or conceiving an atonement theory, as follows:

> What are called atonement theories can be understood ... as narrative redescriptions of the story of Jesus. Atonement theories imply augmented, expanded forms of the story that make clear how it is the story of redemption. *It is by the construction of such augmented forms of the story of Jesus that the soteriological task is carried out.*[25]

Root proceeds to qualify this statement by pointing out that there is both a certain amount of freedom and indeterminacy in soteriology as well as factors within the biblical narrative itself for which a soteriology must account if it is to be considered theologically valid. Root concludes, 'While the patterns in the text may be able to place limits on soteriological construction, they are not sufficiently specific to dictate a particular soteriology.'[26] This flexibility, though not without limits in interpreting the redemptive significance of the life and passion of Jesus Christ as depicted in the biblical narrative, enables us to account for the variety of potentially valid interpretations of the same event – the death of Jesus Christ. For example, Anselm's interpretation of the death of Christ in terms of the repayment of an infinite debt, Gregory of Nyssa's colourful depiction of the deception of the devil, and Schleiermacher's explanation of Jesus Christ's redemptive significance in terms of an elevated God-consciousness all may be valid interpretations of the life and death of Jesus Christ. Although one may be persuaded that one narrative redescription of the story of Jesus Christ is superior to all others, this superiority is incapable of being strictly and conclusively proven, and no one soteriology can adequately and fully explain how the story of Jesus Christ is redemptive.

Soteriology, in Root's description, involves the identification of narrative patterns within the biblical text and the organization of narrative of Scripture as a

---

24   Michael Root, 'The Narrative Structure of Soteriology', *Modern Theology* 2 (1986): pp. 145–58.

25   Root, 'The Narrative Structure of Soteriology', p. 148. John Webster provides an insightful complement to Root's understanding of the task and structure of soteriology by highlighting the character of theology as second-order critical reflection. Webster states, 'A theology of the atonement is ... reflexive upon the evangelical narratives which furnish a primary idiom for the identification and description of Jesus as personal subject and agent. Certainly theology is not itself narrative: it is not story-telling but a second-order exercise, a reflexive, critical account of the Christian [*mythos*]. But as such an exercise it may not supplant the narrative material which forms the object of its inquiry. A theology of the atonement is constantly referred to this *donum*, by which its conceptual representations must be broken down and refashioned.' John Webster, 'Atonement, History and Narrative', *Theologische Zeitschrift* 42 (1986): p. 121.

26   Root, 'The Narrative Structure of Soteriology', p. 154.

whole. This rendering of Scripture in terms of a single, whole and total narrative is the result of a 'canonical construal' in which the interpreter reads the Bible 'as a whole with some kind of unity'.[27] After identifying narrative patterns present in Scripture and organizing the biblical narrative as a unified whole, the theologian must account for three interrelated factors in the construction of his or her soteriology. First, Root claims, 'any soteriology must . . . bring to light patterns in the Christian story which will make clear that story's redemptive character'.[28] This takes place as the narrative patterns present in the story of Jesus are joined with patterns that are potentially present in the life of the reader of Scripture. 'Soteriological interpretation of the Christian story', Root explains, 'must play off, both utilize and reshape, patterns that do or can exist in the reader's life that are like redemption.'[29] As a result of this, one may interpret the saving significance of the life and passion of Jesus Christ, for example, in terms of the repayment of a debt, the bearing of a punishment, the liberation of the oppressed, or the achievement of a specific form of consciousness. Each of these categories or patterns is discernible in common human experience. Even though the story of Jesus is interpreted by way of redemptive patterns present in the life of the reader of Scripture, Root maintains that the particular story of Jesus is not absorbed into a general class of redemptive patterns, which are anthropologically determined.[30] Jesus Christ's redemptive significance is indeed unique. This leads us to the second factor of soteriology.

The narrative pattern of the story of Jesus differs in significant ways from the patterns to which it is similar. Jesus satisfies an infinite debt; he endures the total punishment of God's eschatological wrath; he liberates the oppressed from Satan and death itself, and the consciousness he achieves is perfect, fully potent God-consciousness.[31] This recognition of the unique redemptive significance of Jesus Christ leads to an affirmation of the scandal of particularity. In other words, the redemptive patterns that are highlighted in a soteriology must not be separated from the particular instantiation of these patterns in the singular life and death of Jesus Christ. The redemptive patterns exhibited in the life and passion of Jesus Christ cannot be repeated and are unsubstitutable. Root claims, 'The generality that soteriological interpretation requires need not reduce Jesus to an illustration of a general truth or one realization of a repeatable pattern. The interplay of generality and specificity in narrative allows the story of Jesus in its uniqueness to have

---

27   Ibid., p. 149.
28   Ibid., p. 153.
29   Ibid.
30   Webster makes a similar point when he states, 'The divine act of salvation in Jesus is not to be sublimed into a more general truth of which his historical ministry and death are merely the instantiation. God's saving intention is not simply expressed but actualised in the story of Jesus.' Webster, 'Atonement, History and Narrative', p. 117.
31   Root, 'The Narrative Structure of Soteriology', p. 153.

soteriological significance.'[32] Finally, the emphasis on the uniqueness of Jesus Christ, the inseparability of the redemptive narrative patterns of Scripture and the particular and individual existence of Jesus, and the prohibition of viewing Jesus as an example of a general law or an illustration of a general truth, requires that a soteriology pay attention to the concrete narrative patterns of Scripture.[33] It is therefore impossible to uncover a necessary connection between the story of Jesus and general law or patterns of redemption. As a result, soteriology can never reach the permanence and completion of necessary explanation.

Even though the redemptive significance of the life and passion of Jesus can never be theoretically explained, this is not to say that any soteriological redescription of the story of Jesus through expansion, extension and augmentation may be considered valid. The theologian engaged in the construction of a soteriology must attend to what Root calls 'the seeds of interpretations in [Scripture's] descriptions of events and the patterns that organize those events into a narrative'.[34]

In an earlier essay, 'Dying He Lives: Biblical Image, Biblical Narrative and the Redemptive Jesus', Root elaborates precisely how biblical patterns place limits upon soteriology.[35] His description of these limits directly addresses the difference that exists between Balthasar and Barth in terms of the function of the descent into hell. Root begins by identifying two distinct but interrelated groups of New Testament images that inform an interpretation of the redemptive significance of the life and passion of Jesus Christ. The first group, which Root calls 'liberation' images, 'depicts evil as something humanity undergoes rather than undertakes, suffers rather than commits'.[36] Jesus is portrayed in these images as the victor over the devil, the powers and the principalities, and death itself, which is often personified. Humanity is in bondage to sin, evil, death and the devil, and Jesus' work achieves liberation from this overwhelming oppression. The second group of

---

32   Ibid.

33   Again, Webster's analysis of connection between soteriology and narrative contributes to the argument advanced by Root. Webster highlights the function of narrative as providing an identity-description of a particular historical agent. This stresses the untranslatable character of the gospel narratives, and demands that the theologian must attend to the specific narratives of the gospels and show great care in restating the narrative of Jesus in other terms. Webster writes, 'In a doctrine of the atonement, the personal identity of the atoner is to be rendered in narrative terms, by rehearsing his biography, tracing the movements of his history. And in describing Jesus in this way, we are implicitly refusing any suggestion that his history is less than primordial, and so are asserting that his identity can only be grasped in and with the actualities of his life-story. The more we shift towards the propositional, the more readily we translate out of the temporal categories of the evangelical narratives, the less secure of our grasp of Jesus' *Istigkeit*, of that which made him into what he was. By shifting from the deed to the idea, a doctrine of the atonement for which narrative is not of prime significance fails to convey the insight vouchsafed in the gospel texts.' Webster, 'Atonement, History and Narrative', p. 120.

34   Root, 'The Narrative Structure of Soteriology', p. 154.

35   Michael Root, 'Dying He Lives: Biblical Image, Biblical Narrative and the Redemptive Jesus', *Semeia* 30 (1985): pp. 155–69.

36   Root, 'Dying He Lives', p. 156.

images, which Root designates 'reconciliation', depicts evil and sin not as an external and foreign oppressor, but as something that humanity undertakes and in which it is complicit. Death is not considered as a personified force against which God through Jesus Christ battles; rather, death is the consequence of sin as determined by God (Romans 6:23). Reconciliation through the forgiveness of sins is necessary, and not simply liberation. Reconciliation is focused on the sacrificial character of Jesus' death, and to this we may add interpretations of Jesus' death as bearing the punishment meant for sin, becoming a curse for humanity, and so forth.[37]

Root also identifies a corresponding dual emphasis in the narrative depiction of Jesus' life and passion. This dual emphasis may be described as the power/powerless relation and the activity/passivity relation in the life of Jesus. The narrative depiction of Jesus includes a transition from power to powerlessness and, therefore, from activity to passivity, which takes place in Gethsemane. This transition is essential to the salvific efficacy of Jesus' passion, as salvation is accomplished in Jesus' full participation in the helplessness and powerlessness of those whom he came to save. It is necessary to acknowledge, however, that this transition from power to powerlessness and from activity to passivity is not something that overtakes Jesus without his wilful acceptance. Jesus chooses to be powerless, and in obedience allows himself to be passive. So, in light of Jesus' free adoption of powerlessness and passivity, we must say that his powerlessness is in fact a demonstration of his radical power, and his passivity is his own act. The dual nature of the passion narratives is seen in the concise summary, 'The submissive redeemer is redeemer only as his submission is somehow also his conquering activity.'[38] Root concludes the following about the relationship between the soteriological images of liberation and reconciliation and the depiction of Jesus in the passion narratives:

> The doublesidedness in the relations depicted within the narratives correlates with the two groups of soteriological images discussed above. The patterns that shape these two aspects of the text are interlocking. The liberation images develop the picture of Jesus as the agent of God combating the evils to which God is opposed. The reconciliation images develop the depiction of Jesus as the object of an action of God mediated in some way through Jesus' per-

---

37 The complexity of these interrelated groups of images is seen clearly in two New Testament passages. In Colossians 2:14–15, Paul employs legal imagery to interpret the redemptive significance of Christ's death. God has cancelled the bond that stood against humanity, along with its legal demands, and sets it aside by nailing it to the cross. Paul, then, immediately shifts images and portrays the cross as that event in which God triumphs over the principalities and powers by disarming them and making a public example of them. The narrative of John's apocalyptic vision also presents a clear picture of the interrelatedness of these two groups of images – liberation and reconciliation as Christ is depicted simultaneously as the conquering Lion of the tribe of Judah and the slain Lamb (Rev 5:5–6).

38 Root, 'Dying He Lives', p. 160.

secutors. The duality of soteriological images meshes with a basic double-sidedness in the New Testament narratives.[39]

The implications of the soteriological images, coupled with the passion narratives, for theological reflection on the passion of Jesus Christ are concentrated in the claim that it is precisely Jesus Christ's death that is salvific, enacting both liberation and reconciliation. There is no way open to us for explaining how Jesus' death leads to his new life and to new lives of those who live in him. Death is destruction and non-being, and it is final. Root acknowledges that there are indeed analogies with the transition of life out of death, but these analogies break down, because Christian faith affirms that true life comes out of the particularity and utter finality of Jesus' true death. This claim of true life coming out of true death cannot be explained, and it is therefore not surprising that the biblical narrative does not include a depiction of this transitional event. The gospel narratives move from the burial directly to the empty tomb. Root states, 'The turn from death to life remains hidden in the non-narrated interlude. The hiatus in our understanding is thus paralleled by a hiatus in the narrative.'[40] The inexplicable character of the salvific significance of Jesus' death as the transition from death to life, the liberation of humanity from bondage, and the reconciliation of humanity to God through the forgiveness of sins is a consequence of death as the opposite of life, as destruction and non-being, and as completely final. Root concludes:

> Jesus' powerlessness is true powerlessness, the powerlessness of death, not a false front or a moment in the dialectical rhythm of power. Yet he is the embodiment of the power that redeems. Death as destruction and non-being is the opposite of life; yet it becomes the path to new life. The only way to resolve the tensions is to explain how new life is brought out of death, to bridge the hiatus between Good Friday and Easter. But within the limits set by the biblical views of death and resurrection, we cannot provide such an explanation or bridge.[41]

Root's proposal for considering soteriology as the narrative redescription of the story of Jesus, which augments and expands the story of Jesus in the biblical narrative, and his identification of the limits placed upon soteriology as found in the gospel narratives themselves and the interpretative soteriological images of the New Testament enable us to examine the difference between Balthasar and Barth regarding the descent into hell. The difference lies in the way in which they expand and augment the story of Jesus in their constructive soteriologies.

Barth highlights patterns of judgment and claims that the saving significance of Jesus Christ is best understood in terms of his enduring the ultimate judgment of God on human sin and doing this on our behalf and in our place. Barth also insists

---

39   Ibid., pp. 160–1.
40   Ibid., p. 163.
41   Ibid., p. 164.

that the event of judgment that takes place in Jesus Christ's passion is the revelation as well as the execution of God's righteous judgment and is not an instance of a general class of punishment, penalty or judgment. The descent into hell comes into play in Barth's retelling of the story of Jesus as an intensification of the description of the judgment that Christ endures in his death on the cross. Jesus Christ's death involves entering into the ordeal (*Anfechtung*) and it is from the midst of this experience of separation from and abandonment by God, which is the essence of hell, that Jesus Christ questions his relationship with the Father and cries out to God, asking why he has been forsaken.

Balthasar trades in patterns of evil, suffering and human misery, as well as others, including judgment, punishment and sacrifice. For Balthasar, Jesus Christ's suffering is peerless; it is unique and surpasses all the actual and potential suffering of humanity. And this act of suffering demonstrates the radical nature of God's love, accomplishes human redemption, and frees humanity from the futility of human evil and suffering. The suffering of Jesus Christ is more profound than human suffering, and the eternal Son of God assumes human suffering and takes it into the triune life of God. As a consequence, God triumphs over suffering and death, as death is swallowed up in life.

Balthasar moves beyond Barth by extending the gospel narrative to include a scene of Jesus Christ's descent into hell, which is staged between the cross of Good Friday and the resurrection of Easter Sunday. Barth omits such a distinct scene, and, instead, augments Jesus' dying words from the cross with the profound weight of the confession that Jesus Christ descended into hell.

Both Barth and Balthasar account for the two soteriological images that Root identifies. Both speak of the victorious and triumphant character of Christ's death as being a direct consequence of his vicarious death as sacrifice and sin-bearer. Both also refrain from attempting to explain exactly how new life emerges from the fullness of death. They honour the silence of Scripture by affirming the resurrection as a new act of God, which cannot be explained through rational and historical means. While Barth is in line with Root in maintaining the 'episodic juxtaposition "Good Friday, then Easter"', and locates Jesus Christ's descent into hell in the event of the cross on Good Friday, Balthasar ventures to add a third component to this juxtaposition – Holy Saturday. Balthasar would revise this phrase to read, 'Good Friday, Holy Saturday, then Easter'.

Balthasar concentrates his attention in his soteriology on the hiatus of death in which the Word of God is silent, and about which the biblical narrative does not speak. Yet he does not regard the descent into hell as capable of describing or explaining the transition from death to new life. Rather, he pushes Jesus Christ's experience of death to its furthest limit, and by pointing to his experience of hell accounts for the profound character of the resurrection as a completely new act of God. Balthasar reminds us that Jesus Christ is not raised from the cross, but from death – from the hell of Holy Saturday. He therefore honours the silence of the biblical narrative regarding the movement from cross to resurrection, which corresponds to our conceptual inability to account rationally for or explain the transition from Jesus Christ's death to his new life, and which includes the new lives of those who participate in him. The descent into hell on Holy Saturday is essential to a comprehensive understanding of Jesus Christ's passion and is a necessary complement to the suffering endured by Christ in his death on the cross. Since God is victorious and triumphs and over death and the devil in Jesus Christ's death on the cross and in his being with the dead on Holy Saturday, the descent into hell is also a necessary bridge to the resurrection of Easter Sunday.

Balthasar's extension of the biblical narrative

Given the novelty of Balthasar's soteriology, whose central feature is the claim that the descent into hell is an essential element of a comprehensive understanding of the salvific significance of Jesus Christ's passion, the procedure he follows in reaching and defending such a claim must be examined. In light of the well-documented similarities between Balthasar's and Barth's soteriological reflections, we must account for the difference that exists between them regarding the interpretation of the descent into hell, and, further, we must determine whether Balthasar's particular expansion of the biblical narrative to include the scene of the descent into hell is consonant with Barth's position.

Balthasar engages in theological exegesis located within the life of the Church as he articulates his understanding of the descent into hell and its centrality in his constructive soteriology. There are at least two essential elements of Balthasar's theological exegesis that contribute to our assessment of the biblical character of the descent into hell. The first is Balthasar's affirmation of, and emphasis on, the unity of Scripture. The second is the influence of tradition and the experiences of Christian mystics on his reading and interpretation of Scripture.

For Balthasar, the unity or harmony in Scripture is the result of Scripture's subject matter, Jesus Christ – the Word made flesh. In affirming the unity of Scripture, Balthasar is not in any way denying the diversity of biblical viewpoints and the potential for entirely valid multiple meanings of Scripture. In actuality, given the depth of the mystery of the love of God manifest in the Word of God made flesh, it is necessary to approach this inexhaustible mystery from an endless variety of vantage points.[42] Balthasar does not attempt to impose an artificial unity

---

42 It is important to note that Barth also endorses the possibility of multiple valid interpretations of one biblical text. Given the distinction Barth draws between the words of the Bible and the Word of God in God's revelation, which contains the implication that God must be active in making the human words of the Bible conform to God's own word about himself, divine revelation is not absolutely established. Drawing on the significance of the *analogia fidei* and the relationship between Barth's doctrine of revelation and his theological exegesis, Bruce McCormack acutely observes, 'What God has said through the prophets and apostles to the Church in the past may give hints of what he will say though the same to the Church in our own day, but he is not bound to repeat himself. It is the freedom

upon Scripture, nor does he attempt to discover a unity present as a feature of the biblical text itself.[43] It is Jesus Christ, the genuine subject matter, and the Spirit, his interpreter, who together guarantee the unity of Scripture. Balthasar links the unity in diversity of Scripture with the unity of the Church, which is constituted by many members. 'The New Testament, inspired by the same Holy Spirit who inspires the Church, could therefore have no other structure than the Church: in the multiplicity, a unity; and the living principle of this unity dwells in it only because it first of all (as head) transcends it.'[44]

The most vital consequence of Balthasar's affirmation of the unity of Scripture for our task of exploring the biblical character of the descent into hell is the conclusion that no text can be read in isolation. Balthasar exhibits great freedom in unapologetically bringing a variety of texts together in order to determine the significance of a specific text. Balthasar's theological exegesis is a prime example

---

of God to address himself to the Church in new and different ways through the witness of Scripture which gave rise, in Barth's view, to the possibility that a text could bear a plurality of meanings.' McCormack continues by distinguishing the grounds for Barth's acknowledgement of multiple meanings from the similar conclusion drawn from literary approaches to the Bible. He writes, 'Note well: that Barth could accept the possibility that biblical texts could bear a number of valid meanings had nothing to do with a general literary-critical theory. It had everything to do with his conviction that God is a living agent, who continues to speak anew through these ancient texts.' Bruce McCormack, 'Historical Criticism and Dogmatic Interest in Karl Barth's Theological Exegesis of the New Testament', in *Biblical Hermeneutics in Historical Perspective: Studies in Honor of Karlfreid Froehlich on His Sixtieth Birthday*, ed. Mark S. Burrows and Paul Rorem (Grand Rapids, MI: Wm. B. Eerdmans Publishing Company, 1991), p. 333.

43   Oakes recognizes Balthasar's affinity with narrative and canonical interpretations of Scripture, which stress the Bible's intratextual coherence and intelligibility. Oakes points out, however, that the unity of Scripture and the harmony present between the Old and New Testaments is not simply attributable to the Bible as a unified text; rather, the unity and harmony is established by an extra-textual reality, i.e., the actuality of redemption, which is accomplished by Jesus Christ – the eternal Word of God incarnate. Oakes writes, 'While his work bears crucial affinities with the work of textual and canonical critics, it is absolutely crucial to realize that the harmony he sees obtaining between the two Testaments is primarily *extra*-textual: that is, one that is shaped much more by what Anselm termed *rectitudo* than by what literary critics mean by an integrated text. What I mean by this: that *once one realizes how, in the way our redemption was carried out, "it had to be thus,"* the inner connections between the worlds of the Old and New Testaments will emerge into view. This is admittedly related to the position that the advocates of narrative theology take, but I think it must be distinguished from theirs by its fundamentally *extra-textual* referentiality.' Oakes, *Pattern of Redemption*, p. 186.

Barth too affirms the unity of Scripture on the basis of its proper subject matter. Mary Kathleen Cunningham observes, '[Barth] treats New Testament texts not first as diverse but rather as ultimately cohering because he sees Scripture as a unified witness to Jesus Christ. As he has affirmed in *CD* I/2, "The object of the biblical texts is quite simply the name Jesus Christ, and these texts can be understood only when understood as determined by this object" (p. 727). Barth believes that Scripture is canon, with a unified witness, because of the unity of its object; it is not the case that Scripture as a text is intrinsically one but rather that Scripture is one because Jesus Christ is One.' Mary Kathleen Cunningham, *What is Theological Exegesis? Interpretation and Use of Scripture in Barth's Doctrine of Election* (Valley Forge, PA: Trinity Press International, 1995), p. 70.

44   Balthasar, *The Glory of the Lord* VII, p. 112.

of the practice of using Scripture to interpret Scripture. Two related passages in *Theo-Drama* II provide a definitive statement of Balthasar's insistence on a multiplicity of interpretations of the true subject matter of Scripture, which leads to the necessity of interpreting Scripture by way of Scripture:

> Naturally the standpoint of the word of God must be so total and so rich that it mocks every attempt to tie it down to particular schemata. All we can do is to circle around it, approaching it from countless perspectives. That is evidently why the Spirit inspired the variety of biblical writings. Neither in the forward march of the Old Testament nor in the great synthetic utterances of the New can these writings be 'systematically' shown to coincide, if by 'system' we mean some totality that can be cited, surveyed and evaluated before the judgment seat of human reason.
>
> ... Since God's entire purpose for the world is present in every phase of theo-drama ... the entirety of the word must also be present, at all times, in the individual books and words of Scripture, however much they may characterize one particular aspect, one particular phase. God's word can reveal itself anew from an infinite number of sides, but it cannot be parceled out. Therefore, if we are to proceed theologically, the individual passage can only be properly interpreted within the total context of Scripture, however much effort we must first invest in ascertaining its particular meaning, its special significance, and so forth. (*TD* II, pp. 78–9, 114)

By acknowledging the unity of Scripture, as located in its proper subject matter, and affirming the reality and necessity of multiplicity, we may conclude that Balthasar bases his understanding of the descent into hell on a synthetic reading of Scripture. He will not attempt to construct a doctrine of the descent into hell based upon isolated exegesis of individual passages that have been traditionally considered as referring to the descent into hell, i.e. 1 Peter 3:18–22; 4:6; Romans 10:6–7; Ephesians 4:8–10. In fact, he denies that these passages individually or even collectively are capable of validating a doctrine of the descent into hell. On this point he agrees, to a certain extent, with critics of the confession of the descent into hell who point to the exegetical difficulties present in these texts. Balthasar, however, departs from these critics who call for the removal of the clause 'he descended into hell' because of lack of biblical warrant. Balthasar maintains that the descent into hell is indeed a valid interpretation of Scripture as a whole, if not of specific, individual texts. The validity of the descent into hell, thus, does not depend upon the interpretation of isolated texts; rather, it depends upon rigorous theological reflection on the revelation present in Scripture taken as a whole.[45]

The second feature of Balthasar's theological exegesis to be addressed is the

---

45 It is important to note that Barth also challenges the assumption that a theological doctrine must be grounded on the exegesis of specific biblical texts. Barth affirms a distinction between the practice of biblical exegesis and the task of dogmatics. These two disciplines may not be separated, but neither can they be collapsed into one another. In his discussion of the biblical character of dogmatics, Barth describes the task of dogmatics insofar as the dogmatician must refer to the biblical text, yet must move beyond the specific endeavour of biblical exegesis. See *CD* I/2, p. 821.

relationship between Scripture and tradition. Balthasar places himself, and every biblical interpreter, under the guidance of the history of biblical interpretation, which runs from the Fathers through the medieval period and the Reformation. Balthasar commits himself to learning from the women and men throughout the Church's history who have devoutly approached Scripture and ventured an interpretation.

Balthasar's regard for the importance of the Church's tradition as a complement to Scripture is obvious in his constructive soteriology, and most notably in his interpretation of the descent into hell. Balthasar affirms an asymmetrical relationship between Scripture and tradition, as he does not consider the two as parallel and distinct sources for divine revelation. In one instance, Balthasar describes the relationship between Scripture and tradition with the aid of marriage imagery. He writes, 'The word of scripture is a gift of the Bridegroom to his bride the Church. It is destined for the Church and, in this respect, belongs to her; but it is also the Word of God, the Word of the Head and as such it is above the Church.'[46] Scripture retains authority in theology, even as tradition is affirmed as bearing witness to divine revelation, and even as biblical interpretation must always take place within the life of the Church. Tradition, for Balthasar, is not a source of revelation independent of Scripture; nor is it the natural organic development from Scripture; rather, it is witness to the living presence of Jesus Christ. 'If [the Church] recognizes tradition as a source of the faith alongside scripture', Balthasar states, 'it is far from her intention to evade the authority of scripture by appealing to traditions unknown, perhaps even formed by herself. What she really means is that the letter of scripture can, after the incarnation, only be a function of his living humanity which, in any case, transcends mere literalness.'[47]

In his constructive doctrine of the descent into hell, Balthasar, on the one hand, relies heavily on the traditional readings of the descent into hell and the experiences of Christian mystics. On the other hand, he strongly criticizes traditional interpretations and depictions of the descent into hell. Although Balthasar relies upon the history of theological reflection regarding the descent into hell and upon the 'dark night' experiences of Christian mystics, he does not accept this material blindly. In practice, he does not hesitate in challenging prominent features of the interpretation of the descent into hell common to a host of Patristic divines. He does not reject wholesale the teachings of the Mothers and Fathers of the Church; rather, he appropriates what he can and shapes his teaching into a form that he considers both biblically and theologically warranted.[48]

---

46   Hans Urs von Balthasar, 'The Word, Scripture and Tradition', in *Explorations in Theology*, volume I, *The Word Made Flesh*, trans. A. V. Littledale with Alexander Dru (San Francisco: Ignatius Press, 1989), p. 17.

47   Ibid.

48   Balthasar introduces a section devoted to Jesus' solidarity with humanity in his death by clearly stating his task. He writes, 'What we have said up to now leads us to undertake a critical examination of the theological tradition, as that has developed from the end of the first century until our own day,

Balthasar's specific emphasis on the passivity and objectivity of Christ's experience of death, which he learned from Adrienne von Speyr and with which he approaches Scripture, leads him to critique the portrayal of the descent into hell in the iconography of the Eastern Church. Balthasar asserts that the images of Christ's breaking down the gates of hell and liberating the prisoners, beginning with Adam, illegitimately impose the effects of Easter on the time of Holy Saturday, and transform the victory of Holy Saturday 'which was objective and passive into one that is subjective and active'.[49] Though it is indeed proper to attribute victory and triumph to Christ's solidarity with the dead to the point of his unique vision of hell, this victory takes place precisely in the silence and isolation of Jesus' abandonment and forsakenness.[50]

Balthasar's rejection or radical revision of the traditionally dominant interpretation of the descent as the 'harrowing of hell', which is vividly depicted in the iconography of the Eastern Church, troubles even some of his most his sympathetic readers. Balthasar's insistence on the sheer passivity of the dead Christ, which precludes any form of activity during the time of Holy Saturday, is disconcerting to John Saward because 'it is at odds with the long tradition, theological as well as literary and iconographic, which sees Christ descending as Victor, the Harrower of Hell, the One who alone is "free among the dead"'.[51] Not only does Saward judge Balthasar's interpretation as in conflict with the consensus of tradition; he also claims that it contradicts the clearest testimony to the descent into hell in Scripture, 1 Peter 3:18–22, which asserts that 'the departed soul of Jesus "preaches"'.[52] Saward acknowledges that Balthasar attempts to account for the difference between his account of the passive Christ and the interpretation of the descent into hell that associates activities of liberation and proclamation to Christ during Holy Saturday. Saward also acknowledges the possibility of reconciling the traditional image of Christ as preacher, liberator, and victor, with the Balthasarian image of the passive dead Christ, by claiming that 'it is precisely as passively dead that Christ actively preaches'.[53]

---

without for all that rejecting it completely. We must not only grade the differing value of its affirmations but examine each one in particular in order to re-compose the set in a new way. Certain elements will find themselves definitively laid to one side (such as the mythical accoutrements of a combat in Hades). Others, and above all the soteriological explorations excluded by recent dogmatics in favour of a rigid systmatisation, will be once again placed in the limelight.' *MP*, p. 160.

49 Ibid., p. 180.

50 Balthasar does not completely reject the depiction of the descent and resurrection in the icons of the Easter tradition. He regards the Eastern icons superior to the Western images of Easter, because in the East the risen Christ is accompanied by those whom he redeemed in his death; he is not alone, which is the way he is portrayed in the West. Balthasar affirms this emphasis on the social and communal element of Christ's passion. Jesus Christ died, descended into hell, and was raised *pro nobis* – for us and for the whole world.

51 Saward, *Mysteries of March*, p. 123.

52 Ibid.

53 Ibid.

Fergus Kerr also questions Balthasar's overturning of tradition in his radical revision of the harrowing of hell motif. He acknowledges the potential for reconciling Balthasar and the tradition as Saward proposes, but, even so, he calls Balthasar's procedure into question. He determines that it is at odds with traditional Catholic practice. Kerr specifically challenges Balthasar's position on the descent into hell because he questions the major influence that Speyr's individual mystical experiences has on Balthasar's understanding of the descent into hell. Kerr ends his essay on the relationship between Balthasar and Speyr with the critical conclusion that the 'harrowing of hell' is 'one familiar theological and iconographical topos that von Balthasar radically revises, principally on the strength of von Speyr's private revelations'. Kerr regards this practice as 'not a very traditional way in which to develop Catholic doctrine'.[54] Kerr, however, underestimates the significant role played by Scripture and elements in the Church's tradition in Balthasar's understanding of the descent into hell, and his corresponding criticism of the traditional account of the harrowing of hell. At the same time, Kerr overestimates the impact of Speyr's personal experiences. Although Speyr's influence, as well as the experiences of Christian mystics throughout the history of the Church, is significant and undisputed, it does not exercise monolithic control over Balthasar's soteriology.

Balthasar is not cavalier in his critical treatment of the traditionally held interpretation of the descent into hell in terms of the harrowing of hell. I contend that various factors influence Balthasar's interpretation of the descent into hell and his radical revision of the tradition, and these factors include: the interpenetration of biblical passages, the experiences of Christian mystics (insofar as they are directed toward and reveal the experience of Christ in his suffering), theological reflection on the death of Christ and the descent into hell present in the history of the Church, and the liturgy of the Paschal Triduum.[55] These factors influence Balthasar's interpretation of Scripture and his constructive theology of Holy Saturday, but they

---

54 Fergus Kerr, 'Adrienne von Speyr and Hans Urs von Balthasar', *New Blackfriars* 79 (1998): p. 32.
55 Saward cites the constant refrain of the Byzantine liturgy on Great and Holy Saturday in his attempt to reconcile Balthasar's position with Scripture and the traditional interpretation of the harrowing of hell: 'Going down to death, O Life immortal, Thou hast slain Hell with the dazzling light of Thy divinity . . . Of Thine own will descending as one dead beneath the earth, O Jesus, Thou leadest up the fallen from earth to Heaven.' *The Lenten Triodion* as quoted in Saward, *The Mysteries of March*, p. 123. Balthasar also points to the prohibition of singing alleluias on Holy Saturday, and the lack of a celebration of the Eucharist on Holy Saturday as liturgical support for his position. See also Balthasar's meditations on the Stations of the Cross. In reflecting on the fourteenth station and the burial of Jesus, Balthasar points to the hope of the resurrection but reminds us that we must be patient, for Holy Saturday lies between the cross and the resurrection. He writes, 'Already the Easter question takes shape . . . But Silently. For tomorrow is only Holy Saturday. The day when God is dead, and the Church holds her breath. The strange day that separates life and death in order to join them in a marriage beyond all human thought. The day which leads through hell, and, after all the paths of the world, into a pathless existence.' Hans Urs von Balthasar, *The Way of the Cross*, trans. Rodelinde Albrecht and Maureen Sullivan (New York: Herder and Herder, 1969), p. 30.

function as an aid to his interpretation of Scripture. They do not supplant Scripture's priority or supplement the fullness of God's revelation in Scripture.

Balthasar's radical revision of the traditional account of the descent as the harrowing of hell demonstrates his theological creativity, and at the same time, it enables us to see a hint of Balthasar's tentativeness in his proposals concerning the descent into hell. Balthasar is both bold and self-critically restrained in his novel treatment of the descent into hell. Although he does not deny the spiritual benefits of contemplating the dramatic and joyful encounter between Jesus Christ and the prisoners of the dead, especially the encounter between the second Adam and the first, he insists that this detailed depiction of Jesus Christ's activities in death exceeds what theology can affirm (*MP*, pp. 180–1). Theology must resist the temptation to claim that it knows more that it ought to know, and the Church must follow the dead Christ on Holy Saturday from a distance. Balthasar somewhat matter-of-factly proposes a minimal description of his understanding of Christ's experience of hell on Holy Saturday as he states:

> This experience [of the *poena damni* on Holy Saturday] has no need to be anything other than what is implied by a real solidarity with the inhabitants of Sheol that no redemptive light has brightened. For all redemptive light comes uniquely from the one who was in solidarity until the end. And he can communicate it because he, substitutionally, renounced it. (*MP*, p. 172)

The mandate that the Church must follow from a distance further contributes to our understanding of the complicated issue of Balthasar's reliance on the experiences of Christian mystics in his theological reflection on the descent into hell. Balthasar wants to reclaim for contemporary theology the source of a theology of the passion that 'lies in the great holy figures of Church history' who were given a charism that enabled them to 're-immerse themselves, beyond everything that convention might dictate, in a "contemporaneity" with the Gospel so as to bequeath the legacy of their intimate experience to their spiritual children' (*MP*, p. 39). In regard to the specific topic of the descent into hell, Balthasar highlights what he sees as 'an uninterrupted charismatic re-interpretation of the Cross . . . [which] runs through the centuries of the Church's life' (*MP*, p. 76). He is primarily concerned with 'those charismatic experiences of night and abandonment', which take the form of a struggle against demons in the East and, in the West, the 'comprehension of the "radiant darkness" of the unknown God' and the purification of the soul through the '"tests" of God-abandonment' (*MP*, p. 77). Balthasar contends that in order for these charismatic experiences to contribute to our understanding of Jesus Christ's descent into hell, they must be directed towards participation in Christ and must be conformed to Christ's own suffering. He recognizes grave dangers in certain forms of mysticism, especially the apophaticism that has its source in Psuedo-Dionysius. 'What bothers von Balthasar about itineraries of apophatic ascent', Mark McIntosh observes, 'is that, unless they are reinterpreted in terms of a christomorphic *descent*, they focus attention more immediately on the soul's progress than on the soul's participation in Christ or Christ's own experience of suffering.'[56]

In his notable essay, 'Theology and Sanctity', Balthasar emphatically challenges theologians to utilize mystical experiences of saints, which include participation in the sufferings of Christ. Balthasar inquires, 'Why should we persist in ignoring the detail of these sufferings, making not the least attempt to use, for a better understanding of the faith, these experiences so valuable for the Church?'[57] The theological significance of the 'participation' in the sufferings of Christ lies not in the particular experience of the individual and what this reveals about the spiritual life of the saint; rather, the theological significance lies solely in the light that is shed by this experience on the fullness of Christ's suffering in his death. In order for these experiences to be revelatory of Jesus Christ's inner experiences in his passion, they must be considered as genuine 'participation' in his sufferings. Otherwise, they would only give us insight into the capabilities of humans for suffering, and we cannot simply raise human suffering to the highest degree and, as a result, arrive at the suffering of Jesus Christ. Jesus Christ's suffering is unique, and is qualitatively, and not merely quantitatively, distinct from human suffering. The 'dark night' experiences of Christian mystics, Balthasar insists, mark the relationship between the Church and Jesus Christ – the body and its head. The importance of the experiences of the saints for the Church, Balthasar concludes, is 'the fact that something of the passion is, through the grace of the Head, constantly being made present in the body, and that the body needs to understand what is happening there by relating it to the Head as its source and end'.[58]

Even though Balthasar affirms that the 'dark night' experiences of Christian mystics that are properly ordered towards the experience and suffering of Jesus Christ may indeed enhance our understanding of Christ's own suffering and agony in his death, he insists that we honour the great distance that separates Christ from his followers. This distance remains even in the midst of the Christian mystic's 'participation' in the suffering of Christ. The Church is able to follow Christ only

---

56 Mark A. McIntosh, *Christology from Within: Spirituality and the Incarnation in Hans Urs von Balthasar* (Notre Dame, IN: University of Notre Dame Press, 1996), p. 93. In this illuminating and provocative study, McIntosh explores the relationship between theology and spirituality and argues that Balthasar's christology is best understood as what he calls a 'mystical christology'. In describing Balthasar's christology as a 'mystical christology' McIntosh writes, 'It is a christology "from within". Although it would undoubtedly rank as a "high" christology, one that always assumes the full divinity of Jesus, it is not a standard christology "from above"; that is, its center of gravity is not really the eternal life of the divine Logos. Nor is it a christology "from below," focusing on the critical examination of Jesus' earthly sayings or ministry or sociocultural milieu. Rather von Balthasar develops a christology from within, an analysis of Christ from the perspective of those women and men who have mystically entered *within* the life of Christ.' McIntosh, *Christology from Within*, pp. 1–2.
57 Hans Urs von Balthasar, 'Theology and Sanctity', in *Explorations in Theology*, volume I, *The Word Made Flesh*, trans. A. V. Littledale with Alexander Dru (San Francisco: Ignatius Press, 1989), pp. 199–200.
58 Ibid., p. 200.

at a distance. Balthasar concludes, 'All the experiences of night in both Old and New Testaments [he includes Christian mystics throughout the history of the Church in his discussion of the New Testament] are at best approaches, distant allusions to the inaccessible mystery of the Cross – so unique is the Son of God, so unique is his abandonment by the Father' (*MP*, p. 79).

Balthasar's designation of the 'dark night' experiences of Christian mystics as 'distant allusions', and his consistent appeal to the unique and exclusive character of Jesus Christ's vicarious suffering and death cautions against overstating the influence of Christian mysticism on his theological reflection and construction. We may acknowledge that the testimonies of those graced with the charism of participating in Christ's suffering shape, to a certain extent, his reading of Scripture and the interpretation of Scripture in the history of theology, but we must stop short of crediting these experiences with a form of revelation that lies outside Scripture.[59] On this point I concur with Edward Oakes' evaluation of the relationship between the experiences of Speyr – to these we could add the experiences of a host of Christian mystics – and Balthasar's theology of Holy Saturday. Oakes writes, 'What further access do they [Speyr's mystical experiences of Holy Saturday] give to theologians that is not otherwise available to them from revelation and later reflection on it? I myself am cautious about attributing any direct theological content (in the sense of new revelation) to her experiences.'[60]

By relegating the influence of Christian mysticism to a secondary role in Balthasar's understanding of the descent into hell, we may argue for the principal role played by Scripture. Although Balthasar was undeniably prompted to investigate the Church's confession of the *descensus ad inferna* by witnessing and recording Speyr's experiences of the hell of Holy Saturday, which belong to a great history of Christian mystical experiences, his articulation of a theology of the descent into hell is primarily determined by a synthetic reading of Scripture and by

---

59   This is not to dismiss McIntosh's thesis regarding Balthasar's Christology as 'mystical christology' and his work on the relationship between spirituality and theology. Rather, it is to point out that Balthasar's theology of Holy Saturday is genuinely biblical and involves drawing out conclusions from the biblical text and the logic of redemption as evident in Christ's passion to which the biblical text bears witness. There is not a direct line between Speyr's individual, personal mystical experiences and Balthasar's theology of the descent.

Even though Balthasar chides the Church and theologians for neglecting the experiences of Christian mystics as an important source for reflection on the passion of Christ, he does not, in any way, regard these experiences as normative for theological reflection. His view of the relationship between genuine Christian mysticism and Scripture is clearly seen as he writes, 'Since God's truth is imparted to the soul in scripture, no dialogue between God and the soul, however interior or mystical, ever takes precedence of scripture or replaces it . . . It would be far better for Christian mysticism to recognize in scripture its true canon, instead of diverting into the obscurities of individual psychology. Christian mysticism is scriptural mysticism, that is to say, a special charismatic form of encounter with the word. Its function, direct or indirect, is to convey the revelation of the word to the Church.' Balthasar, 'The Word, Scripture and Tradition', p. 25.

60   Oakes, *Pattern of Redemption*, p. 238, n. 17.

the logic of redemption that is ascertained through theological reflection on Scripture. Balthasar's teaching regarding the descent into hell is most accurately seen as an extrapolation from the logic of the redemption wrought by God in the life and passion of his incarnate Son, Jesus Christ. If in Jesus Christ God has entered into the sinful condition of humanity, freely taken on the sin of the world, and endured the eschatological penalty for this sin, all for the purpose of destroying death and sin and reconciling humanity with himself, then we must faithfully reflect upon the gravity of Jesus Christ's suffering and the condition of the Son of God in his death. And this leads therefore to an affirmation of Christ's encounter with hell during the silence of Holy Saturday.

As we have seen, Balthasar brings various factors into play in his augmentation of the story of Jesus Christ to include the descent into hell of Holy Saturday as a primary scene. All of these factors must be taken into account in order for one to present an adequate description and assessment of Balthasar's theology of Holy Saturday. Balthasar affirms the importance of specific New Testament passages as starting points for theological reflection on Christ's condition in his death, his being among the dead, in short, his descent into hell. Yet, Balthasar readily admits that these passages are thin and, as a result, are incapable of supporting a fully worked out doctrine of the descent into hell. Other elements must be fastened to these 'thin' passages in order bear the weight of a comprehensive theology of Holy Saturday. Balthasar reads these passages in the light of other biblical texts, traditionally held interpretations, accounts of the experiences of Christian mystics, and the liturgical enactment of the Paschal Triduum. The affirmation that Jesus Christ died and was truly dead leads Balthasar to Old Testament depictions of Sheol in order to describe the condition of the dead Christ during the time between the cross and the resurrection. Balthasar then adds to the affirmation that as a true human being Jesus Christ experienced a true human death by calling upon New Testament descriptions of the unique and exclusive character of Christ's person and death, and the corresponding representative and substitutionary construal of Christ's person and death. The death that Christ died goes beyond the death common to all human beings. Jesus Christ dies the sin of the sin-bearer and he does this for the sake of the world. The death and descent of Jesus Christ enacts God's loving and saving will for humanity, and manifests God's desire to enter into an intimate relationship with humanity in order to redeem humanity from within, and not from without as an external bystander.

Balthasar also employs the testimony of Christian mystics throughout the history of the Church, and specifically the testimony of his theological companion Speyr, in his depiction of the internal state of Jesus Christ in his suffering and death. This testimony is used by Balthasar not as a separate source of revelation, which judges and surpasses Scripture; rather, this testimony is valid, according to Balthasar, only insofar as it is considered as a genuine revelation of Jesus Christ, and as a result, enables us to be better readers of Scripture. All of these factors – biblical, traditional and experiential – allow Balthasar to speak with quiet confidence regarding the condition of the dead Jesus Christ on Holy Saturday, in spite of the understandable silence of the gospel narratives and the paucity of biblical passages that refer to Christ's descent into hell – passages about which an interpretative consensus is lacking.

Perhaps the most productive way to account for Balthasar's rationale for proposing such a developed understanding of the descent into hell is to point to various conditional statements that succinctly summarize his position. As we have seen, one may account for Balthasar's creative exposition of the descent into hell by acknowledging Balthasar's reliance on Scripture and by examining his use of Scripture. Admittedly, Balthasar employs a variety of factors in his interpretation of Scripture and in his theological construction, which is based upon Scripture; yet, Balthasar's rationale for affirming the doctrinally essential status of the descent into hell lies in a few basic theological convictions, which he extrapolates from the biblical witness.

Balthasar's stress on the descent into hell is a consequence of his affirmation of God's intimate involvement with the human condition, which is manifested in the solidarity of Jesus Christ with sinful humanity, and, further, in Jesus Christ's substitutionary bearing of the world's sin by standing in the place of sinners. 'If the kenosis, and the form of Jesus' existence in claim, poverty, and self-abandonment that is based upon kenosis, made possible the bearing of the sin of the world', Balthasar asserts, 'this act of bearing can be accomplished only in solidarity with the death that is the lot of all.'[61] The actuality of human redemption is dependent, according to Balthasar, on the reality of God's entering into the situation of sinful humanity. God must directly experience human suffering and death in order for God to take this suffering and death, and the hold that it has on humanity, destroy it, and free humanity for a new life. Balthasar writes:

> If God wished to 'experience' (*zein peira*, cf. Hebrews 2, 18; 4, 15) the human condition 'from within', so as to re-direct it from inside it, and thus save it, he would have to place the decisive stress on that point where sinful, mortal man finds himself 'at his wit's end'. And this must be where man has lost himself in death without, for all that, finding God. This is the place where he has fallen into an abyss of grief, indigence, darkness, into the 'pit' from which he cannot escape by his own powers. (*MP*, p. 13)

The radical extreme to which Jesus Christ goes in his solidarity with sinful humanity is expressed in the soteriological necessity of his 'being reckoned among those who have broken the law' (Luke 22:37), his 'being with the unredeemed dead, in the Sheol of the Old Testament' (*MP*, p. 161), and his suffering for the whole world, which includes even those who reject him (*MP*, p. 172). In its most basic expression, Balthasar's insistence on the essential importance of the descent into hell is an implication of his understanding of God's love. In the end, only the

---

61   Balthasar, *The Glory of the Lord*, VII, p. 229.

radical nature of divine love can account for Jesus Christ's journey to the extreme limit of human suffering and death. If God, in Jesus Christ, is in complete solidarity with humanity, then God, in Jesus Christ, must directly experience everything proper to humanity, up to and including death. If Jesus Christ's person and work are best understood in terms of being 'for us' and 'in our place', then Jesus Christ must endure the wrath of God that is meant for humanity and must die not only the physical death common to all humans, but the death that is best understood as the 'second death'. Jesus Christ must die the second death in the place of humanity so that humans are then spared from it. If the entire world is reconciled and redeemed in the death of Jesus Christ, then God, in Jesus Christ, must take the place of his enemies.[62]

We may conclude that Balthasar's understanding of the descent into hell is consonant with Barth's interpretation of Christ's passion, as articulated in his constructive soteriology. Balthasar, in his explicit treatment of the descent into hell as a distinct and essential element of the passion, takes Barth's concerns and convictions regarding Jesus Christ's vicarious death to their necessary limit. He explores them further than does Barth, without contradicting Barth. The suffering that Jesus Christ endures for us and for our salvation, according to Balthasar, cannot be restricted to the cross of Good Friday. To this suffering must be added the distinct suffering of the dead Christ, and his experience of hell in the pure silence and isolation of Holy Saturday.

Conclusion: the descent into hell and scripture

It is now possible to return to the criticism levelled against the descent into hell by Grudem, which was introduced at the beginning of this chapter. The examination of Barth's and Balthasar's use of Scripture in their treatments of the descent into hell within their constructive soteriologies has made it evident that they would partially agree with Grudem's conclusion that 'the idea of Christ's "descent into hell" is by no means taught clearly or explicitly in any passage of Scripture'.[63] Barth and Balthasar agree that a fully developed doctrine of the descent into hell cannot be achieved from the mere exegesis of a set of isolated passages. This, however, does not necessarily lead to the conclusion that the doctrine of the descent into hell is unbiblical. And here Barth and Balthasar radically depart from Grudem's conclusions. Acknowledging that the descent into hell cannot be grounded exclusively on a few scattered and isolated texts in the New Testament does not require one to endorse Grudem's stronger conclusion that the idea of the descent into hell is not taught in Scripture at all.[64] The doctrine of the descent into

---

62   See Barth's exegesis of John 3:16 in *CD*, IV/1, pp. 70–8.
63   Grudem, 'He Did Not Descend into Hell', p. 112.
64   Ibid.

hell, both Balthasar and Barth claim, is not the product of the exegesis of isolated biblical passages; rather, it is the logical consequence of a synthetic reading of Scripture, and rigorous reflection on the implications of the *pro nobis* character of Jesus Christ's life and passion.

The descent into hell, though not explicitly and fully taught in Scripture, has initial warrant in specific biblical texts. These texts may act as starting points for theological reflection on the descent into hell, and one must add to these texts in order to offer interpretations of them that account for the profound character of Jesus Christ's vicarious death and the unique condition of the incarnate Son of God in his death. It ought to be clear that both Balthasar and Barth would challenge Grudem's definitive judgment that 'there would be all gain and no loss if [the clause "he descended into hell"] were dropped from the Creed once for all'.[65] Nothing would be gained and potentially everything would be lost, according to Barth and Balthasar, if the descent into hell were to be removed from the Church's confession of faith and deemed off limits to dogmatic theology. Admittedly, there must be rigorous theological, biblical and historical reflection regarding the proper interpretation of the descent into hell – not every interpretation is acceptable – but a theology that lacks a treatment of the descent into hell is incomplete and fails to treat adequately the profound character of Jesus Christ's vicarious life and passion.

For Barth, the cry of dereliction, which indicates the severity of Jesus Christ's death in God-abandonment, demands that the Church and her theology reflect upon the condition of Jesus Christ in his death, and endorse the confession that he descended into hell. The elimination of the descent into hell from the Church's confession makes it impossible for the theologian to do justice to the narrative depiction of Jesus Christ's death in God-abandonment in the gospels and to the interpretation confessed and proclaimed in the apostolic Church and theologically articulated by the apostle Paul. Thus, for Barth, affirmation of and reflection on the descent into hell is not only warranted by Scripture; Scripture demands it. If one is to reflect theologically on the passion of Christ with the seriousness with which it is both narratively depicted and apostolically interpreted, then one must rigorously examine the meaning of Jesus Christ's death in God-abandonment, which includes his encounter with, or descent into, hell.

Balthasar, it may be argued, takes up Barth's conviction regarding the signifi-cance of interpreting Jesus Christ's death as the 'second death' and expands this conviction by articulating a full understanding of the descent into hell. Balthasar treats explicitly what is implicit in Barth's reflections on the passion of Christ. Whereas Barth refrains from treating the descent into hell as an event proper to Holy Saturday, the time between Christ's death and resurrection, Balthasar faith-fully and creatively expands the biblical narrative to include the 'event' of Christ's descent into hell on Holy Saturday as an essential element of Christ's passion. The result of his imaginative expansion of the biblical narrative is not an extra-biblical

---

65 Ibid., p. 113.

doctrinal addition; rather, it is a doctrine that attends not simply to the words of the biblical text, but attends to the profound, mysterious and inexhaustible reality to which the biblical text bears witness. Balthasar's understanding of the descent into hell is indeed substantiated by Scripture, as it is the product of serious theological reflection on the reality to which Scripture points, namely, God's intimate and redemptive involvement with the sinful world.

The construction of a doctrine of the descent into hell need not be explicitly grounded upon specific biblical texts; rather, it must rely upon a reading of Scripture as a whole. A doctrine of the descent into hell must incorporate a theological interpretation of Scripture and must bring theological convictions to the interpretation of specific biblical texts. A doctrine of the descent into hell may only be the result of rigorous theological reflection on the portrayal of Jesus Christ in the gospels, the interpretation of life and death of Jesus Christ, which was articulated and proclaimed by the apostles, and the precursors to Jesus Christ present in the history and literature of Israel. A doctrine of the descent into hell is both an appropriate and necessary extrapolation from Scripture, which bears witness to the logic of redemption. This redemptive logic, as determined by God, is manifested in God's presence and activity in the life and passion of Jesus Christ. Jesus Christ, in his passion, bears the sin of the world, endures the wrath of God as the rightful penalty for this sin, and by being abandoned and forsaken by God encounters and experiences the isolation and pains of hell. All of this effects the redemption of humanity and the reconciliation of humanity to God. Therefore, we may conclude that far from being a dispensable article of the Church's confession, the descent into hell is essential to a rich and thorough understanding of the salvation wrought in the event of the passion of Jesus Christ attested in Holy Scripture.

CHAPTER FOUR

The descent into hell and the Trinity

After examining the biblical character of the descent into hell, it is necessary to address the relationship between the descent into hell and other doctrines. Since no one doctrine stands in isolation, free from the influence of other doctrines, it is imperative to explore the mutual influence that various doctrines have upon one another. In order to demonstrate the importance of the descent into hell for a comprehensive interpretation of the passion of Jesus Christ and an adequate soteriology, we must examine the consistency and coherence of the doctrine of the descent into hell with other doctrines.

For our purpose of exploring the function of the descent into hell in the theologies of Barth and Balthasar, the interrelation between the descent into hell and the doctrine of the Trinity will prove to be most productive and instructive. We will examine both the function of the Trinity as the ground for the descent into hell and the effect of the descent into hell on the Trinitarian life of God. In order to highlight and clarify the positions held by Balthasar and Barth, I will incorporate an examination of Jürgen Moltmann's creative work on the relationship between the cross and the life of the triune God. This will bring the proposals of Barth and Balthasar into greater relief. If we were to place these three positions on a continuum, Balthasar would lie between Moltmann and Barth as he attempts to account for the essential elements of both positions, while, at the same time, distancing himself from both at significant points. At the end of the day, however, Balthasar stands closer to Barth. In short, Moltmann will function as a way of clarifying the positions of Balthasar and Barth.

Jürgen Moltmann's theology of the cross and the descent into hell

Jürgen Moltmann's reflection on the descent into hell and his construction of a doctrine of the Trinity as based on the particularity of Jesus Christ's abandonment on the cross share many important elements with Barth and Balthasar. It is, however, the significant differences that distinguish Moltmann from Barth and Balthasar that prove to be most suggestive in our evaluation of the significance of the doctrine of the descent into hell for contemporary theology.

Moltmann's assertion that all theology must be a theology of the cross runs throughout his extensive body of work. In his groundbreaking work, *The Crucified God*, Moltmann affirms the conviction that all theology must begin with the crucifixion of Jesus Christ:

> The death of Jesus on the cross is the *centre* of all Christian theology. It is not the only theme of theology, but it is in effect the entry to its problems and answers on earth. All Christian statements about God, about creation, about sin and death have their focal point in the crucified Christ. All Christian statements about history, about the church, about faith and sanctification, about the future and about hope stem from the crucified Christ . . . When the crucified Jesus is called the 'image of the invisible God', the meaning is that *this* is God, and God is like *this* . . . The nucleus of everything that Christian theology says about 'God' is to be found in this Christ event. The Christ event on the cross is a God event . . . What happens on the cross manifests the relationships of Jesus, the Son, to the Father, and vice versa. The cross and its liberating effect makes possible the movement of the Spirit from the Father to us. The cross stands at the heart of the trinitarian being of God; it divides and conjoins the persons in their relationships to each other and portrays them in a specific way . . . Anyone who really talks of the Trinity talks of the cross of Jesus, and does not speculate in heavenly riddles.[1]

The cross, according to Moltmann, is the centre not only of all Christian theology; it is also the centre of God's history. The cross is the centre of the life or history of Jesus Christ, and since Christian faith confesses that the history of Christ is the history of God, then the cross must be the centre of God's history as well. This confession of the identification of Jesus Christ's history with the history of God is intelligible, according to Moltmann, only in Trinitarian terms.[2]

Moltmann follows Luther in his understanding of the descent into hell. The descent into hell, according to Moltmann and Luther, describes the agony and suffering of Jesus Christ that begins in the garden of Gethsemane and continues through the arrest, trial and crucifixion, culminating in the cry of dereliction – the cry of the God-forsaken Son.[3] Jesus Christ's passion, which Moltmann identifies as the descent into hell, is framed by two appeals by Jesus to God. The first is Jesus' request, or demand, for the removal of the cup of suffering that awaits him. The second, which follows upon God's response to the first, is the desperate cry from the cross of the abandoned Son.

Moltmann asserts that God rejects Jesus' plea for the removal of the cup of suffering that will lead to separation from God. In ignoring or rejecting this plea, the Father withdraws from, forsakes and abandons the Son. It is precisely this failure to hear Jesus Christ's request, or, more strongly, the Father's deliberate

---

1   Jürgen Moltmann, *The Crucified God: The Cross of Christ as the Foundation and Criticism of Christian Theology*, trans. R. A. Wilson and John Bowden (Minneapolis: Fortress Press, 1993), pp. 204–7.

2   See Jürgen Moltmann, *The Future of Creation: Collected Essays*, trans. Margaret Kohl (Philadelphia: Fortress Press, 1979), p. 81.

3   Moltmann agrees with Luther's assessment of the suffering of Christ in his descent into hell, which extends from Gethsemane to Golgotha. See Jürgen Moltmann, *The Trinity and the Kingdom: The Doctrine of God*, trans. Margaret Kohl (Minneapolis: Fortress Press, 1993), p. 77. See also Jürgen Moltmann, *Jesus Christ for Today's World*, trans. Margaret Kohl (Minneapolis: Fortress Press, 1994), p. 144.

rejection of the Son's plea, that leads to Jesus Christ's experience of the 'second death'. This experience is expressed in his refusal to address God as his Father in his desperate cry from the cross to God who has abandoned him. Moltmann, moreover, links the cry of dereliction to the relationships within the triune life of God.

> If we take the relinquishment of the Father's name in Jesus' death cry seriously, then this is even the breakdown of the relationship that constitutes the very life of the Trinity: if the Father forsakes the Son, the Son does not merely lose his sonship. The Father loses his fatherhood as well. The love that binds the one to the other is transformed into a dividing curse. It is only as the One who is forsaken and cursed that the Son is still the Son. It is only as the One who forsakes, who surrenders the other, that the Father is still present. Communicating love and responding love are alike transformed into infinite pain and into the suffering and endurance of death . . . On the Cross the Father and the Son are so deeply separated that their relationship breaks off.[4]

Moltmann interprets the words and events of Gethsemane and Golgotha as announcing the introduction of a rift or division into the divine life. The Father's silence in the face of the pleading of Son in Gethsemane, and the subsequent forsaking and abandoning of the Son by the Father on Golgotha, leads to an alteration of the life of God from unity to division, and the transformation of the love of God – between the Father and the Son – into pain and suffering. Moltmann concludes:

> Here [in the descent into hell when the Son loses the Father and the Father loses the Son] the innermost life of the Trinity is at stake. Here the communicating love of the Father *turns into* infinite pain over the sacrifice of the Son. Here the responding love of the Son *becomes* infinite suffering over his repulsion and rejection by the Father. What happens on Golgotha reaches into the innermost depths of the Godhead, putting its impress on the trinitarian life in eternity. [my emphasis][5]

Interpretations of Jesus' prayer in Gethsemane

Since Jesus' request in Gethsemane and God's horrific rejection of this request are determinative for Moltmann, it will be productive to examine closely the distinguishing features of Moltmann's and Barth's respective theological interpretation of Jesus' prayer in Gethsemane.[6] Here we will determine whether the scene in

---

4   Moltmann, *The Trinity and the Kingdom*, pp. 80, 82.
5   Ibid., p. 81.
6   Balthasar has his own reading of what takes place in Gethsemane, which is very close to Barth's. In a rich passage where Balthasar addresses the connection between Gethsemane, Golgotha and the resurrection, we have a typical summary of Balthasar's vision of the gospel. He writes, 'On the one hand; in the contrast between the two wills of the Father and the Son on the Mount of Olives, and in

Gethsemane displays perfect obedience of the Son to the Father and the alignment of wills, or, alternatively, the crushing imposition of the Father's will on the powerless Son. The exegesis of the scene of Jesus in Gethsemane immediately before his arrest is significant for Trinitarian reflection on the descent into hell, because it highlights the importance of the category of obedience for both Barth and Balthasar. Both Barth and Balthasar consider the descent into hell as the furthest limit of Jesus Christ's life of pure human obedience, as well as the final outcome of the mysterious obedience of the eternal Son to the Father.[7] The events of Gethsemane, according to Barth and Balthasar, manifest the unity of the Father's will with the Son's and do not represent the forcing of the Father's will upon the acquiescing Son, as if it were alien to the Son's true will. This comparison will also enable us to see how Barth upholds the unity of the Godhead even in the midst of Jesus Christ's death in God-abandonment, in contrast to Moltmann's affirmation of a rift that is introduced into the divine life as the Son is abandoned and forsaken by the Father, which, in turn, places the life of the Trinity in jeopardy.

For Barth, the garden of Gethsemane forms a turning point in the gospel story. Gethsemane marks a transition from Jesus Christ in his activity to his being acted upon. Gethsemane is the link between Jesus Christ's temptation in the wilderness and his death on the cross. Barth claims that in the story of Gethsemane, 'it is now shown where the victory which Jesus won in the temptation in the wilderness leads, that the end will involve the death of the victor' (*CD* IV/1, p. 264). The story of Gethsemane also presents a compressed account of the events of Good Friday. Gethsemane 'speaks of a passion of Jesus, but of a passion which has to do

---

the abandonment of the Son by God on the Cross, the drastic counterposing of the divine Persons in the economy became visible. On the other hand; for the individual who thinks this out more deeply, this very opposition appears as the supreme manifestation of the whole, integrated saving action of God whose internal logic (*dei*: Mk 8:31, and parallels; 9:31 and parallels; 10:34 and parallels) is once again disclosed in the inseparable unity of the Cross and the Resurrection. John gives this Trinitarian mystery its most concise expression, by coining, from the materials of the Old Testament, the phrase, "The Word became flesh". This formula allows us to understand the man Jesus – his life, death and resurrection – as the fulfillment of the living Word of God of the old covenant, shows the event of Jesus to be the definitive, superabundant consequence of the event of God himself, and interprets the Son's Resurrection as God's take-over of power in his own world, the fundamental breakthrough of the Kingdom.' *MP*, pp. 203–4.

7   Barth describes Jesus Christ's obedience not in terms of his fulfilment of moral requirements; rather, his obedience lies in his unwavering commitment to his mission. Barth writes, 'If we ask where the sinlessness, or (positively) the obedience of Christ, is to be seen, it is not enough to look for it in this man's excellences of character, virtues or good works. For we can only repeat that the New Testament did not present Jesus Christ as the moral ideal, . . . Jesus Christ's obedience consists in the fact that He willed to be and was only this one thing with all its consequences, God in the flesh, the divine bearer of the burden which man as a sinner must bear.' *CD* I/2, p. 156. For a brief discussion of the mystery of obedience in God see *CD* IV/1, pp. 193–7.

Balthasar's emphasis on the link between Jesus Christ's obedience, his mission and his descent into hell characterizes his understanding of Jesus Christ's saving death and descent into hell that runs through his entire theological work. See Balthasar, 'The Descent into Hell', p. 411.

strictly with the establishment of His definitive willingness for the real passion which comes upon Him immediately after' (*CD* IV/1, p. 264). As described in the judicial language and concepts employed by Barth, Gethsemane depicts the inauguration of the 'reversal in which the Judge becomes the judged' (*CD* IV/1, p. 264).

Moltmann, as we have seen, understands God's response to Jesus' plea to be spared from dying a death that includes separation from the Father as one of silence, or more forcefully, rejection. He proceeds to interpret the ultimate acceptance by Jesus of the cup of suffering that he must drink, which is expressed by Jesus' statement, 'Not what I will, but what thou wilt', as Jesus' forced acquiescence to the Father's will in contradiction to his own. Jesus is overpowered by the will of the Father and reluctantly accepts the ineluctability of the events to come.

Barth also takes the urgency and earnestness of Jesus' prayer in Gethsemane seriously. For Barth, the Father's response to Jesus' petition is precisely the actual events that follow. The answer or sign that Jesus receives is simply the actuality of the events leading up to and including his death. Even the future reality of the resurrection is withheld from Jesus, for the resurrection discloses the meaning of his suffering and death. In order for his suffering and death to be comprehensive and salvific, the saving meaning of them must be hidden from him. Jesus is given the same sign as others, the sign of Jonah who was three days and nights in the whale's belly. For Jesus, the only sign or answer to his prayer is his death, in which the Son of man will be three days and three nights in the heart of the earth. 'God will give His answer to the prayer only in this inconceivable, this frightful event, and not otherwise' (*CD* IV/1, p. 268). The frightful thing about the answer given by God is that in the death of Jesus Christ, 'the will of God was done as the will of Satan was done. The answer of God was identical to the action of Satan . . . the coincidence of the divine and the satanic will and work and word was the problem of this hour, the darkness in which Jesus addressed God in Gethsemane' (*CD* IV/1, p. 268).

Barth acutely interprets the movement from the request made by Jesus in prayer to the Father to his acceptance of the Father's response. Barth insists that the content of Jesus' petition – that the cup might pass from him – is not the will of Jesus in isolation from or in contrast to the will of God. The passing of the cup, according to Barth, 'would have been the will of Jesus if it had corresponded to the real will of God' (*CD* IV/1, p. 269). Jesus indeed wished that the passing of the cup might have been the real will of God. He did not, however, set his will that the cup might be removed against the real will of God, and then when it was clear that he would be forced to drain the cup of God's wrath, relent and abandon his will in favour of God's.[8] Unlike Moltmann, who considers Jesus' suppression of

---

8 Barth writes, '[Jesus] did not think out and choose some other possibility. He did not reject the impending reality. He did not establish some other direction of His own will. He did not refuse that which forced itself upon Him in view of what lay ahead. He made His request to God only with a view

his own will and his reluctant acceptance of the Father's will as involving self-contradiction, Barth sees in Jesus' acceptance of the cup a clear affirmation of Jesus' obedience and the unity of his will with God's. This act typifies his entire life, which is one of complete obedience. Jesus' declaration, 'Thy will be done', according to Barth, 'is not a kind of return of willingness to obey, which was finally forced upon Jesus and fulfilled by Him in the last hour; it is rather a readiness for the act of obedience which He had never compromised in His prayer' (*CD* IV/1, p. 270).

Barth concludes that Jesus' prayer in Gethsemane does not represent a desperate situation in which the Son's one true desire is rejected by the Father and the Son is overpowered by the alien will of the Father; rather, Jesus' prayer leads to his empowerment. In confidently and not hesitantly proclaiming 'Thy will be done', Jesus 'renewed, confirmed and put into effect, His freedom to finish His work, to execute the divine judgment by undergoing it Himself, to punish the sin of the world by bearing it Himself, by taking it away from the world in His own person, in His death' (*CD* IV/1, p. 271). The events that unfold upon the heels of Jesus' assent to the Father's will fulfil precisely the mission that constitutes his identity. Commenting on the passage in the gospel according to John that parallels the scene in Gethsemane depicted in the synoptic gospels, Barth comes to the very strong, and perhaps unsettling, conclusion that the Father in fact carries out the real will of the Son by refusing to remove the cup. In John 12:27, Jesus says to himself, 'Now is my soul troubled. And what shall I say? "Father, save me from this hour?" No, for this purpose I have come to this hour.' In light of Jesus' internal dialogue recorded here, Barth concludes: 'If the Father was the Father of Jesus, and Jesus His Son, He could not save Him from this hour. That would have been not to hear his prayer. For Jesus had come to this hour in order that the will of God should be done in this hour as it actually was done' (*CD* IV/1, p. 272).

These distinctive interpretations of the petitionary prayer of Jesus in Gethsemane illustrate significant differences in interpreting Jesus Christ's death in God-abandonment, his descent into hell and the impact of this horrifying event on the eternal life of God. For Moltmann, Gethsemane depicts an opposition and conflict of wills – the will of the Son, Jesus Christ, and the will of his Father. In the end, the Father refuses the desire of the Son, and the Father's will prevails over the Son's. The Son, in response, renounces his own will and is forced to accept the will of the Father. For Barth, the petitionary prayer of Jesus in Gethsemane does not indicate a conflict of wills; rather, it clearly depicts a unity of wills. Throughout his entire obedient life Jesus' will is to do the will of his Father. The death in God-abandonment that Jesus endures after requesting that it be spared him is not something that is forced upon him. Rather, it is something that he willingly endures and accepts as the only possibility.

---

to some other possibility which might be God's own will, and not with any particular bias in this or that direction.' *CD* IV/1, p. 269.

Jesus Christ's death and descent into hell and change in the life of God

Connected with Moltmann's depiction of a clash of wills in Gethsemane is the way in which he attributes change to the divine life, change that is a consequence of the events of the passion. When Jesus refuses to refer to God as Father in his death cry, Moltmann concludes that the relationship between the Father and the Son is fractured. According to Moltmann, in the event of Jesus Christ's death in God-abandonment the Son ceases to be the Son and the Father ceases to be the Father. Moltmann asserts: 'The love that binds the one to the other is *transformed* into a dividing curse', and 'Communicating love and responding love are alike *transformed* into infinite pain and into the suffering and endurance of death [my emphasis].'[9] Moltmann's insistence that the events of the passion, which may be rightfully interpreted as the descent into hell, introduce an actual break in the relationship between the Father and Son, by transforming love into curse, pain and suffering, sets him at a great distance from both Barth and Balthasar.

In order to give Moltmann a fair reading, we must acknowledge that he attempts to uphold the unity of the Father and the Son, even in the midst of the broken relationship between them. Moltmann attempts to do this based upon the unity of wills as evident in Gethsemane. In *The Crucified God*, Moltmann comments on Galatians 2:20, 'The Son of God, who loved me and gave himself for me':

> According to this it is not just the Father who delivers Jesus up to die godforsaken on the cross, but the Son who gives himself up. This corresponds to the synoptic account of the passion story according to which Jesus consciously and willingly walked the way of the cross and was not overtaken by death as by an evil, unfortunate fate. It is theologically important to note that the formula in Paul occurs with both Father and Son as subject, since it expresses a deep conformity between the will of the Father and the will of the Son in the event of the cross, as the Gethsemane narrative also records. This deep community of will between Jesus and his God and Father is now expressed precisely at the point of their deepest separation, in godforsakenness and accursed death of Jesus on the cross. If both historical godforsakenness and eschatological surrender can be seen in Christ's death on the cross, then this event contains community between Jesus and his Father in separation, and separation in community.[10]

This is Moltmann at his best. It is, however, inconsistent with what he says elsewhere about the 'breakdown of the relationship that constitutes the very life of the Trinity', and the deep separation between the Father and Son on the cross, which leads to their relationship breaking off. The 'community of wills' of which Moltmann speaks in *The Crucified God* simply does not jibe with his interpretation of Gethsemane in *The Trinity and the Kingdom*. Here Moltmann interprets Jesus'

---

9   Moltmann, *The Trinity and the Kingdom*, p. 80.
10   Moltmann, *The Crucified God*, p. 243.

declaration, 'Not what I will, but what thou wilt', not as an affirmation of the unity of wills between Father and Son; rather, he reads it as a restraint of Jesus' will in the face of the overpowering will of the Father. Moltmann writes, 'It is only by contradicting his very self that Jesus clings to fellowship with the God who as Father withdraws from him.'[11]

Balthasar is especially helpful at this point, as he draws the unity of wills displayed in Gethsemane back into the eternal decision made by the undivided Trinity regarding humanity's salvation. Jesus does not accept something that contradicts his own will; rather, he accepts in obedience the fulfilment of the decision made by the Trinity, in which he was intimately involved. 'What was accepted by the Son in naked obedience on the Mount of Olives', Balthasar writes, 'ultimately goes back to a decision made by the entire Trinity for the sake of man's salvation' (*TD* IV, p. 500). Although Balthasar insists that the atoning death of Jesus Christ is both something that he actively accepts and something that is placed upon him from without, he maintains that this does not take place against his will or without concern for his will. Jesus Christ's atoning death, according to Balthasar, is grounded in the radical character of God's love, which manifests itself in the love of the Father *and* the love of the Son. The twofold love of God – the love of the Father who lays the burden on the Son, and the love of the Son who bears this burden – presupposes 'the loving decision made by the Trinity, in which the Holy Spirit of love is just as involved as the Father and Son, guaranteeing and fulfilling the unanimity of their love in the deadly abandonment of the Cross' (*TD* IV, p. 501).

In his treatment of the work of Jesus Christ under the rubric of the royal office, Barth claims that the passion, far from consisting in the transformation of love into curse, pain and suffering, and far from indicating a contradiction in the relationship between God the Father and Jesus Christ the Son, actually indicates the culmination of the love and unity of Father and Son and announces the coronation of Jesus Christ as the royal man (*CD* IV/2, p. 252). For Barth, the passion is the fitting outcome or fulfilment of Jesus Christ's life and ministry. The darkness that surrounds the cross is, in fact, the radiance of the glory of God. The abandonment of the Son by the Father involves, in fact, the unity and love of the Father and the Son.

> In [Jesus Christ's] passion the name of the God active and revealed in Him is conclusively sanctified; His will is done on earth as it is done in heaven; His kingdom comes, in a form and with a power to which as a man He can only give a terrified but determined assent. And in the passion He exists conclusively as the One He is – the Son of God who is also the Son of Man. In the deepest darkness of Golgotha He enters supremely into the glory of the unity of the Son with the Father. In that abandonment by God He is the One who is directly loved by God. This is the secret that we have to see and understand. And it is

---

11   Moltmann, *The Trinity and the Kingdom*, p. 76.

not a new and specific secret. It is the secret of the whole. Nor is it a closed secret. It is a secret which has been revealed in the resurrection of Jesus. (*CD* IV/2, p. 252)

Though Barth approaches the fear and terror of Jesus Christ in the face of his death seriously and refuses to detract from the authenticity of Jesus' sorrow, he also emphasizes the strength of Jesus' resolve and his unhesitating assent to the will of the Father, which coincides with the culmination of his mission. It is instructive to notice also that Barth acknowledges the unity of the Father and the Son in the midst of the darkness of the cross and the unbroken love of God for Jesus Christ, even in the midst of abandonment and forsakenness. Barth attributes the truth of these claims to the light shed on the cross by the resurrection. The unity of Father and Son, and the love of God for Jesus Christ, are not established in the resurrection, for they are unceasing and unbroken. The climax and glory of Jesus Christ's life is located not in the resurrection; rather, it is found in his death as a criminal and in the midst of criminals at the hands of the executioner, and, further, in his abandonment and forsakenness by God.

The mystery of Jesus Christ's passion, in which he suffered, was crucified and died for humanity, lies in the person and mission of the one who died. In Jesus Christ, the eternal God gives himself, in the mode of his eternal Son, to act and suffer humanly for the reconciliation of the world to himself. The suffering and death of Jesus Christ are not the suffering and death of an innocent and pure human being, a mere creature; rather, they involve the 'humiliation and dishonouring of God Himself' (*CD* IV/1, p. 246). The question that follows is whether in allowing himself to be subject to humiliation, suffering and death, God has entered into contradiction with himself and lost himself as God. To the suggestion that the death of Jesus Christ, in which he is forsaken and abandoned by God, transforms the unity of God into disunity and places the very life of God into jeopardy, Barth responds with an unequivocal No!

Although Barth portrays God's enduring the judgment for sin in the death of Jesus Christ on the cross in all its starkness and locates the most essential meaning of the incarnation in the cry of dereliction, he insists that God never enters into contradiction with himself, never abandons his deity, and never relinquishes his triunity. 'God gives Himself', Barth writes, 'but He does not give Himself away' (*CD* IV/1, p. 185).[12] It is only by maintaining the unity of God, and the constancy of God in the incarnation and passion, that the death of this particular person in

---

12 Barth does speak of God's radical love as reckless self-giving for the sake of sinful humanity – God's enemies – but he stops short of attributing cleavage to the divine life on the basis of the events of the passion. In his exegesis of John 3:16, Barth concludes that the giving of the Son involves great risk. 'In giving [the Son] – and giving Himself –' Barth writes, '– [God] exposes Him – and Himself – to the greatest danger. He sets at stake His own existence as God . . . in this act God loved the world so much, so profoundly, that it did in fact consist in the venture of His own self-offering, in this hazarding of His own existence as God.' *CD* IV/1, p. 72.

this particular place can effect the reconciliation of the world with God. It is the unity of God and the presence of the integrity of God even in his lowliness and humiliation that enables Jesus Christ's death – his dying the second death – to be the means by which God defeats death and destroys sin. Barth points to the integrity of God in the suffering and death of the incarnate Son when he exclaims, 'In this humiliation [the passion, torture, crucifixion and death of this one Jew – Jesus Christ] God is supremely God, in this death he is supremely alive, He has maintained and revealed His deity' (*CD* IV/1, pp. 246–7). Further, Barth insists that it is precisely this passion and death that effects the world's reconciliation with God; it marks a decisive turning point in the history of the world and in the relationship between God and the world. Barth concludes:

> This human passion does not have just a significance and effect in its historical situation within humanity and the world. On the contrary, there is fulfilled in it the mission, the task, and the work of the Son of God: the reconciliation of the world with God. There takes place here the redemptive judgment of God on all men. To fulfil this judgment He took the place of all men, He took their place as sinners. In this passion there is legally re-established the covenant between God and man, broken by man but established by God. On that one day of suffering of that One there took place the comprehensive turning in the history of all creation – with all that this involves. (*CD* IV/1, p. 247)

In a very similar manner, Balthasar vigorously affirms the unbroken unity of the persons of the Trinity, even in the midst of Jesus Christ's death in God-forsakenness and God-abandonment, which is followed by the isolation of his descent into hell. This affirmation of the unbroken unity of the Trinity is necessary, according to Balthasar, for a proper interpretation of the cross and descent into hell.

> The depths of God's abandonment of the Son on the Cross can be understood only through the unique and lasting relationship of the Son of God, even and precisely in his abandonment ['The hour is coming and is already here when you will leave me all alone. But I am not alone, for the Father is with me' (John 16:32)]. In the whole 'economy' of the Incarnation, the divine intimacy of the Father and Son in the Holy Spirit *assumes only another modality*, occasioned by the absorption of human, sinful alienation in this intimacy, as a new expression of their selfless, surrendering love. The return of the Son to the Father who has raised him from the dead is nothing other than the transparency of this *modality of alienation* in what it already is in truth: the eternal intimacy of divine love. [my emphasis][13]

In contrast to Moltmann, who speaks of a 'transformation', a 'becoming' and a 'turning into', Balthasar speaks of the alienation or abandonment of the cross as another 'modality' of the divine intimacy of Father, Son, and Holy Spirit.

---

13   Hans Urs von Balthasar, 'Eschatology in Outline', in *Explorations in Theology*, volume IV, *Spirit and Institution*, trans. Edward T. Oakes, S.J. (San Francisco: Ignatius Press, 1995), p. 436.

Balthasar maintains that Jesus Christ's experience of God-abandonment on the cross, which reaches its peak in the isolation and desolation of the descent into hell, reveals the absolute character of God's love, and, further, demonstrates that this love is properly understood only if it is understood as Trinitarian love. The fullness of God's Trinitarian love is manifested in the complete identification of the Son of God with sinful humanity. And this identification, which enacts the reconciliation of the world with God and the redemption of humanity, carries the eternal Son of God to hell. It is precisely in his identification with sinful and lost humanity that Jesus Christ reveals that God is absolute, sovereign love. Jesus, by accompanying sinful humanity to their inevitable destination of isolation and desolation, reveals 'that God, as all-powerful, is love, and as love is all-powerful'.[14]

Balthasar draws the further conclusion that God's absolute love is whole within God's very life. This conclusion is significant because it enables Balthasar to affirm the severity of Jesus Christ's death in God-abandonment and God-forsakenness, and his being taken to the depths of hell, while, at the same time, denying that God's love is transformed into dividing curse and suffering, as Moltmann does. Balthasar writes:

> [God] is this [as all-powerful is love, and as love is all-powerful] intrinsically in the mystery of his Trinity, which can be explained only by the total opposition – between being with God and being abandoned by God – within God himself. This mystery can reveal itself in its full reality as accompanying the sinner only *sub contrario*, in secret, because otherwise it would not have revealed itself as reality. But because in this God (and God is God only as eternal and living) reveals himself as love, he cannot have become love merely by virtue of the emancipation of the creature; he has no need of the world and its ways in order to become himself; but manifests himself, precisely in the cross of Christ, in his abandonment by God and descent into hell, as the one he always was: everlasting love. As the three in one, God is so intensely everlasting love, that within his life temporal death and the hellish desolation of the creature, accepted out of love, can become transmuted into an expression of love.[15]

Therefore, according to Balthasar, Jesus Christ's death in God-abandonment and his descent into hell do not indicate a transformation of God's Trinitarian love into separation, curse, suffering and pain, as Moltmann suggests; rather, they are accounted for by the radical character of God's absolute love and the mystery of God's Trinitarian life, which allows for great distance within the very life of God. In Balthasar's proposal, God's love is not changed or transformed into the curse of forsakenness, the pain of separation, the suffering of death, and the isolation of

---

14 Hans Urs von Balthasar, 'Why I am Still a Christian', in Hans Urs von Balthasar and Joseph Ratzinger, *Two Say Why: Why I am Still a Christian and Why I am Still in the Church*, trans. John Griffiths (London: Search Press; Chicago: Franciscan Herald Press, 1973), p. 52.

15 Ibid., pp. 52–3.

abandonment; rather, these authentic elements of human death, both physical and spiritual, are 'transmuted into an expression of love'.[16]

The descent into hell and God's love

In a manner that is similar to Balthasar's grounding God's work of reconciliation (which includes incarnation, passion, death, and descent into hell) in the radical character of God's Trinitarian love, Barth also understands God's presence in Jesus Christ as based upon God's absolute love. Barth, as we have seen, maintains that God acts in complete consistency with himself in the event of the incarnation, which necessarily includes Jesus Christ's death in God-abandonment. Barth writes:

> As God was in Christ, far from being against Himself, or at disunity with Himself, He has put into effect the freedom of His divine love, the love in which He is divinely free. He has therefore done and revealed that which corresponds to His divine nature. His immutability does not stand in the way of this. It must not be denied, but this possibility is included in His unalterable being. He is absolute, infinite, exalted, active, impassible, transcendent, but in all this He is the One who loves in freedom, the One who is free in His love, and therefore not His own prisoner. (*CD* IV/1, pp. 186–7)

Barth demands that we refrain from assigning attributes to God apart from God's self-revelation in Jesus Christ. Otherwise, an invalid restriction is placed upon God. God then becomes constrained by his divine nature. Thus, we must begin with God's revelation in Jesus Christ and then describe divine attributes on the basis of this revelation. We must recognize that Barth upholds the doctrine of divine immutability by insisting that the incarnation, in which God becomes that which he had not previously been, has been accounted for in God's unalterable being, which God has determined for himself. There is no change in God in the event of the incarnation. Immutability, however, along with infinity, impassibility and transcendence, is subordinate to or determined by God's freedom and God's love.

The significance of God's being as self-determined being lies in ensuring that God's loving in freedom is neither arbitrary nor capricious. God determines the precise form that his free loving will take; God is not driven by whim or fancy. Also, God is not bound by any human conception of divine nature. To guard against viewing God's action in Jesus Christ as something that is arbitrary and removed from God's eternal identity, Barth insists that the incarnation and passion can be understood correctly only in terms of obedience. The humility of Jesus Christ, Barth reads the New Testament as teaching, 'is an act of obedience, not a capricious choice of lowliness, suffering and dying' (*CD* IV/1, p. 193). Because of

---

16 For a fine analysis of the differences between the proposals of Moltmann and Balthasar see Anne Hunt, *The Trinity and the Paschal Mystery: A Development in Recent Catholic Theology* (Collegeville, MN: The Liturgical Press, 1997), pp. 164–71.

the hypostatic union, this obedience on the part of Jesus Christ is not merely human obedience to God; it also reflects the mystery of obedience within the very Trinitarian life of God. The freedom in which God, in the mode of the eternal Son, becomes lowly, journeys to the far country, identifies with the plight of his lost brother, and ultimately experiences the hell of the second death, is a freedom that is grounded completely in God's eternal decision to be God for humanity and to reconcile and redeem humanity in this particular way. It is, to repeat, not a freedom that is arbitrary, capricious or indifferent.

> If God made use of His freedom in this sense [in Jesus' way into the depths, into the far country], then the fact that the use of this freedom is an act of obedience characterises it as a holy and righteous freedom, in which God is not a victim driven to and fro by the dialectic of His divine nature, but is always His own master. He does not make just any use of the possibilities of His divine nature, but He makes one definite use which is necessary on the basis and in fulfilment of His own decision. (*CD* IV/1, p. 194)

Here Barth suggests that God makes use of his freedom in a way that is necessary as it takes place on the basis of and for the fulfilment of God's own decision.[17]

The event of the incarnation, which, as we have consistently contended, includes the passion and the descent into hell, takes place both in necessity and in freedom. It is necessary insofar as it is grounded in the eternal love of God, which defines God's essence, being and nature, and insofar as it is the definitive enactment of God's decision in electing to be for humanity and for humanity to be for himself.[18] It is free, however, because it takes place in sheer grace; it does not contribute to God's divinity, nor does it complete something that is lacking in God. God is complete in the love that exists within his eternal triune life. In the following passage from §28.2, 'The Being of God as the One who Loves', in *Church Dogmatics* II/1, Barth sets forth his position that God's love for humanity and the world, which manifests itself in the way of reconciliation into the far country

---

17 Barth explores the content of this decision in his creative and seminal discussion of the doctrine of election. For obvious reasons, a full discussion of Barth's teaching regarding this doctrine lies beyond the scope of this study. We may simply point to two related theses that Barth defends regarding the content of God's decision, which is the basis for and is fulfilled by the reconciliation wrought in the life-history of Jesus Christ. Barth states: 'The doctrine of election is the sum of the Gospel because of all words that can be said or heard it is the best: that God elects man; that God is for man too the One who loves in freedom. It is grounded in the knowledge of Jesus Christ because He is both the electing God and elected man in One. It is part of the doctrine of God because originally God's election of man is a predestination not merely of man but of Himself. Its function is to bear basic testimony to eternal, free and unchanging grace as the beginning of all the ways and works of God.' *CD* II/2, p. 3. Barth fills out further what is involved in God's election of humanity as he states: 'The election of grace is the eternal beginning of all the ways and works of God in Jesus Christ. In Jesus Christ God in His free grace determines Himself for sinful man and sinful man for Himself. He therefore takes upon Himself the rejection of man with all its consequences, and elects man to participation in His own glory.' *CD* II/2, p. 94.

18 See *CD* IV/1, p. 213.

travelled by the Son, is sheer grace, yet may be described as necessary as well. God's love for humanity and the world is necessary not because God is somehow incomplete without the world or apart from loving the world, nor is God bound by some external demand. Rather, God's love for humanity is necessary because it corresponds to God's self-determined nature. Barth writes the following regarding the extravagance of God's love and the fellowship-creating nature of God's love for humanity:

> God's loving is necessary, for it is the being, the essence and the nature of God. But for this very reason it is also free from every necessity in respect of its object. God loves us, and loves the world, in accordance with His revelation. But He loves us and the world as He who would still be One who loves without us and without the world; as He, therefore, who needs no other to form the prior ground of His existence as the One who loves and as God. Certainly He is who He is wholly in His revelation, in His loving-kindness, and therefore in His love for us. He has not withheld Himself from us, but given us Himself. Therefore His love for us is His *eternal* love, and our being loved by Him is our being taken up into the fellowship of His eternal love, in which He is Himself for ever and ever. All the same it is a 'being taken up.' It is not part of God's being and action that as love it must have an object in another who is different from Him. God is sufficient in Himself as object and therefore as object of His love. He is no less the One who loves if He loves no object different from Himself. In the fact that He determines to love such another, His love overflows. But it is not exhausted in it nor confined or conditioned by it. On the contrary, this overflowing is conditioned by the fact that although it could satisfy itself, it has no satisfaction in this self-satisfaction, but as love for another it can and will be more than that which could satisfy itself. While God is everything for Himself, He wills again not to be everything merely for Himself, but for this other. (*CD* II/1, p. 280)

God's love, which manifests itself in Jesus Christ's identification with sinful humanity to the point of experiencing hell and dying the second death, is grounded in the completeness, vitality and abundance of God's eternal love. God's love for humanity and the world, which leads to God's decision to take upon himself the consequences of humanity's sin and, in turn, to exalt humanity to the position of participation in his eternal glory, is utterly free and does not in any way indicate a deficiency in God's being.

Balthasar agrees completely with Barth on this issue, as he also affirms the self-sufficiency of God. 'God in himself', Balthasar writes, 'must be life, love, an eternal fullness of communion, who does not need the world in order to have another to love' (*TD* III, p. 529). At the same time, Balthasar speaks of God's love for the world as a manifestation or overflowing of the reckless self-giving of God's absolute love. According to Balthasar, the Johannine formula 'The Word became flesh' 'shows the event of Jesus – his life, death and resurrection – to be the definitive, superabundant consequence of the event of God himself' (*MP*, pp. 203–4).

Both Barth and Balthasar affirm God's complete self-sufficiency and the fullness of God's eternal Trinitarian love, which rules out any notion of need or deficiency within God's triune life and entails that creation, covenant, incarnation, crucifixion and descent into hell be considered sheer gift and utterly free. These shared affirmations separate them from Moltmann. In *The Trinity and the Kingdom*, Moltmann describes the nature of God's divine love on the basis of an analysis of a general conception of human love. This analysis includes two elements that are significant for our discussion. First, God's love is, by definition, both engendering *and* creative love. This means that God's love is not complete in the Father's generation of the Son and the spiration of the Holy Spirit, and the corresponding vital, dynamic, inner-Trinitarian love of the Godhead. God must move beyond merely love for like, which is the case in God's inner-Trinitarian love, and must engage in love of one who is essentially different, the Other. Creation of the world therefore becomes a necessary element of God's love. If God did not create the world, then God would not be love, and as a result God would contradict himself and no longer be God, for God is love. In his proposal for a Christian panentheism Moltmann writes:

> Creation is a fruit of God's longing for 'his Other' and for that Other's free response to the divine love. That is why the idea of the world is inherent in the nature of God himself from eternity. For it is impossible to conceive of a God who is not a creative God. A non-creative God would be imperfect compared with the God who is eternally creative. And if God's eternal being is love, then the divine love is also more blessed in giving than in receiving. God cannot find bliss in eternal self-love if selflessness is part of love's very nature.[19]

Although there is some similarity between Moltmann and Balthasar in regard to understanding God's love as essentially self-giving love, Balthasar insists that this love is complete in the self-giving of the Father to the Son, the response of gratitude of the Son towards the Father, and the bridging of the 'distance' between Father and Son by the Holy Spirit. The vitality and dynamism of God's inner-Trinitarian life is real and complete; otherwise, Balthasar warns, one is forced to conclude that God must become involved in the temporal processes of the created world in order to satisfy a deficiency in his love and in order to become complete. God then requires something external to himself in order to be God. Balthasar maintains that creation and the temporal world process are grounded in God, but he denies that creation and the world process are in any way necessary for God.[20]

Balthasar asserts that God is not bound by God's nature; rather, as revelation demonstrates, God is sovereign in respect to his nature. God is free to 'do what he will with his own nature' (*TD* II, p. 256). God's freedom with respect to his nature, even with respect to his nature as love, means that it is improper to attribute either

---

19   Moltmann, *The Trinity and the Kingdom*, p. 106.
20   See *TD* IV, p. 327.

necessity or chance to God. The generation of the Son and the creation of that which is not God are not the necessary outcomes of God's eternal nature, nor are they the result of chance or God's whimsy. The generation of the Son and the creation of the world are, for Balthasar, in accordance with or consequences of God's nature, yet we must remember that for Balthasar, as it was for Barth, God is in control of his nature and is not bound by it. Balthasar's insistence that God is not bound by any necessities of his nature supports his claim that creation, covenant, incarnation and passion are concrete enactments and manifestations of God's absolute free love, and are not necessary elements of God's development – the process of God's becoming fully God. Balthasar writes:

> In generating the Son, the Father does not 'lose' himself in order thereby to 'regain' himself; for he *is always* himself by giving himself. The Son, too, is always himself by allowing himself to be generated and by allowing the Father to do with him as he pleases. The Spirit is always himself by understanding his 'I' as the 'We' of Father and Son, and by being 'expropriated' for the sake of what is most proper to them. (Without grasping this there is no escape from the machinery of Hegelian dialectic.) (*TD* II, p. 256)

The second element of Moltmann's understanding of love that places him at odds with both Barth and Balthasar is his assertion that suffering is an essential element of love. Moltmann not only argues for the possibility of the suffering of God; he proposes that God *must* suffer in order to be consistent with himself. 'Creative love', Moltmann asserts, 'is always suffering love.'[21] In the same way that God must create in order to be consistent with himself as love, God also must suffer in order to be fully God, because love by definition is suffering love. Given his methodological starting point of the cross of Jesus Christ, Moltmann concludes:

> The sole omnipotence which God possesses is the almighty power of suffering love . . . This is the essence of divine sovereignty . . . the self-sacrifice of love is God's eternal nature . . . the cross of Christ is not something that is historically fortuitous, which might not have happened. God himself is nothing other than love. Consequently Golgotha is the inescapable revelation of his nature in a world of evil and suffering . . . God is love; love makes a person capable of suffering; and love's capacity for suffering is fulfilled in the self-giving and the self-sacrifice of the lover. Self-sacrifice is God's very nature and essence.[22]

By defining God's essence as self-sacrifice and by insisting that love is necessarily suffering love, Moltmann places God in subjection to the world's suffering. God's suffering with and for the world becomes necessary for God's very life. God and the world are now considered as being subject to one process – God becomes a

---

21 Moltmann, *The Trinity and the Kingdom*, p. 59.
22 Ibid., pp. 31–2.

victim who suffers alongside human victims. Moltmann minimizes the significance of viewing the sufferings of Jesus Christ on the cross as a bearing of sin, a suffering of the consequences of sin, and the enactment of atonement by bearing sin away. Rather, Moltmann emphasizes God as suffering alongside human beings, especially in the form of innocent suffering. He writes:

> Suffering reaches as far as love itself, and love grows through the suffering it experiences – that is the signpost that points to true life. The universal significance of the crucified Christ on Golgotha is only really comprehended through the theodicy question. The history of Christ's sufferings belongs to the history of the sufferings of mankind, by virtue of the passionate love which Christ manifests and reveals.[23]

These sufferings, of both God and human beings, contribute to the fulfilment of God; they enable God to reach eternal bliss, which he lacks within his inner-Trinitarian love.

By identifying Jesus Christ's sufferings with the sufferings of humanity and God's suffering with the sufferings of Christ, Moltmann fails to distinguish sufficiently between God and the world process. He describes the suffering of God univocally. Moreover, he makes God's life dependent upon the suffering of Christ on the cross and his descent into hell. 'The pain of the cross', Moltmann writes, 'determines the inner life of the triune God from eternity to eternity.'[24] It is this claim that the suffering of Christ is necessary for the constitution and actualization of the Trinity that separates Moltmann from both Balthasar and Barth. Although Balthasar, as we have seen, claims that the incarnation, life, death and descent into hell do not leave the inner-Trinitarian relationships unaffected, he does not consider the sufferings of Christ as necessary for God or determinative for God's actualization. For Moltmann, the cross constitutes God's triune being, while for Balthasar, the cross and the descent into hell fully reveal God's triune being. Also, Balthasar speaks in a careful and qualified manner regarding divine suffering, as we will see below. This further distinguishes his position from Moltmann's.

Both Balthasar and Barth uphold the freedom of God as a non-negotiable element of a Christian doctrine of God as triune, and insist that we must refrain from lumping together the internal divine process – processions – with the process of salvation history – missions.[25] God is indeed love, according to Barth and Balthasar, but God's love is entirely free. God has no need to create or to suffer. For Moltmann, however, God's love must be creative love, and creative love must be suffering love. Although Moltmann recognizes the problems involved with entangling God in the world process as he writes, 'In order to understand the

---

23   Ibid., p. 52. For a detailed discussion of Moltmann's rejection of giving primacy to view of the cross that considers it as a sacrifice for sin or as bearing the judgment for sin see Moltmann, *The Crucified God*, pp. 178–87.

24   Moltmann, *The Trinity and the Kingdom*, 161.

25   See *TD* IV, pp. 319–28.

history of mankind as a history *in* God, the distinction between the world process and the inner-trinitarian process must be maintained and emphasized.'[26] It is very difficult to see how Moltmann is able to follow his own admonition. Given Moltmann's suggestion that God must create in order for his love to be fulfilled, and, further, that God must suffer in order for his love to be genuine, it is difficult to see how Moltmann avoids Balthasar's charge that the God he describes is 'entangled in the world process and becomes a tragic, mythological God' (*TD* IV, 322).

In his detailed and highly critical essay on Moltmann's understanding of the doctrines of the Trinity and Creation, Paul Molnar points to two primary flaws in Moltmann's theological construction. The first is Moltmann's failure to think analogically, his attempt to understand the suffering of Christ and the eternal inner-Trinitarian love from a single perspective. This leads to a confusion of God's inner-Trinitarian life and the world process and makes God dependent upon the world for his existence. The second flaw, identified by Molnar, is Moltmann's failure to uphold the distinction between the immanent and economic Trinity, which Molnar, in agreement with Barth and Balthasar, considers imperative to an authentically Christian doctrine of God and to a proper interpretation of Jesus Christ's death and descent into hell. Molnar writes:

> Moltmann honestly believes that the historical event of the cross and the heart of the triune God can be understood together in a single perspective. If they can, then there is no distinction between the immanent and economic Trinity. And there is no God independent of the world; there is only a God who can be seen from within the world's perspective as one who is subject to suffering love. The perspective (whether conceived relationally or not) would dictate the nature of God's love and freedom and to that extent would become that which is truly 'almighty.' Here God can no longer be free in the traditional sense, i.e., in the sense that He does not exist as one who stands in need.[27]

In the following two sections, we will address these fatal flaws of Moltmann's understanding of the relationship between the passion of Jesus Christ, which includes or can be described as his descent into hell, and the Trinity. In order to answer the question of whether God suffers as result of the cross and descent into hell and to determine the content of this suffering, it is necessary first to address the significance of maintaining a proper relationship between the immanent and economic Trinity.

---

26   Moltmann, *The Trinity and the Kingdom*, p. 107.

27   Paul Molnar, 'The Function of the Trinity in Moltmann's Ecological Doctrine of Creation', *Theological Studies* 51 (1990): pp. 687–8.

The descent into hell and the immanent and economic Trinity

Whereas both Barth and Balthasar depart from Karl Rahner's dictum that the economic Trinity is the immanent Trinity and vice versa, Moltmann offers a variation of this identifying statement. Barth's and Balthasar's view may be described as affirming unity in distinction and distinction in unity. The economic Trinity and the immanent Trinity do not refer to two separate trinities, but at the same time, they are not to be conflated. There is significant theological rationale for maintaining the distinction but not separation between the two modalities of the one eternal Trinity. This distinction ensures the freedom of God, upholds the transcendence of God, and safeguards God's independence from the world, by refusing to depict God as being subject to the historical process of creation.[28] Moltmann, in contrast, challenges the distinction between the immanent Trinity and economic Trinity and considers a strong notion of the immanent Trinity – defined as God's existence in and of himself apart from the world – as flawed theological thinking, because it fails to account adequately for God's intimate involvement in the world and, as a result, introduces an arbitrary element into God's loving relationship to the world.[29] Moltmann's so-called Christian panentheism unabashedly affirms the mutual or reciprocal relationship between God and the world, which includes the assertion that the process of God's involvement in the world constitutes the triune being of God. Moltmann's modification of Rahner's dictum would account for this progressive and eschatological element of the relationship between the world and God. Instead of stating that the immanent Trinity is the economic Trinity and vice versa, Moltmann claims that the economic Trinity becomes the immanent Trinity. Moltmann concludes:

> The economic Trinity completes and perfects itself to [the] immanent Trinity when the history and experience of salvation are completed and perfected. When everything is 'in God' and 'God is all in all', then the economic Trinity is raised into and transcended in the immanent Trinity. What remains is the eternal praise of the triune God in his glory.[30]

---

28 In his call for a renewal of a doctrine of the immanent Trinity in contemporary theology, Paul Molnar defends the bold claim that the neglect of the doctrine of the immanent Trinity leads to grave theological problems, which pervade every aspect of theological inquiry. 'What is the purpose of a doctrine of the immanent Trinity?' Molnar asks, 'Broadly speaking it aims to recognize, uphold and respect God's freedom. Without theoretical and practical awareness of this freedom all theological statements about the significance of created existence become ambiguous and constitute merely human attempts to give meaning to creation using theological categories.' Paul D. Molnar, 'Toward a Contemporary Doctrine of the Immanent Trinity: Karl Barth and the Present Discussion', *Scottish Journal of Theology* 49 (1996): p. 311.

29 See Moltmann, *The Trinity and the Kingdom*, p. 151.

30 Ibid., p. 161.

Moltmann's rationale for blurring the distinction between the immanent Trinity and the economic Trinity results from his commitment to constructing the doctrine of the Trinity with the cross as the principal and exclusive starting point.

> I myself have tried to think through the theology of the cross in trinitarian terms and to understand the doctrine of the Trinity in the light of the theology of the cross. In order to grasp the death of the Son in its significance for God himself, I found myself bound to surrender the traditional distinction between the immanent and the economic Trinity, according to which the cross comes to stand only in the economy of salvation, but not within the immanent Trinity.[31]

Balthasar shares Moltmann's commitment to a Christocentric starting point for the doctrine of the Trinity. According to Balthasar, 'We know about the Father, Son and Spirit as divine "Persons" only through the figure and disposition of Jesus Christ' (*TD* III, p. 508). This conclusion is indicative of a principle regarding 'personhood' operative throughout *Theo-Drama* III and present in each volume of the *Theo-Drama*, i.e., 'theological persons cannot be defined in isolation from their dramatic action' (*TD* III, p. 508). Even though Balthasar agrees with the commonly held assumption that 'it is only on the basis of the economic Trinity that we can have knowledge of the immanent Trinity and dare to make statements about it' (*TD* III, 508), he draws two significant conclusions from this assumption, one of which sets his position directly against Moltmann's.

First, Balthasar cautions against the search for and employment of *vestigium trinitatis*. Since God reveals himself as triune in the particular life history of Jesus Christ, analogies for the Trinity outside of Christianity have minimal theological significance. According to Balthasar, 'Such analogies lack the "economic" basis and can easily appear as a mere collection of cosmological principles that does not get any farther than tritheism, or else they stay at the level of modalism' (*TD* III, p. 508).[32] Balthasar's second conclusion directly addresses the point of contention between Moltmann's position and his own. Although Balthasar affirms that the economic Trinity is the interpretation of the immanent Trinity, and the immanent Trinity is known only on the basis of the economic Trinity, he insists that the economic Trinity must not be identified with the immanent Trinity. The immanent Trinity, according to Balthasar, ontologically grounds and supports the economic Trinity. Correspondingly, the immanent Trinity is known only on the basis of the economic Trinity. The grave theological danger of identifying the economic Trinity with the immanent Trinity, according to Balthasar, is the risk that the 'immanent, eternal Trinity would threaten to dissolve into the economic'. As a result of this,

---

31   Ibid., p. 160.

32   Balthasar heeds his own admonition to proceed with caution in employing analogies of the Trinity as he asserts the theological significance of the two traditional models of the Trinity, i.e., the psychological model, advanced by Augustine and the West, and the social or communal model, articulated by the Cappadocians and the East. These models must be held together, or the result will be either modalism or tritheism. See *TD* III, pp. 526–7.

'God would be swallowed up in the world process – a necessary stage, in this view, if he is fully to realize himself' (*TD* III, p. 508).

On the one hand, Balthasar maintains the distinction between the immanent Trinity and the economic Trinity, by insisting that the two must not be confused nor made identical. On the other hand, he refrains from driving a wedge between the immanent Trinity and the economic Trinity. He shares Moltmann's concern to avoid separating the immanent and economic Trinity in such a way that the passion of Jesus Christ – the events of the economy of salvation – leaves the immanent Trinity unaffected. Balthasar's understanding of the relationship between the immanent Trinity and the economic Trinity emphasizes both unity in distinction and distinction in unity. He avoids a hasty identification as well as a careless separation. The difference between Balthasar and Moltmann regarding the relationship between the immanent Trinity and the economic Trinity may be clarified in the light of Molnar's criticism that Moltmann attempts to understand the event of the cross and the heart of the triune God together in a single perspective. This dissolves the distinction between the economic and immanent Trinity and strips God of his freedom and independence.

Maintaining a relationship of both distinction and unity in terms of the immanent and economic Trinity is important both for a proper understanding of God and for a proper understanding of soteriology. Failure to distinguish between the immanent and economic Trinity jeopardizes God's freedom and sovereign independence from the creature. God's love is also called into question, as an identification of the immanent and economic Trinity leads to the conclusion that God becomes love only in God's relationship to the world. If God is not fully love within the eternal triune life, and if God becomes entangled in the world process, then the actuality of redemption is also at stake because God too would be in need of redemption.

Barth shares Balthasar's commitment to maintaining the distinction between the immanent and economic Trinity. Barth emphatically endorses the distinction between the immanent and economic Trinity in support of his argument for the indirectness of God's revelation – the indirectness of human knowledge of God's Word – which includes a denial of the revelatory character of the humanity of Jesus Christ *per se*. In order to avoid the twin dangers of making God a predicate of humanity or making humanity requisite in God's nature, Barth insists that a clear distinction must be maintained between the immanent and economic Trinity.

> It is not just good sense but absolutely essential that along with all older theology we make a deliberate and sharp distinction between the Trinity of God as we may know it in the Word of God revealed, written and proclaimed, and God's immanent Trinity, i.e., between 'God in Himself' and 'God for us,' between the 'eternal history of God' and His temporal acts. In so doing we must always bear in mind that the 'God for us' does not arise as a matter of course out of the 'God in Himself,' that it is not true as a state of God which we can fix and assert on the basis of the concept of man participating in His revelation, but that it is true as an act of God, as a step which God takes

> towards man and by which man becomes the man that participates in His
> revelation . . . we must know God as the One who addresses us in freedom, as
> the Lord, who does not exist only as He addresses us, but exists as the One
> who establishes and ratifies the relation and correlation, who is also God before
> it, in Himself, in His eternal history. (*CD* I/1, p. 172)

Barth's commitment to the indirectness of revelation – revelation as both veiling
and unveiling – compels him to employ the traditional distinction between the
immanent and economic Trinity – God *in se* and God *pro nobis*.[33] We misinterpret
Barth, however, if we conclude from his strong insistence on the distinction
between the immanent and economic Trinity that he considers God's relation to
the world as distant and accidental. It is precisely because God exists in eternal
love in himself that God is able to draw intimately close to humanity and draw
humanity into an intimate relationship of fellowship with himself.

> In [the] triunity of His essence God loves both as and before He loves us; both
> as and before He calls us to love. In this triunity of His essence God is eternal
> love. In Himself He is both the One and the Other. And He is this, not in any
> reciprocal self-seeking, indifference, neutrality or even enmity, but in the self-
> giving of the Father to the Son and the Son to the Father which is accomplished
> in the fact that He is not merely the Father and the Son but also the Holy
> Spirit, and therefore as the Father is wholly for the Son, and as the Son wholly
> for the Father. In virtue of His trinitarian essence God is free and sovereign
> and competent and powerful to love us. He can and may and must and will
> love us. He does in fact love us. And He makes Himself the basis of our love.
> In so doing, He does not place us merely in an external and casual fellowship
> with Himself, but in an internal and essential fellowship in which our existence
> cannot continue to be alien to His but may become and be analogous. (*CD* IV/
> 2, p. 757)

The acknowledgment of the relationship of the immanent and economic Trinity as
one of distinction in unity and unity in distinction, moreover, provides a third
alternative to two unacceptable positions regarding God's relationship to the world.
On the one hand, if the immanent Trinity, or God's transcendence, is emphasized
at the expense of the economic Trinity, or God's immanence, then God becomes a
distant observer, barred from living in communion with creation, and, further,
incapable of fully revealing himself and effecting reconciliation and redemption by
bearing the consequences of human sin and evil. On the other hand, if the economic
Trinity is emphasized at the expense of the immanent Trinity, then God becomes a

---

33   See also Barth's discussion of the being of God as the one who loves in freedom. In order for
God's love for the world to be free and gracious, God's love must be complete in the loving relations
of the loving God as Father, Son, and Holy Spirit. Barth advances the following thesis in *CD* II/1, §28
'The Being of God as the One who Loves in Freedom': 'God is who He is in the act of His revelation.
God seeks and creates fellowship between Himself and us, and therefore He loves us. But He is this
loving God without us as Father, Son and Holy Spirit, in the freedom of the Lord, who has His life
from Himself.' *CD* II/1, p. 257.

mythical character caught up in the vagaries of historical existence. In this case, God would be equally in need of redemption as creation. To be both redeemer and redeemed, however, is self-contradictory (*TD* III, p. 529).

The mystery of the unity in distinction of the immanent and economic Trinity provides a way for holding together the truths of both previous views without falling prey to the hazards of depicting God as a distant observer or as a vulnerable mythical god trapped in the movement of history. In respect of an understanding of God's relationship to the world and God's presence in the drama of salvation, Balthasar presents three elements of a proper understanding of the relationship between the immanent and economic Trinity.

First, God must exist in a fully complete life of love within himself in order for his decision to create and redeem the world to be a free decision. As it is a free action, God is then able to become intimately involved in the world without becoming entangled in the world.

Second, the unity of the immanent and economic Trinity enables God truly to enter into the world in the person of the eternal Son. Balthasar writes, 'The Son of the Father "became like us in all things except sin", and in a true sense he acts alongside us before the Father, through the Spirit who mediates between himself and the Father, between heaven and earth' (*TD* III, pp. 529–30). It is the Spirit who bridges the great distance between the Father and the Son, and it is the distance between Father and Son that encompasses the distance between heaven and earth, and all inner-worldly distance. The distance between heaven and earth, Balthasar proposes, 'is to be seen as an expression of this ... all-embracing distinction [between Father and Son]' (*TD* III, p. 530).

This leads us to the third element of Balthasar's understanding of the proper relationship between the immanent and economic Trinity. It is only by affirming the relationship between the immanent and economic Trinity as one of distinction in unity, and not one of identification nor separation, that the death and descent into hell of Jesus Christ may be regarded as redemptive. A proper understanding of the immanent and economic Trinity enables us to affirm that 'God can simultaneously remain in himself and step forth from himself'. By stepping forth from himself, God 'descends into the abyss of all that is anti-divine; God does nothing anti-divine – the sinner does – but he can experience it within his own reality. This is Christ's descent into hell, into what God has utterly cast out of the world' (*TD* III, p. 530). Balthasar links the absolute obedience of Jesus Christ to the Son's absolute response or grateful receptivity to the gift of the Father's generation. The processions within the immanent Trinity act as the ground for the missions within the economic Trinity. The mission of Jesus Christ is not identical with the procession of the Son; rather, it is an extension of the procession, or is a form or modality of the eternal procession.[34] 'Because he is triune', Balthasar

---

34 John O'Donnell offers a clarifying description of the significance of Balthasar's Trinitarian thinking: 'Balthasar wants to stress that the cross is a separation of Father and Son, but the dramatic

concludes, 'God can overcome even what is hostile to God within his eternal relations' (*TD* III, p. 530).

In proposing that the immanent Trinity must be considered as the necessary ground for the saving events of the passion, by highlighting the 'trinitarian substructure' of soteriology, Balthasar does not minimize the salvific significance of the historical events of the passion, nor does he deny the real impact of these events on the eternal life of God – the immanent Trinity. Balthasar insists that the events of Jesus Christ's death on the cross and his descent into hell on Holy Saturday actually effect the world's reconciliation to God and do not merely illustrate or manifest a constant state of affairs. Even though Balthasar claims that, 'by way of the Incarnation, death and Resurrection, [God] can truly and not just in seeming become that which as God he already and always is' (*MP*, p. 208), and, further, that in the resurrection 'the extreme distance between Father and Son, which is endured as a result of the Son's taking on of sin, changes into profound intimacy; but it always *was* such because the distance was a work of trinitarian loving obedience' (*TD* IV, pp. 361–2), he demands that we acknowledge the salvific efficacy of the historical events of death and descent of Jesus Christ. It is only by maintaining a proper relationship between the immanent and economic Trinity that one can affirm that the events of Good Friday and Holy Saturday effect the world's salvation.

God must not be thought of as being unaffected by the passion of Jesus Christ, which is a hazard of separating the immanent from the economic Trinity. At the same time, God must not be seen as being determined by and a victim of the world process, which follows from an identification of the immanent and economic Trinity, or by absorbing the immanent Trinity into the economic Trinity. Balthasar's understanding of the relationship between the immanent and economic Trinity grounds his conviction that it is precisely in Jesus Christ's descent into hell that the salvation of humanity is accomplished.

> Good Friday is not just the same as Easter: the economic Trinity objectively acts out the drama of the world's alienation ... we should say that God, desiring to reconcile the world to himself (and hence himself to the world), acts dramatically in the Son's Cross and Resurrection. This dramatic aspect does not entangle the immanent Trinity in the world's fate, as occurs in

caesura that rends the heart of God on Calvary has already been embraced from all eternity by the divine Trinity. For from eternity the Father has given himself away to the Son, has risked his being on the Son, and from eternity the Son has been a yes to the Father, a surrender of obedience. Thus the Father's risk of himself on the Son creates a space for the Son. The Father separates himself from himself, so that the Son can be. But this separation is also bridged over in eternity by the Holy Spirit, the communion of love of the Father and the Son. Hence according to Balthasar, there is both a separation and a union within the divine life which makes possible the separation and the union of the cross-event. The dramatic action of the economic Trinity is made possible and embraced within the primordial drama of the eternal Trinity.' John O'Donnell, *The Mystery of the Triune God* (London: Sheed & Ward, 1988), p. 65.

mythology, but it *does* lift the latter's fate to the level of the economic Trinity, which always presupposes the immanent. This is because the Son's eternal, holy distance from the Father, in the Spirit, forms the basis on which the unholy distance of the world's sin can be transposed into it, can be transcended and overcome by it. The dramatic interplay between God and the world is enacted in the temporal acts of the concrete Christ-event and its consequences . . . Within the Son's absolute, loving obedience (which persists in the realm of the immanent Trinity), according to which he walks into an utter forsakenness that surpasses the sinner's isolation, we find the most radical change from eternal death to eternal life, from the absolute night of the Spirit to the Spirit's absolute light, from total alienation and remoteness to an unimaginable closeness. (*TD* IV, p. 362)

Here we clearly see that for Balthasar, on the one hand, God's being is not determined or constituted by the historical events of the passion; but, on the other hand, God does not hover above the events of the passion, without being affected by them. We also see that God enacts his reconciling will in the very limit of the Son's forsakenness by the Father, in the unsurpassed isolation of Jesus Christ's passive plunge into the depths of hell. It is here where sin and its consequence – eternal death – are defeated and radically transformed into eternal life. God effects the reconciliation and redemption of humanity in Jesus Christ's death and descent into hell, and the saving significance of the cross and the descent into hell is revealed only in the resurrection.

The resurrection, according to Balthasar, is both abrupt *and* organic; it comes as a great shock to the dead Christ, and it is intrinsic to his death and being among the dead.

By going all the way to the outermost alienation, God himself has proven to be the Almighty who also is able to safeguard his identity in nonidentity, his being-with-himself in being lost, his life in being dead. And so the Resurrection of Christ and of all who are saved by him can be seen as the inner consequence of his experience of Holy Saturday. There is no 'reascent' after the descent; the way of love 'to the end' (John 13:1) is itself love's self-glorification.[35]

Though the resurrection itself does not effect human salvation, it is the culmination of the self-revelation of the triune God. The fullness of the Trinity is seen only in the glorious light of the resurrection. 'The decisive revelation of the mystery of the Trinity is not', Balthasar maintains, 'something which precedes the *Mysterium Paschale* itself . . . that revelation is prepared in the counterposition of the wills on the Mount of Olives and by the divine abandonment on the Cross, yet only with the Resurrection does it come forth openly into the light' (*MP*, pp. 212–13).

---

35   Balthasar, 'The Descent into Hell', p. 413.

The descent into hell and divine suffering

The second fatal flaw of Moltmann's understanding of the relationship between the cross and the Trinity, as pointed out by Molnar, is closely related to his collapsing of the distinction between the immanent and economic Trinity. If there is no distinction between the immanent and economic Trinity – between God and the world – then the nature of the triune God and the suffering of Jesus Christ on the cross must be seen from a single perspective. As a result, suffering must be attributed univocally to humanity and to God, in his eternal nature. By grounding all theology exclusively in the cross, and by attempting to overcome the traditional notion of God's *apatheia*, Moltmann insists that suffering is an essential element of God's nature. If God is to be defined as love, then suffering must be in God, for God's love is necessarily suffering love. God does not merely identify with human suffering, or take on human suffering, through the incarnation and death of Jesus Christ; rather, suffering is *in* God. As we have noted, Moltmann asserts that the cross determines and constitutes the Trinitarian life of God. 'God's relationship to the world', Moltmann writes, 'has a retroactive effect on his relationship to himself . . . The pain of the cross determines the inner life of the triune God from eternity to eternity.'[36] In his interpretation of the cross and its effect on the 'inner' life of God, Moltmann ascribes distinctive types of suffering to each member of the Trinity. There are specific types of suffering proper to the Father, Son, and Holy Spirit.

> The suffering and dying of the Son, forsaken by the Father, is a different kind of suffering from the suffering of the Father in the death of the Son . . . The Son suffers dying, the Father suffers the death of the Son. The grief of the Father here is just as important as the death of the Son. The Fatherlessness of the Son is matched by the Sonlessness of the Father, and if God has constituted himself as the Father of Jesus Christ, then he also suffers the death of his Fatherhood in the death of the Son.[37]

By presenting a bold depiction of God's suffering, suffering which is proper to God and is essential to God's nature, Moltmann ascribes human characteristics – pain, suffering and death – to God univocally and risks reducing our understanding of God to something that is crudely anthropomorphic. John Thompson perceptively identifies the problem with Moltmann's account of the suffering of God.

> Perhaps the chief criticism which is to be made of Moltmann's theology is that his innovation lies in making the cross an inner, divine experience. Suffering is not simply something with which God identifies in becoming man in Jesus Christ, but rather suffering is in God himself . . . One of the chief defects of his whole theological approach is an almost total unawareness of the problem

---

36   Moltmann, *The Trinity and the Kingdom*, p. 161.
37   Moltmann, *The Crucified God*, p. 243.

of applying human predicates to God. Or, to put it otherwise, he fails to see that in applying suffering to God he is in danger of using this term not in an analogical way but in an illegitimate, univocal manner.[38]

Barth and Balthasar share Moltmann's insistence that a proper understanding of the Trinity must account for God's saving involvement in the cross and resurrection. Both challenge the traditional commitment to God's *apatheia* and affirm the need to speak of God and suffering. Nevertheless, both depart from Moltmann's straightforward attribution of suffering to God and insist that the suffering of God may be affirmed only analogically.

In a representative passage in the *Church Dogmatics*, Barth goes so far as to allow suffering to be applied to the Father.

> It is not at all the case that God has no part in the suffering of Jesus Christ even in His mode of being as the Father. No, there is a *particula veri* in the teaching of the early Patripassians. This is that primarily it is God the Father who suffers in the offering and sending of His Son, in His abasement. The suffering is not His own, but the alien suffering of the creature, of man, which He takes to Himself in Him. But He does suffer it in the humiliation of His Son with a depth with which it never was or will be suffered by any man – apart from the One who is His Son. And He does so in order that, having been borne by Him in the offering and sending of His Son, it should not have to be suffered in this way by man. This fatherly fellow-suffering of God is the mystery, the basis, of the humiliation of His Son; the truth of that which takes place historically in His crucifixion. (*CD* IV/2, p. 357)

At least two things must be highlighted in this passage.

First, Barth insists that the suffering that God experiences in the humiliation of the Son – the passion of Jesus Christ – is not suffering that is proper to his divinity; rather, this suffering is an alien suffering, suffering that is proper to human beings as creatures. In the incarnation and death of Jesus Christ, God makes human suffering and death his own. God, in the mode of the eternal Son, identifies with human suffering and death, and draws it into the very life of God, with the sole redemptive purpose of eliminating suffering, eradicating sin, and defeating death.

The second key element of this passage is Barth's proposal that the suffering of God in the humiliation of the Son exceeds the potential and possible suffering of any human being. The depth to which the Son of God plunges in his death in God-abandonment, his dying the second death, his descent into hell, surpasses that of any one human being. In fact, the suffering of the incarnate Son surpasses the collective suffering of all human beings if they were indeed handed over to the consequences of their evil and sin. It is only by way of this unique and immeasurable suffering that the death and descent into hell of Jesus Christ can effect the reconciliation of humanity to God, the destruction of human persons as

---

38   John Thompson, *Modern Trinitarian Perspectives* (New York: Oxford University Press, 1994), p. 63.

sinners, the defeat of sin, death and the devil, and the redemption of human persons to a future as new creatures.

In enduring the alien suffering of the creature in its most extreme form of the fullness of the wrath of God, God spares humanity from being subject to the divine rejection to which they have been sentenced because of their sin. For the sake of the election, salvation and life of humanity, God has determined for himself reprobation, perdition and death (*CD* II/2, pp. 162–3). In electing himself to be God for humanity and in electing humanity to be for himself, God elects the rejection of humanity and elects completely the consequences of sin and evil. God elects this not as an enhancement of his own being, nor as an means of redemption for himself, as is potentially the case in Moltmann's theology; rather, God elects humanity's rejection in order to manifest his gracious love and to effect his reconciling and redemptive will.

> If we would know what it was that God elected for Himself when He elected fellowship with man, then we can answer only that He elected our rejection. He made it His own. He bore it and suffered it with all its most bitter consequences. For the sake of this choice and for the sake of man He hazarded Himself wholly and utterly. He elected our suffering (what we as sinners must suffer towards Him and before Him and from Him). He elected it as His own suffering. This is the extent to which His election is an election of grace, and an election of love, an election to give Himself, and an election to empty and abase Himself for the sake of the elect. Judas who betrays Him He elects as an apostle. The sentence of Pilate He elects as a revelation of His judgment on the world. He elects the cross of Golgotha as His kingly throne. He elects the tomb in the garden as the scene of His being as the living God. That is how God loved the world. That is how from all eternity His love was so selfless and genuine. (*CD* II/2, pp. 164–5)

Since the alien creaturely suffering, which God identifies with and takes to himself, is elected by God as the means by which humanity is saved and his being as love is fully revealed, God is not bound by nor subject to this extreme form of suffering, which includes the nadir of hell, the second death of God-abandonment. God reigns from the cross and is fully alive in the death of the incarnate Son. God remains sovereign even, or especially, in his intimate involvement with the human contradiction of sin, evil, suffering and death. '[God] makes His own the being of man in contradiction against Him', Barth writes, 'but He does not make common cause with it. He also makes His own the being of man under the curse of this contradiction, but in order to do away with it as He suffers it. He acts as Lord over this contradiction even as He subjects Himself to it' (*CD* IV/1, p. 185).

Balthasar's position on this matter is similar to Barth's. Balthasar, though resisting Moltmann's proposal of ascribing suffering directly to God's eternal triune life, which also includes referring univocally to the suffering of God and the suffering of humanity, asserts that theology must speak of the suffering of God as the result of Jesus Christ's passion, but he demands that talk of divine suffering must be analogical. Balthasar is unwavering in his commitment to the historic formula 'one of the Trinity has suffered'.[39] This formula must be upheld for a proper understanding of the salvific significance of the death and resurrection of Jesus Christ. In a terse response to Rahner's critique that in attributing suffering and death to a member of the Trinity he violates the Chalcedonian formula by confusing the divine and human in Jesus Christ, Balthasar writes, 'I cannot see how the *pro nobis* of Christ's Cross and Resurrection can avail for us if the one who was crucified and risen is not "one of the Trinity"' (*TD* V, p. 13). Balthasar denies the specifics of Rahner's charge of 'Neo-Chalcedonianism' and instead presents his position as thoroughly in line with the rules set forth at Chalcedon, though moving to a certain extent beyond Chalcedon. Rahner's refusal to affirm the statement 'one of the Trinity has suffered' and his mistaken portrayal of Balthasar's Christology as Monophysite betrays his own commitment to a form of Antiochene Christology, which is seen in his assertion that only the humanity of Jesus suffered and died.[40]

Balthasar insists that if we are to follow Chalcedon's teaching of the hypostatic union of humanity and divinity in Jesus Christ, without 'separation', then we must speak of the Son of God taking on or experiencing suffering and death in the hypostatic union. In a way similar to Barth, Balthasar maintains a real *communicatio idiomatum*, and, as a result, insists that Jesus Christ in his divine–human unity suffered and died: the human suffering of Jesus is appropriated by the eternal Son of God through the hypostatic union.[41] 'If we are to follow biblical revelation', Balthasar asserts, 'we must not split the Son of God in the exercise of his mission into the one who carries out his mission on earth and the one who remains unaffected in heaven, looking down at the "sent" Son. For he is One: he is the eternal Son dwelling in time' (*TD* III, p. 228). Gerard O'Hanlon insightfully summarizes the significance of Balthasar's Christological commitments to his understanding of the suffering of God:

> From his repeated emphasis on the ontological, personal identity of the Logos as the subject who unites the two distinct natures in Christ, [Balthasar] will refuse to limit the change and suffering which Christ experiences to his human nature alone. This is the advance on Chalcedon and its traditional interpretation which Balthasar proposes. The tendency to consider the human nature of Christ as an *instrumentum conjunctum* which does not affect the divine person he sees

---

39 Balthasar treats Jesus' mission and the formula regarding the suffering of a member of the Trinity in the following, 'Jesus truly fulfills the universal mission entrusted to him in that the *commercium* becomes a real exchange of places; anthropologically this is not possible if it is simply man who suffers on the other's behalf: it is only possible if *"unus ex Trinitate passus es"* both in his human nature and in his divine person for it is only by virtue of his divine person that he can enter into the desperate situation of a free human being vis-à-vis God, in order to transform it from a dead-end to a situation full of hope.' *TD* III, p. 239.

40 See *TD* IV, pp. 273–84.

41 See Barth's discussion of Jesus Christ as 'Very God and Very Man', in *CD* I/2, pp. 132–71.

as Nestorian in character. And so he is anxious to insist on a more than merely logical *communicatio idiomatum*, to accept that the formula 'one of the Trinity has suffered' does indeed mean that God has 'suffered', albeit mysteriously. But why 'mysteriously'; why not say univocally that God suffers? Because – and here we find Balthasar's respect for Chalcedon – there *is* an enduring and incommensurable difference between God and the world, between the divine and human 'unmixed' natures of Christ. Any facile attribution of change and suffering to God, based on the fact that the person of Christ is affected by his human nature, represents a failure to maintain the distinction between the natures; it is a relapse into monophysitism and results in a mythical notion of God.[42]

Balthasar moves from his Christological commitment that the one Jesus Christ, in his divine–human unity, suffered and died, which enables him to affirm that 'one of the Trinity has suffered', to a hypothesis regarding the potential for suffering in God's triune life. 'If it is possible for one Person in God to accept suffering', Balthasar writes, 'then evidently it is not something foreign to God, something that does not affect him. It must be something profoundly appropriate to his divine Person, for – to say it once again – his being sent (*missio*) by the Father is a modality of his proceeding (*processio*) from the Father' (*TD* III, p. 226).

Although Balthasar criticizes Moltmann for speaking univocally regarding human suffering and divine suffering, for identifying the internal divine processions with salvation history, and for locating the suffering and forsakenness of the cross directly in the Trinitarian life of God, he insists that we must not distinguish to the point of separation the saving mission of Jesus Christ and the procession of the Son from the Father (*TD* IV, p. 322). While Moltmann's position includes the danger of identifying missions and processions, Balthasar worries that Barth risks espousing the latter position of separating God's internal processions from God's economic mission, and, as a consequence, stops short of affirming that the events of the passion really affect the internal life of God.[43]

In addressing the question of whether there is suffering in God, Balthasar maintains that although it is improper to ascribe suffering directly to God's internal being, we must affirm that there is something analogous to suffering in God, even if human language and conceptuality break down in the face of such a statement. Balthasar proposes that it is the reckless self-giving of intra-Trinitarian divine love that is analogous to suffering, or more properly, which can develop into suffering. Balthasar states, 'There is something in God that can develop into suffering. This suffering occurs when the recklessness with which the Father gives away himself (and *all* that is his) encounters a freedom that, instead of responding in kind to this magnanimity, changes it into a calculating, cautious self-preservation' (*TD* IV, pp. 327–8).

In summary, both Balthasar and Barth refrain from attributing suffering directly

42   O'Hanlon, *The Immutability of God*, p. 43.
43   See *TD* V, pp. 236–9, 243–6.

to God, in contrast to Moltmann's radical reinterpretation of God's being and his emphasis on the essential pathos of God. Balthasar, more than Barth, ventures to describe how the events of Jesus Christ's passion really affect God's internal Trinitarian life, and he does this by attempting to walk along the narrow way between, on the one side, baldly asserting that God suffers and experiences pain, and on the other side, maintaining a philosophically precise definition of God's *apatheia*, which neglects the depiction of God in the biblical text. A complete investigation into whether Balthasar fully succeeds in navigating between the Scylla of mythologically and anthropomorphically entangling God in the world process and the Charybdis of maintaining an unbiblical picture of a distant and unapproachable God lies beyond the scope of this study.[44] It is my inclination, however, that Balthasar often drifts dangerously close to the shoals guarding the former forbidden shore. Whereas Barth is very cautious in his treatment of the effect of the passion of Jesus Christ on the eternal life of the triune God, Balthasar boldly asserts that the death of Jesus Christ and his descent into hell do not leave God's triune life unaffected. However, Balthasar does not specify exactly how God is affected. At this point, Balthasar strongly criticizes Moltmann for going too far, because he depicts God in such a way that God is caught up in the world process. God, according to Balthasar's interpretation of Moltmann, becomes a tragic, mythological god. At the same time, Balthasar criticizes Barth for being unwilling to affirm that the passion of Jesus Christ somehow affects God's eternal triune life. It seems that one could argue that Balthasar's strong criticism of Moltmann betrays the risks of his own position. In other words, Balthasar recognizes that his own position moves towards Moltmann's, and he therefore is compelled to critique Moltmann as an attempt to preserve his own view. If this is an accurate portrayal of Balthasar, then we could say that he needs Barth's modesty as a corrective, and as a means of safeguarding his own position from the hazards that he rightly recognizes in Moltmann, and towards which his own position drifts.

In sum, we may affirm that Balthasar is ever aware of the perilous position that he feels he must take, and we may conclude our discussion of the question of suffering and pain in God with Balthasar's own description of the theological 'knife edge' upon which God's action in Jesus Christ forces theology to stand.

---

44 John Thompson points out a potential critical distinction between Balthasar and Barth on this issue, which was mentioned above. This distinction highlights a potential risk present in Balthasar's theology towards allowing God to be affected too directly by the history to the point of affirming an enriching change in God that is a consequence of the cross. Thompson writes, 'Balthasar parts company with Barth at one point. For him the cross in some measure affects God, who experiences "enrichment" thereby . . . Barth sees God's true nature revealed in the cross of Jesus Christ where suffering and death do not alter him but are potentialities of his triune being. Balthasar, on the other hand, sees a reciprocal relationship between God and the world which means a change in God. This latter, however, is not to be regarded as affecting his essential deity, but analogous to human love, is an "evermore" of the same. Barth's view is to be preferred since Balthasar's could be seen as an expansion of or growth in God, though this is clearly not his intention.' Thompson, *Modern Trinitarian Perspectives*, pp. 57, 58. For a full discussion of this matter see, O'Hanlon, *The Immutability of God*, pp. 35–40, 80–7, passim.

> There is only one way to approach the trinitarian life in God: on the basis of what is manifest in God's kenosis in the theology of the covenant – and thence in the theology of the Cross – we must feel our way back into the mystery of the absolute, employing a negative theology that excludes from God all intramundane experience and suffering, while at the same time presupposing that the possibility of such experience and suffering – up to and including its christological and trinitarian implications – is grounded in God. To think in such a way is to walk on a knife edge: it avoids all the fashionable talk of 'the pain of God' and yet is bound to say that something happens in God that not only justifies the possibility and actual occurrence of all suffering in the world but also justifies God's sharing in the latter, in which he goes to the length of vicariously taking on man's God-lessness. The very thing that negative ('philosophical') theology prohibits seems to be demanded by the *oikonomia* in Christ: faith, which is beyond both yet feels its way forward from both, has an intuition of the mystery of all mysteries, which we must posit as the unfathomable precondition and source of the world's salvation history. (*TD* IV, p. 324)

Fundamentally for Balthasar, the issue of the possibility and actuality of suffering or pain in God must be addressed from within an exploration of the mystery of God's love. The events of the passion, in which 'one of the Trinity has suffered', must be grounded in the mystery of the reckless self-giving of God's love, in which the Father generates the Son, the Son exists in grateful receptivity, and the Spirit is the bond of mutual love, which bridges the 'distance' between the Father and the Son. This is the mystery to which the events of the passion point and upon which they are grounded. The question of the suffering of God is always secondary for Balthasar to the primary issue of the mystery of God's love, God's being as love revealed in the cross, descent into hell, and resurrection, and the salvation of humanity wrought in these events.[45] The deep mystery of God's Trinitarian love and the corresponding mystery of God's radical love for the world, which perdures even in the face of wilful rejection, lie at the heart of all discussions regarding the relationship between the passion of Jesus Christ and the triune life of God. It is the great mystery of this twofold love alone that shines light on the deep darkness of the suffering and death of the incarnate Son of God in Jesus Christ. One must speak deliberately and not rashly about pain and suffering in God, yet, one must speak all the same. The gospel demands that we speak of suffering and death in

---

45 Hunt observes, 'Von Balthasar, while coming within a hair's breadth of attributing suffering to God, assiduously avoids such an attribution. Suffering and death *ad extra* are not attributed univocally to God *ad intra*. Von Balthasar attributes no more than something *analogous* to suffering to the divine being. He argues that the grounds for the possibility of what takes place *ad extra* are to be found in God *ad intra*. In other words God does not become what God was not: God is, in the paschal mystery, what God is eternally. The crux of the matter, as von Balthasar would persuade us, is that in and through the paschal mystery all creation is incorporated into God's trinitarian love, that love alone is credible, that the mystery we behold in the paschal mystery is not the mystery of God's suffering but the mystery of God's inexhaustible and ever-creative love.' Hunt, *The Trinity and the Paschal Mystery*, pp. 167–8.

God because it proclaims that God loves the world in such a way that his Son must suffer and die, and it is precisely in the suffering and death of the Son that God himself takes the place of sinful humanity bears humanity's sin and bears it away.[46] For Balthasar, the eradication of sin and the defeat of death take place in the silence and isolation of Jesus Christ's passive descent into the depths of hell. This event also reveals the mystery of the unsurpassable fullness of God's radical love. At the very point where the Word of God is silent, suffers and dies – the descent into hell of Holy Saturday – the Word reveals God's ever greater Trinitarian love to those who receive it in faith (*MP*, p. 65).

Alan Lewis' *Between Cross and Resurrection: A Theology of Holy Saturday*

As a way to enhance our treatment of Barth, Balthasar and Moltmann, it will be beneficial to address briefly Alan Lewis' constructive exploration of the descent into hell, published posthumously as *Between Cross and Resurrection: A Theology of Holy Saturday*. Lewis' significant work is the most comprehensive constructive treatment of the doctrine of Holy Saturday and the descent into hell. It is also notable as it presents a detailed analysis of Barth and then offers Moltmann (with Eberhard Jüngel) as moving beyond Barth in significant ways, which Lewis argues are faithful extensions of Barth's theology. There is much to be commended in Lewis' explication and analysis of Barth's method, christology, innovative doctrine of election and his passion-centred theology, all of which contribute considerably to a constructive doctrine of the descent into hell. The difficulty with Lewis' impressive work is his contention that Moltmann in fact moves in directions that are necessary and faithful expansions and extensions of Barth's position. This, I contend, is a difficult if not impossible case to make.

One of Lewis' concerns with Barth stems from his reading of Barth's emphasis on God's freedom and the effect of this emphasis on the genuineness of God's revelation in the passion of Jesus Christ. Lewis agrees with Moltmann's hesitancy in distinguishing between the immanent and economic Trinity, as he shares Moltmann's concern to insist that the events of this world are consequential, even constitutive, for the eternal life and being of God. In Lewis' estimation, Barth perpetuates a dangerous dualism by distinguishing between the immanent and economic Trinity; this, Lewis concludes, leads to a depiction of a God who is aloof and detached from the events in creation. This concern regarding a dualistic picture of God and the world is confirmed, according to Lewis, by Barth's consistent identification of God as the 'one who loves in freedom'. Lewis is concerned,

---

46 For two profound passages which treat the depth of God's radical love for sinful humanity – a love that involves God's bearing humanity's sin and the grave consequences of this sin – see Hans Urs von Balthasar, *Convergences: To the Source of Christian Mystery*, trans. E. A. Nelson (San Francisco: Ignatius Press, 1983), pp. 120–33; and *MP*, pp. 139–40.

following Moltmann's lead, with the troubling possibility that incarnation and passion are not decisively revelatory of the being of God, and that God could have chosen not to love humanity in this way. Lewis writes:

> God's unconditioned otherness over against creation, without which God would not be God, is not compromised but fulfilled by the love of God for creation, which leads to actions of self-involvement in our createdness and brokenness. God's love is free, the exercise and not surrender of lordship even in the extremities of abandonment and contradiction in our far country. But does this sovereign freedom mean that behind God's actual decision to love, elect, and assume our humanness there stands an open choice, a freedom *not* to love us, a possibility in God's immanence to be other than the loving, self-humiliating God revealed in the economy? If there is no such freedom, what of God's unconditioned lordship? If there is such freedom, is God's love toward us not contingent and capricious – a possibility actually chosen but which might not have been?[47]

Lewis concludes that Barth risks this troubling conclusion of capriciousness and contingency of God's love, because Barth is so intent on 'safeguarding God's own freedom'.[48] For Lewis, the firmness with which Barth asserts God's freedom, self-sufficiency and independence leads to the unsettling conclusion that the self-giving and suffering love displayed in the passion of Jesus may not be fully revelatory of the eternal being of God. God might actually be other than the one who manifests himself in the cross of Christ.

Although Lewis wants to be generous in his reading of Barth, and is consistently careful and perceptive in his interpretation of Barth, his suggestion that Barth risks depicting God as capricious and untrustworthy is off the mark. Barth explicitly rejects the notion that divine freedom entails arbitrariness. In fact, as we have seen, Barth describes God's love as free and necessary. God's love for creation is indeed free, but it is not capricious, arbitrary or indifferent. In his revolutionary reconstruction of the Reformed doctrine of predestination or election, Barth clearly rejects any thought of God's election being anything other than it actually is and any suggestion that God's election might be overturned or reversed. Barth writes:

> The justification of the sinner in Jesus Christ is the content of predestination in so far as predestination is a No and signifies rejection. On this side, too, it is eternal. It cannot be overthrown or reversed. Rejection cannot again become the portion or affair of man. The exchange which took place on Golgotha, when God chose as His throne the malefactor's cross, when the Son of God bore what the son of man ought to have borne, took place once and for all in fulfilment of God's eternal will, and it can never be reversed. There is no condemnation – literally none – for those that are in Christ Jesus ... Predestination means that from all eternity God has determined upon man's

47   Alan Lewis, *Between Cross and Resurrection: A Theology of Holy Saturday* (Grand Rapids, MI: Wm. B. Eerdmans Publishing Co., 2001), p. 209.
48   Ibid.

acquittal at His own cost. It means that God has ordained that in the place of the one acquitted He Himself should be perishing and abandoned and rejected – the Lamb slain from the foundation of the world. There is, then, no background, no *decretum absolutum*, no mystery of the divine good-pleasure, in which predestination might just as well be man's rejection. (*CD* II/2, p. 167)[49]

Lewis affirms the freedom of God, but his definition differs significantly from Barth's. It is Lewis's delineation of freedom, which he learned from Moltmann, that demonstrates his break with Barth's theology. There is indeed a break here, even though Lewis asserts that his position – and Moltmann's as well – is faithful to Barth's commitments. This break is seen as Lewis writes:

God is free, not as one who could do otherwise, but as *the* one above all who can do *no* other. Self-bound to one sole way of being, God is committed, necessarily but thus freely, to the cognate course of action. God's lordship in bowing to the contradiction of the godless cross and godforsaken grace does not reside, as Barth occasionally and illogically asserts, in a prior self-sufficiency and secure immutability, but – as he more often understood and later followers more emphatically underscored – in the uncoerced impulse to self-consistency: love's determination not to be deflected from its purposes but to flourish and perfect itself through willing self-surrender. What judges us as burdensome imperative illuminates God as free but binding indicative: the truth – for our Creator and therefore for ourselves – that only one who gives up life discovers and fulfils it. On such a basis alone can we understand how the cross and grave truly reveal God's inmost triune life.[50]

As we have seen, Barth rejects any suggestion that divine love must 'perfect itself' through self-surrender. God, for Barth, is indeed self-sufficient and independent. God does not love the world out of ontological necessity. We have also seen that although Balthasar is willing to move beyond Barth and to press Barth regarding the effect of historical events on the eternal life of God, Balthasar joins Barth in

---

49   For an astute treatment of the ontological significance of Barth's doctrine of election see Bruce McCormack's essay, 'Grace and Being: The role of God's gracious election in Karl Barth's theological ontology'. McCormack's conclusion regarding the free self-determination of God demonstrates that Lewis' concern is ill founded. God is not other than who he is as revealed in the passion of Jesus Christ. McCormack writes, 'The eternal act of establishing a covenant of grace is an act of Self-determination by means of which God determines to be God, from everlasting to everlasting, in a covenantal relationship with human beings and to be God in no other way. This is not a decision for mere role-play; it is a decision which has ontological significance. What Barth is suggesting is that election is the event in God's life in which he assigns to himself the being he will have for all eternity. It is an act of Self-determination by means of which God chooses in Jesus Christ love and mercy for the human race and judgment (reprobation) for himself. Choosing reprobation for himself in Jesus Christ means subjecting himself as the incarnate God to the human experience of death – and not just to any death, but to spiritual death in God-abandonment.' Bruce McCormack, 'Grace and Being: The role of God's Gracious Election in Karl Barth's Theological Ontology', in *The Cambridge Companion to Karl Barth*, ed. John Webster (Cambridge: Cambridge University Press, 2000), p. 98.

50   Lewis, *Between Cross and Resurrection*, pp. 211–12.

rejecting any implication that calls into question God's fullness and sufficiency. Barth and Balthasar together affirm that divine love does not perfect itself through self-surrender, nor does divine love need such perfecting.

A further problem with Lewis' treatment of divine love and divine freedom is his frank statement that God and human beings are under the same obligation for life and fulfilment. What is essential for human beings is essential for God. This essential truth, according to Lewis, is that 'only one who gives up life discovers and fulfils it'. Again, as our examination of Barth and Balthasar has determined, God does not give himself for humanity, does not enter into the full reality of suffering, death and hell as the necessary means to self-fulfilment. Rather, God's self-giving and self-surrender is for humanity and humanity's salvation; it is for the life of the world.

An additional indication of Lewis' movement away from Barth is his agreement with Moltmann's assertion that the cross and the descent into hell lead to a break in the life of God. Lewis views the descent into hell as an event that 'ruptures God's own life'.[51] Lewis also invites us to consider the Trinitarian life of God as a loving community that 'endures death in the radical separating of the Father and the Son'.[52] Lewis considers his assertions of rupture in the divine life and separation between the Father and the Son as ontological implications of Jesus' death and descent into hell. He faults Barth for 'illogically' refusing to embrace these ontological implications. Though Lewis repeatedly portrays Barth's hesitancy to go along with Moltmann as illogical, Barth has clear reasons for stopping where he does, and, as we have seen, he has very good theological reasons to do so.

Lewis engages in an direct comparison of Barth and Moltmann on the relationship between God's eternal life and temporal events and he sides with Moltmann and his eschatological emphasis. Lewis writes:

> [God's] identity is so mediated through activity and time that God's eternal life and being will not be complete until the end of time, when all that God has to do is finally done. If, therefore, for Barth, eternity makes space for time, for Moltmann, conversely, the temporal adds to and enriches the eternal. God not only makes time but shares in it, so that through historical involvement the divine life experiences increments of Godhead: greater glory, deeper joy, fuller being.[53]

As we have seen, both Barth and Balthasar reject the proposal offered by Moltmann that the event of the cross and descent into hell adds to and enriches the eternal life of God, in the sense that it constitutes the Trinity. Although it is accurate to read both Barth and Balthasar as proposing that the Trinity grounds and manifests itself in the event of the cross and descent into hell, both resoundingly reject any

---

51   Ibid., p. 214.
52   Ibid.
53   Ibid., p. 218.

suggestion that the Trinity is constituted by the cross and descent into hell. As we have seen, Balthasar distances himself from Moltmann, while at the same exploring the mystery of the assertion that the cross and the descent into hell do not leave the Trinity unaffected. In this exploration, Balthasar speaks of enrichment or addition to the Trinity, but he does so cautiously, deliberately avoiding the suggestion that the cross and descent into hell constitute the Trinity. Lewis, I suggest, would have been much better served by examining Balthasar's proposal regarding the 'enrichment' of the Trinity, which is nicely summarized by Guy Mansini:

> In the first place, the 'enrichment' in question is predicated of the persons, not of the divinity. In the second place, Balthasar wants to say that this is not a becoming like an earthly becoming, not a passage from potency to act, but rather a matter of a supraworldly Trinitarian 'event.' In the third place, the enrichment is a gratuitous enrichment; that is, it is so to speak a contingent means by which the persons glorify one another, a means enfolded in an eternal conversation, glorification, and enrichment that takes place among the persons, and would take place, whether the world existed or not, and whether the world was redeemed in the way that it in fact is or not.[54]

In short, although Lewis indeed offers a remarkable constructive proposal of a doctrine of the descent into hell, his championing of Moltmann as a necessary and faithful extension to Barth is curious and difficult to support. As we have made clear, Moltmann is at odds with Barth, and his proposals cannot be sustained on Barthian soil. In fact, Balthasar steps forward as one who can push and challenge Barth regarding the relationship of the cross and the descent into hell in a way that takes Barth's concerns into account while avoiding the theological pitfalls of Moltmann.

Conclusion: the descent into hell and the Trinity

The comparison of Moltmann's position with the similar positions of Barth and Balthasar enables us to see clearly the theological significance of what is at stake in viewing the Trinity through the lens of the descent into hell and, correspondingly, in grounding the descent into hell in the Trinitarian life of God.

First, the descent into hell must be considered as an essential aspect of Jesus Christ's life of pure obedience to the will of the Father. The journey that Jesus travels in complete obedience to God, to be exact, has its destination in the descent into hell. Although we must emphasize the passivity of Jesus in his descent into hell – his being taken to the realm of the dead as a genuinely dead human being – we must stress that his being taken to hell is not something that contradicts his own will. Rather, it is an element of his will to obey and trust God completely. In

---

54   Guy Mansini, O.S.B. 'Balthasar and the Theodramatic Enrichment of the Trinity', *The Thomist* 64 (2000): p. 506.

fact, given the Trinitarian ground for the descent into hell, Jesus' wilful acceptance of what will befall him in the passion – including his descent into hell – is the acceptance of the eternal saving decision made by the triune God, a decision in which he was intimately involved as the eternal Son.

Considering the descent into hell as the consequence of the Son's obedience to the Father and as the implementation of the saving mission that constitutes his identity leads to our second conclusion. The descent into hell, though expressing the severity of the Son's death in God-abandonment and God-forsakenness, does not jeopardize the unity of the Godhead. The unity and integrity of God, both Barth and Balthasar insist, is upheld in the descent into hell. God does not cease to be God in the distance that separates the Son from the Father in the descent into hell, as Moltmann suggests; rather, God manifests the mystery of his divinity in identifying with human sinfulness and in his bearing his own judgment against human sin, in order to effect human reconciliation and redemption.

A third conclusion stipulates that the descent into hell be considered as a consequence of God's perfect freedom and not as a divine necessity. The descent into hell is not necessary for God's self-actualization, nor is it necessary for God's love to be fulfilled. God is completely actualized in and of himself, and God's love is complete in the internal loving relationship of the triune Godhead. It is only this understanding of the descent into hell that can guarantee God's independence from the world and can uphold the theological conviction that God's creation that which is not God is a gracious act, and, correspondingly, that God's activity in reconciling the world to himself and redeeming humanity through the event of the passion of Christ is sheer grace, uncoerced, unmerited, and the product of the abundance of God's love.

One qualification of this specification is that there is a way in which we must affirm the necessity of God's love and, therefore, the necessity of the death and descent into hell of Jesus Christ. This affirmation of 'necessity' follows from the conviction that God's activity is never arbitrary or capricious; rather, it is consistent with God's being or identity and, therefore, is an instance of God's self-revelation. Again, Barth contributes to this point through his discussion of God's primal decision of election, in which God determines himself to be God for humanity and for humanity to be for God. Balthasar, as we have seen, speaks of the 'necessity' of the descent into hell as a consequence of the reckless self-surrender which characterizes the event of God. The descent into hell, following Barth and Balthasar, is an instance of God's self-revelation, and is not, as Moltmann proposes, a necessary element of God's self-constitution.

Fourth, when speaking of the suffering of God one must emphasize the alien character of this suffering as well as the saving purpose of this suffering. The suffering of God is genuine, because Jesus Christ suffers, dies and descends into hell in his divine–human unity. Yet the suffering is alien, because it is creaturely suffering that the Logos incorporates into the divine life as a result of the hypostatic union and the *communicatio idiomatum*. One must tread lightly in a discussion of the suffering of God. On the one hand, one must unhesitatingly affirm God's participation in the suffering and death of Jesus Christ, because this is what Scripture demands. On the other hand, one must always speak analogously regarding the suffering of God. Otherwise, one risks applying human categories univocally and uncritically to God, and this is theologically unacceptable.

The rationale for attributing suffering to God is the significant distinction between Moltmann's position and the common position of Barth and Balthasar. God suffers solely in order to reconcile humanity to himself and in order to redeem humanity by enduring the fullness of God's wrath – God's judgment on human sin. God does not suffer in order to enhance his own being, or as Moltmann suggests, in an act of self-redemption. The suffering that God endures, therefore, is precisely the suffering that is the result of human sin and evil. The death of Jesus Christ, both Barth and Balthasar demand, must be understood as atoning and must employ the difficult categories of expiation and propitiation. The death of Jesus Christ, and the suffering of God in this death, is understood properly only as being 'for us and for our salvation' and, further, as being done in the place of humanity. God is not, as Moltmann risks suggesting, a victim who suffers alongside humanity; rather, God deliberately takes on the suffering of the world in order to identify with it and, further, in order to overcome it.

I am not, however, suggesting that suffering may be understood only as the consequence of sin, because this would neglect the actuality of the atrocities of innocent suffering. God, through Jesus Christ, identifies with the innocent suffering of the world, and by doing so offers genuine hope to those who are victims of this arbitrary, random and innocent suffering. The suggestion that I am making is that Moltmann's view of the suffering of God does not adequately account for the vicarious character of the life and death of Jesus Christ, and therefore presents a view of God in which God is a victim alongside the human victims of innocent suffering. In such a case, God becomes an empathetic fellow sufferer rather than one who, through his suffering, deals effectively with suffering and overcomes it.

The fifth and final conclusion insists that the descent into hell is understood properly only if it is seen in the light of God's absolute love. The descent into hell must be grounded in the superabundant Trinitarian love of God, which defines God's essence, being and nature. In this respect, the descent into hell is an instance of God's self-revelation, in which God reveals himself as love. Secondly, the descent into hell must be seen as a consequence of God's mysterious, absolute and ever-gracious love for humanity. God's love for the world is seen clearly in God's endurance of everything that is anti-divine, and this takes place precisely in the mode of the eternal Son and his experience of hell in the divine–human unity of Jesus Christ. How does God love the world? God loves the world and humanity by experiencing death in the absence of God and entering hell so that humanity is freed from having to perish, freed from the sentence of the second death, and freed for a future that may be described with words whose meaning lies beyond the capabilities of human language, i.e. a future that is eternal life.

In the end, the relationship between the descent into hell and the Trinity must be grounded on the mystery of God's absolute Trinitarian love and God's corresponding love for humanity. The descent into hell is the manifestation of the mysterious and superabundant love of the triune God, in which we see the splendour of God's beauty and the grandeur of God's glory.

CHAPTER FIVE

The descent into hell and discipleship

The third aspect of a constructive doctrine of the descent into hell addresses the impact of the descent into hell on Christian discipleship. In order for our treatment of the doctrine of the descent into hell to be complete, a discussion of the shape of Christian existence in the indirect light of the descent into hell must be added to the discussion in the previous two chapters regarding the descent into hell and Scripture, and the descent into hell and the doctrine of the Trinity.

An examination of the impact of the descent into hell on Christian discipleship is an essential element of a comprehensive constructive doctrine of the descent into hell, because the truth of Christian doctrine must not be separated from Christian practice and a lived faith. Theological doctrines and convictions give rise to and are informed by specific ethical practices. We must emphasize that doctrinal statements and ethical practice cannot be divorced. Truth is not simply something believed and propositionally affirmed; truth is also something done and lived (John 3:21). Let it suffice to say that I shall presume that doctrines must function in such a way as to give shape to Christian existence. Moreover, vital faith in the doctrinal assertion that Jesus Christ bore the sins of the world, endured the punishment for sin on the cross and faced the loneliness of extreme separation from God in his descent into hell, *pro nobis* – for us, for others and for me – gives rise to authentic discipleship, which is characterized by genuine self-giving love for all.

In our discussion of the relationship between the descent into hell and the Trinity in the previous chapter, we returned again and again to the theme of God's absolute love. We concluded that the descent into hell is understandable only as a manifestation of the reckless self-giving of the triune God's superabundant love, and, furthermore, that this love is directed to all humanity, which consists of sinners, God's enemies, and those who wilfully reject this love. In this chapter, we will explore the qualifications of Christian discipleship as it is determined by the descent into hell and the understanding of God's love that is manifested there. We will ascertain the contours of Christian discipleship and the defining characteristics of Christian love from the divine love revealed in the descent into hell.

God's love as non-violent enemy-love and the shape of discipleship

In his comparison of the constructive atonement teachings of T. F. Torrance, Hans Urs von Balthasar and Karl Barth, George Hunsinger asserts the following as a way both to distinguish Barth from Torrance and Balthasar, and to argue implicitly for the superiority of Barth's position:

> More than von Balthasar . . . and to some extent than Torrance, Barth stresses the atonement as the justification of the ungodly. Enemy-love in Karl Barth's theology is the heart of the gospel. It is not only a decisive category for understanding God's love as revealed in the cross of Christ, but also for Christian discipleship as grounded and called forth by that love.[1]

Although I do not take issue with Hunsinger's compelling account of Barth's understanding of Jesus Christ's passion, God's non-violent enemy-love and Christian discipleship, I want to suggest that he has overlooked Balthasar as a crucial ally.[2] I am not convinced that Barth stresses the atonement as 'justification of the ungodly' more than Balthasar. Balthasar, I will demonstrate, shares Barth's conviction that the passion of Jesus Christ manifests God's radical love for humanity, that this love is not coercive or triumphalistic, and, further, that this love is directed to all human beings – sinners, enemies and those who reject this love. I contend that Balthasar's contribution to an understanding of both God's love and Christian love as non-violent love for the enemy is a direct consequence of his particular understanding of the descent into hell and the essential role played by the descent into hell in his soteriology. Therefore, Balthasar's teaching regarding the descent into hell has both doctrinal and ethical ramifications that are complementary to Barth's teaching.

As Hunsinger concentrates his attention on Barth's view of the cross in his description of God's love as non-violent enemy-love, I will focus on Balthasar's view of Jesus Christ's descent into hell, in order to contribute to an understanding of divine love and human love that the believer is summoned to embody in the call to discipleship. An exploration of the relationship between the descent into hell

---

1   George Hunsinger, 'The Politics of the Nonviolent God: Reflections on René Girard and Karl Barth', *Scottish Journal of Theology* 51 (1998): p. 77.

2   I must make it clear from the outset that I will not specifically address the complicated issues of pacifism, violence, just war theory, and the political embodiment of non-violence. There is generally recognized ambiguity in both Barth and Balthasar regarding political non-violent resistance, and the issue of the Christian's involvement in war and the military organization of the state. For example, see Karl Barth, *The Epistle to the Romans*, translated from the sixth edition by Edwyn C. Hoskyns (London: Oxford University Press, 1933), p. 471, 'A Church which knows its business well will, it is true, with a strong hand keep itself free from militarism; but it will also with a friendly gesture rebuff the attentions of pacifism.' Although Barth insists that Christians cannot help but be pacifists in practice, he will not allow pacifism to be absolutized. Balthasar also acknowledges the complexity and ambiguity of violence and political struggle. 'The Christian politician and sociologist must have a realism that comes from a sober assessment of earthly power relationships, . . . the boundaries of the use of force are not easily identifiable.' *TD* IV, pp. 485–6. My purpose in this chapter is to describe the context within which the question of pacifism, just war, Christian military involvement and so forth must be addressed, rather than work out in detail the social and political ramifications of non-violent enemy-love, the casuistry of non-violence, if you will. Let it suffice to say that I will argue that for both Barth and Balthasar, the social, political, and ethical issue of violence and non-violence must be handled within the context of the crucified Messiah, who died and descended into hell for us and for all. My concern in this chapter is the relationship between the doctrine of the descent into hell and Christian discipleship and theological existence; I am not attempting to construct a social ethic on the basis of the descent into hell.

and Christian discipleship in Balthasar's thought will complement Barth's conviction regarding God's love and the corresponding non-violent love for the enemy commanded by God of all disciples of Jesus Christ. An examination of Balthasar's position will enhance our understanding of God's radical love and sharpen our view of the shape of Christian discipleship that this love calls forth and supports.

Hunsinger begins his analysis of the relationship between Barth's view of the atoning work of Jesus Christ on the cross and Christian discipleship and ethics with a concise description of Barth's treatment of the cross, where God takes the place of humanity, who exist as God's enemies in disobedience and rebellion. Motivated by his radical love, God endures the penalty for human sin and offers his life for the life of the world.[3]

> In the cross God does not meet his enemies with malice, retaliation or crushing force. He meets them with the mystery of suffering love. He not only treats them with restraint, but offers himself up for them all. He presents himself as a living sacrifice, saving them from their self-inflicted destruction by suffering the condemnation they deserve. He does not repay evil for evil, but overcomes evil with good, even to the point of setting at stake his own existence. The politics of God thus reveals itself as the politics of nonviolent love.[4]

God's merciful love grounds God's intervention on humanity's behalf, which involves enduring the punishment and wrath that was properly meant for sinful humanity, who are disobedient covenant breakers and have moved from being God's partners to being his enemies. In the event of the self-giving love of God, in which God takes the penalty for sin upon himself, atonement is made and humanity

---

3 Hunsinger directs our attention to a significant passage from *CD* IV/1 where Barth provides an exegesis of John 3:16. At the core of Barth's exegesis lies the description of God's activity in the cross as involving great risk to God – God hazards his own existence as God. This radical and reckless self-giving by God is for the life of his creatures and partners, who stand in opposition to him as his enemies. See *CD* IV/1, pp. 71–8.

See also a passage in *CD* II/2 where Barth describes God's action in the death of Jesus Christ as the enacting of God's self-giving, non-violent love for humanity, whom Barth identifies as the 'disobedient' and as the enemies of God. Barth writes, 'The rejection which all men incurred, the wrath of God under which all men lie, the death which all men must die, God in His love for men transfers from all eternity to Him in whom He loves and elected them, and whom He elects as their head and in their place. God from all eternity ordains this obedient One in order that He might bear the suffering which the disobedient have deserved and which for the sake of God's righteousness must necessarily be borne. Indeed, the very obedience which was exacted of Him and attained by Him was His willingness to take upon Himself the divine rejection of all others and to suffer that which they ought to have suffered . . . That the elected man Jesus had to suffer and die means no more and no less than that in becoming man God makes Himself responsible for man who became His enemy, and that He takes upon Himself all the consequences of man's action – his rejection and his death. This is what is involved in the self-giving of God. This is the radicalness of His grace . . . He elects Jesus, then, at the head and in the place of all others. The wrath of God, the judgment and the penalty, fall, then, upon Him. And this means upon His own Son, upon Himself: upon Him, and not upon those whom He loves and elects "in Him," upon Him, and not upon the disobedient.' *CD* II/2, pp. 123, 124.

4 Hunsinger, 'The Politics of the Nonviolent God', p. 78.

is reconciled to God. Human persons no longer exist as enemies of God; they are reinstated as God's covenant partners.

Hunsinger identifies two elements of Christian ethics and discipleship that follow from Barth's account of the character of God's love as manifested in the atoning death of Jesus Christ.

First, since God's love is love for the sinner, the disobedient, the rebellious, and the enemy, this love is not a response to some aspect inherent to human persons *qua* human persons. 'God does not love us because we are lovable', Hunsinger writes; 'we are lovable because God loves us.'[5] God's love is prevenient and creative. In loving sinful humanity, God takes the initiative (1 John 4:9–10), and God's love is such that it removes obstacles that would otherwise impede humanity's reception of this love. By removing anything that gets in the way of his love, God also enables humanity, through the creative power of the Holy Spirit, to respond to God's love by freely loving him in return. God's love transforms enemies into friends, and as a result, human beings are able to love God and one another.

Second, non-violent enemy-love is not an abstract ideal within which we are to understand God's love and human love. Rather, non-violent enemy-love is intelligible only on the basis of the particular and concrete event of Jesus Christ's passion, in which God's radical non-violent love for the enemy is enacted and revealed. God's love is utterly free, and God alone determines the defining characteristics of this love. God's non-violent enemy-love, according to Hunsinger, 'is not grounded in any plausibility structure other than the one it provides for itself. It cannot be explained or comprehended by any principle other than its own self-disclosure.'[6] One need not, and indeed cannot, look for ratification of the ethic of non-violent enemy-love in some universal ethical norm, principle, or system. The viability and intelligibility of the human practice of non-violent enemy-love depends entirely upon God's love as enacted in Jesus Christ's atoning death on the cross, where he bore the world's sin, endured the wrath of God, and died a death in God-abandonment so all might live. In sum, '[Christians] are commanded to love their enemies', Hunsinger writes, 'not because they are to conform to an abstract if noble principle, but because they know and may never forget that this is exactly how God has loved them.'[7]

Hunsinger identifies three elements of Christian discipleship as non-violent enemy-love: Christian discipleship as non-violent enemy-love reflects God's love, is judged by the cross, and is empowered by God's love. The ethic of non-violent enemy-love must reflect God's love and as God's love, God's being, or else it will appear as an arbitrary human ethical convention, which stands alongside other ethical alternatives to be or not to be chosen by the individual at the conclusion of

---

5   Ibid., p. 79.

6   Ibid., p. 80.

7   Ibid., p. 81.

deliberation. Non-violent love for the enemy is not a human ethical system or ideal chosen by the autonomous ethical agent; rather, it is the obligation of Christian disciples who have been summoned and commissioned by God. This type of love, moreover, is not a burden imposed upon the individual; rather, it is a gift, and it is through acceptance of this gift and obedience to this calling that the individual lives in perfect freedom. Furthermore, it is a valid obligation for disciples only because it is the exact way that God's love is manifested in the life and death of Jesus Christ. In the same way that disciples could not be expected to bear their own cross if Jesus Christ did not in fact bear the weight of his own cross, disciples of Jesus Christ could not be compelled to love their enemies in a non-violent manner if this was not in fact the way in which God in Jesus Christ loves all humanity. Hunsinger concludes that the ethic of non-violent enemy-love is a reflection of God and, therefore, is an essential aspect of obedient discipleship, because, as Barth writes, 'God does not stand in the far distance high above this ethics, but it is his divine nature to exist in the sense of this ethics, this ethics being only a reflection of his own being' (*CD* IV/1, p. 191).

It is significant to notice that perhaps Barth's clearest description of Christian discipleship and New Testament ethics as non-violent enemy-love comes within the section, 'The Judge Judged in Our Place' in *Church Dogmatics* IV/1, which played such a central role in our examination of Barth's view of the passion and the content of divine wrath in Chapter one. The ethic of non-violent love for all, including and especially for the enemy, is entailed, according to Barth, in a version of the atonement that emphasizes its penal, representative and substitutionary character. Barth devotes a small print section to the shape of New Testament ethics in the light of Jesus Christ's taking the place of sinners in his passion. Barth concludes this section with the following:

> Under the compelling power of our consideration of the One who was and acted for us as One accused and condemned and rejected, we are given the admonition: 'Who, when he was reviled, reviled not again; when he suffered, he threatened not; but committed himself to him that judgeth righteously; who his own self bare our sins in his own body on the tree, that we being dead to sins should live unto righteousness' (1 Peter 2:22f). From this we learn that we are not to oppose evil, as we are tempted, by repaying it with evil. Christians who know that He did this for them belong to Him. In their opposition to evil and evil men they have to comport themselves as these words demand. From this there follows quite naturally the supreme command to love our enemies. Jesus Christ fought His enemies, the enemies of God – as we all are (Rom 5:10, Col 1:21) – no, He loved His enemies, by identifying Himself with them. Compared with that what is the bit of forbearance or patience or humour or readiness to help or even intercession that we are willing and ready to bring and offer in the way of loving our enemies? But obviously when we look at what Jesus Christ became and was for us, we cannot leave out some little love for our enemies as a sign of our recognition and understanding that this is how he treated us His enemies. It is indeed a very clear commandment of God which points us in this direction from the cross of shame. (*CD* IV/1, p. 244)

Christian discipleship as non-violent enemy-love, Barth and Hunsinger insist, follows directly from a view of the atonement that emphasizes the work of Jesus Christ as being something 'on our behalf' and 'in our place'. It is important to notice that non-violent enemy-love does not preclude or neglect a strong opposition to both evil and evil people. Non-violent enemy-love that is called forth and supported by Jesus Christ's suffering love, is not marked by naive sentimentality or simplistic optimism; rather, it exhibits resolve in its strong opposition to evil in all its forms – structural, institutional, personal and so on. Evil and evil people are to be resolutely opposed, yet the manner in which evil is opposed must be determined by God's mysterious and all-powerful suffering, self-giving and non-violent love.

Next, Hunsinger observes that even though disciples are to emulate the characteristics of Jesus Christ's suffering love on the cross, as they embody the ethic of non-violent enemy-love, disciples are not to be considered as reiterating or duplicating Christ's work. Jesus Christ's work is perfect, complete and fully effective. This work lacks nothing. Given this description of discipleship, it must be said that Barth's understanding of an ethic of enemy-love departs from the tradition of the *imitatio Christi*. Jesus Christ's work and the work of his disciples are related indeed, but they are not identical. Jesus Christ bears the cross alone, and his disciples are to bear their own crosses, not his.[8] In this respect, the ethic of enemy-love is best seen as a following after Jesus Christ rather than an imitation of him.[9]

Closely related to the preference for the category following after rather than imitation is the affirmation that Christian discipleship is not something that is achieved through the power and abilities of the individual disciple. Affirming that discipleship involves following Jesus Christ from a distance therefore does not mean that the disciple's activities are external to Christ's activities. The disciple and his activities are never strictly independent. Following after Christ involves the participation of the disciple in Jesus Christ. Hunsinger observes, 'No one of us can love our enemies in the way that is required merely by relying on our own resources, nor are we expected to do so. The needed power is received only as it is continually sought by the believer and given by Christ in the ongoing history of their relationship.'[10]

---

8   Barth writes, 'The cross of Jesus is His own cross, carried and suffered *for* many, but *by* Him alone and not by many, let alone by all and sundry . . . the suffering which comes on Christians, the cross to which they are nailed, the death which they have to die, is always *their* suffering, *their* cross, *their* death, just as the salvation which accompanies it is *their* salvation, won for them and brought to them in the suffering and cross and death of Christ on their behalf. Their cross corresponds to the death of Christ. It is not a repetition or re-presentation, of the cross of Christ.' *CD* IV/2, pp. 600, 601.

9   For a brief discussion of the *imitatio Christi* see *CD* IV/2, pp. 533–4. For an insightful examination of discipleship and ethics examined within the category of following after Christ from a distance and not imitating him, see Gene Outka, 'Following at a Distance: Ethics and the Identity of Jesus', in *Scriptural Authority and Narrative Interpretation*, ed. Garrett Green (Philadelphia: Fortress Press, 1987), pp. 144–60.

10   Hunsinger, 'The Politics of the Nonviolent God', p. 83.

Hunsinger describes the relationship between Jesus Christ and the disciple in terms of 'participation', 'fellowship' and 'witness'. Christian non-violent enemy-love is possible and actual only insofar as the believer participates in the eternal life of God and the love of God for the world. This participation is possible because Jesus Christ as the crucified One is present to Christian faith, and the Christian exists in a relationship of fellowship with Jesus Christ crucified. Barth asks what gives New Testament ethics such as humility, love and prayer for and solidarity with one's enemies, and responding to evil with good their direction, dynamic and pull. His answer is that the New Testament ethic non-violent enemy-love exists solely as a response to Jesus Christ's summons and commission to genuine discipleship. The disciples in the New Testament, and therefore all disciples of Jesus Christ, are compelled 'to enter into and remain in fellowship with the Crucified' (*CD* IV/1, p. 190). Hunsinger concisely defines the fellowship of the believer with Jesus Christ as follows: 'The fellowship of the Christian with Christ takes the form of mutual indwelling. As the Christian lives in Christ, and Christ in the Christian, the Christian comes to participate in what Christ does.'[11]

Hunsinger then moves from the notions of participation and fellowship to the category of witness. In the *koinonia* relationship of union and communion between Jesus Christ and the believer, the believer participates in the eternal life of God and, in turn, bears witness to Jesus Christ, or, more accurately, shares in the self-witness of the living crucified Christ.[12] Moreover, this involvement in the self-witness of Jesus Christ leads to the suffering of the disciple, a suffering that must be understood as a participation in the suffering of Christ. The suffering of the Christian, seen through the lenses of participation, fellowship and witness, is understood properly, Barth asserts, as a participation of the Christian in the passion of Jesus Christ's cross.

Hunsinger immediately qualifies Barth's assertion that the believer participates in the passion of Jesus Christ's cross by insisting that for Barth the relationship between the believer and Christ is marked by both intimacy and great distance. The relationship between the Christian and Jesus Christ is an asymmetrical relationship. Jesus Christ is always prior and superior to the believer. Jesus Christ's work is unique and proper to him as the incarnate Son of God; the work of the Christian is a genuine human work. They are related, but they are neither identical nor equal.[13] The suffering of the Christian is both similar and severely dissimilar

---

11   Ibid.

12   Ibid.

13   Barth describes the relationship between Jesus Christ and the Christian who bears witness to him as follows: 'If the true being of the Christian consists in the life of Christ in him and his life in Christ, then it follows that the principle which controls Christian existence, provisionally formulated, consists in the community of action determined by the order of the relationship between Christ and the Christian. We have in view divine–human action in divine–human sovereignty when we speak of the being and life of Christ, and human action and human freedom when we speak of the being and life of the Christian. Christ engaged in a work, and in perfect fellowship with Him so, too, is the Christian called

to the unique suffering of Jesus Christ. Although we may speak of a 'correspondence' between the believer's suffering and Christ's, in no way may we consider the suffering of the believer as a repetition, re-presentation, or completion of Christ's cross. The sufferings of Christians function as an aspect of their vocation as witnesses to Jesus Christ and his cross; they are not repetitions of his unique cross. Hunsinger firmly concludes, 'Neither in their fellowship with Christ in his sufferings, nor in their expressions of enemy-love in this fellowship, do Christians repeat, contribute to, or augment the redemptive work of Christ on the cross.'[14]

We may draw at least the following four conclusions from our examination of Hunsinger's analysis of Barth's articulation of an ethic of non-violent enemy-love.

First, the ethic of non-violent enemy-love is not arbitrary, nor is it a human ethical construct or system that stands alongside competing ethical alternatives. Therefore, it is demanded of all disciples, who live in obedience and conformity to Jesus Christ. The ethic of non-violent enemy-love is not a human ideal; rather, it is a reflection of God's being as absolute love.[15] It is intelligible only in the light of and on the basis of God's love for the world and as this love is enacted in Jesus Christ's death on the cross.

Second, disciples as followers of Christ from a distance do not rely upon their own abilities and powers in their response to the command of enemy-love requisite to their call to discipleship. Human beings are incapable of genuine Christian non-violent enemy-love if forced to depend upon their own will and strength. The ethic of non-violent enemy-love is possible only through the participation and fellowship of the Christian with Jesus Christ. The Christian's love for the enemy is a participation in God's love for the world.

---

by Him. The latter works, but he does so in perfect fellowship with the working of Christ. Everything else which takes place in this relationship, and especially the giving of Christ and receiving of the Christian, takes place relatively to this community of action, within the context and in furtherance and consequence of it. And since the fellowship as a fellowship of action takes place in this definite and irreversible order, the action, work or activity of Christ unconditionally precedes that of man called by Him, the Christian, and that of the latter must follow. Their fellowship of life thus finds realisation as a differentiated fellowship of action in which Christ is always superior and the Christian subordinate. Hence the principle controlling Christian existence, which is our specific concern, will always necessarily result from the fact that the Christian, as he lives in Christ and Christ in him, exists in this fellowship of action and its order.' *CD* IV/3.2, pp. 597–8.

14   Hunsinger, 'The Politics of the Nonviolent God', p. 84.

15   Barth writes, 'In its ethics the New Testament is speaking in terms of necessity, not of chance or arbitrariness, if in all these sayings [regarding humility, love and prayer for the enemy, etc.] – as in those concerning the lowly existence of the man Jesus as the Son of God – we have to do with a reflection of the New Testament concept of God. If in fellowship with Christ Christians have to be μιμηταὶ θεοῦ (Eph 5:1), if the τελειότης, the fulfilment of the being and essence, of their heavenly Father is the measure and norm of their own τελειότης (Mt 5:48), then in its original and final authority and compulsion the demand addressed to them is necessarily this and no other. The περισσόν, the special thing which is commanded of and has to be done by them as distinct from the publicans and Gentiles, is that which marks them out as the children of the Father in heaven, the περισσόν of God Himself cannot be lacking in His children.' *CD* IV/1, p. 190.

Third, through the fellowship of the Christian with Christ the believer bears witness to Christ and participates in Christ's own self-witness. Bearing witness to the living Christ who was crucified leads to the suffering of the Christian. This suffering involves a participation in Jesus Christ's unique suffering in the passion and is intelligible only in the shadow of Christ's cross. The suffering of the Christian, however, is similar and dissimilar to the suffering of Jesus Christ. The suffering of the disciple in no way repeats or completes the suffering of Jesus Christ.[16]

Finally, the activity of Christian non-violent enemy-love, though rightly understood as a participation in God's eternal love, is a genuine human activity. It is freely performed in obedience to God through the power of the Holy Spirit. The Christian does not act as a conduit that functions as a link between God's love and the world.[17]

---

16 See Barth's discussion in *CD* IV/3.2 of the similarity and dissimilarity between the suffering of the Christian and the suffering of Christ in his discussion of the Christian in affliction. Barth writes, '[The Christian] necessarily has his share in the suffering of Christ, and in his own place and manner is brought under the shadow of His cross. We repeat that in his own place and manner he is brought under the shadow of His cross, and not therefore under the great affliction and passion of Jesus Christ Himself, not under a fellow-suffering of the atoning suffering endured once and for all by the one Son of God and Son of Man, not under the task and claim to achieve again by what he endures that which He achieved for all times and men, not under the dreadful, isolated responsibility in which He did it, not under the final and supreme extremity which this fulfilment entailed for Him, not under the agony of the question of Mark 14:34: "My God, my God, why hast thou forsaken me?" Even in the last extremity the Christian realises that he is spared this question, this affliction and passion, because it has been borne by the suffering of this One. And he must realise this if he is to avoid that wild exaggeration. On the other hand, he certainly does suffer, and has to do so, as a witness of the suffering of this One. He has to bear the lesser, yet for him no less severe and bitter, suffering which inevitably overtakes those appointed to be witnesses to this One. This suffering of his is suffering in reflection and analogy to the suffering of the one man of Gethsemane and Golgotha. It is suffering under the shadow of His cross. And in this secondary form appropriate to His follower and disciple, it is suffering in real fellowship with Him and with His suffering.' *CD* IV/3.2, p. 637.

17 Barth writes, 'Christian love is not a kind of prolongation of the divine love itself, its overflowing into human life which man with his activity has to serve as a kind of channel, being merely present and not at bottom an acting subject ... the work of the Holy Spirit consists in the liberation of man for his own act and therefore for the spontaneous human love whose littleness and frailty are his own responsibility and not that of the Holy Spirit. Christian love as a human act corresponds indeed to the love of God but is also to be distinguished from it. It is an act in which man is at work, not as God's puppet, but with his own heart and soul and strength, as an independent subject who encounters and replies to God and is responsible to Him as His partner.' *CD* IV/2, p. 785. For an insightful discussion of Barth's criticism of viewing the Christian as an 'instrument' and the parallel view of infused and acquired virtue see: Gene Outka, *Agape: An Ethical Analysis* (New Haven and London: Yale University Press, 1972), pp. 233–8.

The descent into hell and the ethic of non-violent enemy-love

There are many themes present in Balthasar's understanding of Christian discipleship that resemble Barth's treatment of discipleship and New Testament ethics.
Balthasar shares Barth's position that Christian love and existence are measured by
the passion of Jesus Christ and that this love and theological existence are possible
for the disciple only insofar as the believer, through the power of the Holy Spirit,
participates in God's eternal love in fellowship with Christ crucified.

> The truth that provides the yardstick for faith is God's willingness to die for
> the world he loves, for mankind and for me as an individual. This love became
> manifest in the dark night of Christ's crucifixion. Every source of grace – faith,
> love, and hope – springs from this night. Everything that I am (insofar as I am
> anything more on this earth than a fugitive figure without hope, all of whose
> illusions are rendered worthless by death), I am solely by virtue of Christ's
> death, which opens up to me the possibility of fulfillment in God. I blossom
> on the grave of God who died for me. I sink my roots deep into the nourishing
> soil of his flesh and blood. The love that I draw in faith from this soil can be
> of no other kind than the love of one who is buried.[18]

The standard against which Christian faith and existence are measured is nothing
other than the self-giving and suffering love of God present in Jesus Christ's death
on the cross, his burial, his descent into hell and his being raised from the dead on
the third day in accordance with Scripture. Genuine Christian existence and genuine
Christian love are possible only insofar as the believer participates in the very
person of the Crucified who has been buried. By employing organic imagery
reminiscent of the 'vine and the branches' imagery in John 15, Balthasar stresses
the necessity of abiding in Christ and being empowered to love others only on the
basis of this intimate relationship with Christ.[19]

God in Jesus Christ dies for the world he loves, and those whom God loves and
for whom Jesus Christ dies are sinners, and as sinners they are enemies of Christ
and of God. Balthasar insists with the same intensity as Barth that the death of
Jesus Christ is a death on behalf of and in the place of God's enemies, and that in
this death atonement is made and the enemies of God are transformed into God's
covenant partners. An essential aspect of understanding Jesus Christ's death as a
superabundant atonement, according to Balthasar, is that Jesus dies out of love for
his enemies.

> It is obvious that, in his atoning work, Jesus dies *out of love*. He dies essentially
> 'for' us. 'Greater love has no man than this, that a man lay down his life for

---

18   Hans Urs von Balthasar, *The Moment of Christian Witness*, trans. Richard Beckley (San Francisco:
Ignatius Press, 1994), pp. 26–7.
19   Perhaps the most prominent means by which one participates in and is nourished by the 'flesh and
blood' of Jesus Christ – the 'God who died for me' – is the Eucharistic self-offering of Christ. See *TD*
IV, pp. 389–406.

his friends,' says Jesus to his disciples (John 15:13); and these 'friends' are what Paul calls the 'enemies' of Jesus since they are sinners: 'One will hardly die for a righteous man . . ., but God shows his love for us in that while we were yet sinners Christ died for us' (Romans 5:7f). We were sinners, that is, 'in rebellion against God' (*asebeis*), hopelessly 'incapable' (*asthenes*) of extricating ourselves from the situation (Romans 5:6). So we are not friends but sinners and 'enemies' (cf. Romans 8:7). (*TD* IV, pp. 500–1)

Balthasar also affirms that one gift of discipleship is the participation of the believer in the cross and resurrection of Jesus Christ. Although Balthasar does not contradict Barth's conviction that an understanding the suffering of disciples as a participation in the passion of Jesus Christ in no way attributes repetition, re-presentation, extension or completion to the disciples' suffering, he ventures to explore the intercessory role of the disciple further than does Barth.[20] Balthasar maintains the dissimilarity but dares to explore the similarity with the seriousness that he thinks Scripture requires. Balthasar insists that the suffering of Jesus Christ is complete and sufficient; yet he maintains that Christ has made room for the believer and the Church to share in his suffering and work. Balthasar interprets the gospel as suggesting that the disciple, in a mysterious manner, participates in the *pro nobis* character of Jesus Christ's passion. The participation of the believer in Christ in this manner is not due to a deficiency in the work of Christ; rather, it is the result of Christ's mercy and grace and his making room for the believer, which leads to great intimacy between Christ and his Church. Balthasar, we must emphasize, does not rashly or uncritically propose that disciples function as co-reconcilers with Christ. He recognizes the need to proceed slowly, with caution and hesitation, as the New Testament demands.

> Discipleship brings with it the gift of participation in the Cross and Resurrection of Christ, and this points to a final element. This participation is bound to extend itself, albeit in a secondary manner, to the *pro nobis* of Christ's Paschal Mystery. We have to speak of this with reticence, as does the New Testament itself. But is there not something frightening in what Jesus says to the Sons of Zebedee when, unsuspecting, they say that they can drink of the cup that he will drink (Mark 10:39f)? Is it not disconcerting to hear Paul say, unabashed, that he is crucified together with Christ (Galatians 2:19) and that he bears Christ's wounds (Galatians 6:17)? He is quite aware, of course, of the vast gulf between Christ's crucifixion and his own (1 Corinthians 1:13) and wants to know and preach nothing but the Cross of Christ (1 Corinthians 2:2). There is closeness *and* distance here, as is shown by the phrase 'I complete what is lacking in Christ's afflictions' (Colossians 1:24). The sufferings of the God-man are all-sufficient, but within those sufferings a place has been left for the disciples; thus Jesus predicts that those who are his will share his destiny (John 16:1–4; Matthew 10:24f). 'Through grace', a fellowship of suffering and resurrection is created, and this fellowship only has meaning if the *pro nobis* is

---

20 Barth speaks in highly qualified terms when he addresses the possibility that human suffering and death share the *pro nobis* quality of Jesus Christ's suffering and death. See *CD* IV/2, p. 605.

> extended to the participants. The metaphor of the vine brings us as close as we
> can get to uttering its meaning: the man who lives *en Christoi*, from the root
> and stem of Christ, will bear fruit. (*TD* IV, pp. 387–8)

The meaning and effectiveness of the suffering of the disciple depend upon this
suffering being taken up into the suffering of Jesus Christ. Balthasar acknowledges
the mystery of the distance and closeness that characterize the participation of the
believer's suffering in Jesus Christ's suffering, as he is taken into fellowship with
the crucified and risen Christ. The suffering of the disciple indeed 'bears fruit', yet
the power for producing fruit comes from Christ, as the disciple lives in Christ and
Christ lives in the disciple. 'Those who abide in me and I in them', the Johannine
Christ says, 'bear much fruit, because apart from me you can do nothing' (John
15:5). The disciple and his suffering bear fruit, but this fruit is produced not by the
power of the disciple, but by the power of Christ through the fellowship of the
disciple with Christ.

In *The Moment of Christian Witness*, Balthasar describes the shape of the
Christian life primarily in terms of martyrdom – surrendering one's life for Christ's
sake even to the point of death.[21] Balthasar insists that this willingness to give up
one's life for others is properly understood as the form of Christian existence only
if it conforms to the death of Jesus Christ. The willingness of the Christian to die
for the sake of others is not, Balthasar demands, a 'humanistic ideal' or an
'arbitrary sacrifice', which is pursued on the basis of the individual's judgment.
Rather, the willingness to surrender one's life for others has meaning only if seen
through the lens of the cross. Furthermore, one dies not as a result of one's own
initiative and for the sake of heroism, but solely because God has deemed it
necessary. Christian self-sacrifice is both possible and meaningful only as it is
based upon the peerless and perfect self-sacrifice of Jesus Christ in his passion.[22]

---

21 Balthasar begins this book with a quotation from *Lumen Gentium*, chapter V, 'The Call to
Holiness', that speaks of martyrdom as an aspect of enemy-love, as having its source in the death of
Jesus Christ, and as bearing witness to Jesus Christ. 'Since Jesus, the Son of God, manifested his
charity by laying down his life for us, no one has greater love than he who lays down his life for Christ
and his brothers (cf. 1 Jn 3:6; Jn 15:13). From the earliest times, then, some Christians have been called
upon – and some will always be called upon – to give this supreme testimony of love to all men, but
especially to persecutors. The Church therefore considers martyrdom as an exceptional gift and as the
highest proof of love. By martyrdom a disciple is transformed into an image of his master who freely
accepted death on behalf of the world's salvation; he perfects that image even to the shedding of blood.
Though few are presented with such an opportunity, nevertheless all must be prepared to confess Christ
before men, and to follow him along the way of the cross through the persecutions which the Church
will never fail to suffer.' Vatican II, *Lumen Gentium: Dogmatic Constitution of the Church* 42 as cited
in Balthasar, *The Moment of Christian Witness*, p. 13.
22 It is significant to note that Balthasar demands that all Christians must base their lives on the death
of Christ and must engage in self-giving love for others to the point of being willing to die for others.
This is not merely the mandate to be followed by fanatics and saints alone. All disciples are to take up
their own cross, renounce all that they have, and follow Christ. This is the fundamental requirement for
disciples. It is from this common obligation that the particular mission of individual disciples is

Balthasar recognizes that Christians do not have exclusive rights to the designation of martyr. There are numerous examples of individuals exhibiting human courage in the face of suffering and death. The virtuous traits of heroism and courage are exhibited daily in all walks of life.[23] Balthasar makes the stronger point that not only do many non-Christians persevere and endure in the face of various forms of oppression, but also many non-Christians suffer martyrdom specifically at the hands of Christians. As a result, Balthasar demands that we refrain from uncritically praising and honouring Christian martyrs without acknowledging the other worldly forms of courage and heroism in the face of suffering, for which Christianity is often culpable. We must refrain from exclusively celebrating the lives and deaths of Christian martyrs; rather, we must recognize the solidarity between Christian martyrs and all humans who suffer and endure oppression, even to the point of death. Furthermore, we must avoid identifying ourselves with the glory of Christian martyrs as we commemorate their suffering and death. Rather, we must recognize that all glory belongs to God and to Jesus Christ, for it is out of love for God and for the sake of Christ that true martyrs suffer and die.

Although Balthasar recognizes and honours instances of humanistic martyrdom, he insists that we must distinguish genuine Christian martyrdom from every other form of self-sacrifice and self-offering, no matter how heroic and courageous. According to Balthasar, the Christian martyr 'does not die for an idea, even for the highest – not for human dignity, freedom, or solidarity with the oppressed (though all of these may be included and play a role). He dies with someone who has died for him in advance.'[24] The Christian dies out of love for Jesus Christ, and in response to his vicarious life and death.

> The Christian really believes that his life is based on the vicarious death: not only his physical life but also his spiritual life, his life before God, the ultimate meaning of his existence. The Christian is indebted to another. And how else can he seriously acknowledge this debt than by following the same path as his Lord, since he has been very expressly told in advance that the same thing will happen to the servant as to his master and to the pupil as to his teacher. This is the distinctive, special characteristic of the Christian martyr: he is 'crucified with Christ,' and the giving up of his life is an act of proper response, of self-evident gratitude.[25]

---

determined. 'It is by no means true', Balthasar writes, 'that only a few very radically-minded Christians need to base their faith on the death of Christ, while the majority may remain content to let just a little of the transfiguring supernatural light illuminate their natural lives ... It is all part of the disciples' attempt to follow Christ by giving up their lives out of love for the world and in obedience to God who so loved the world that he gave his only Son that the world might be saved through him.' Balthasar, *The Moment of Christian Witness*, pp. 34, 35–6.

23 Balthasar, *New Elucidations*, pp. 283–4.
24 Ibid., p. 286.
25 Ibid.

It is significant to notice that Balthasar links genuine Christian martyrdom to a view of Jesus Christ's life and passion that emphasizes its vicarious character – Jesus Christ lived and died 'on our behalf' and 'in our place'. The Christian martyr bears witness 'to the unabridged, integral New Testament faith, whose core is the *pro nobis* of the Creed'.[26] The Christian dies not for himself, but 'for' others and 'for' Jesus Christ, who died for the whole world.

The *pro nobis* character of Jesus Christ's life and passion is integrally related to the disciple's sacramental dying with Christ (Romans 6:3–4) and to the disciple's daily dying to self and determination to live for Christ. The death of Jesus Christ affects all human deaths and lives, and the believer, through baptism, is granted the grace to participate in this death in a distinctive manner. This special participation of the baptized, however, does not mean that the saving effect of Jesus Christ's death is restricted to the baptized. Jesus Christ's death *pro nobis* is primary, and the believer's sacramental dying with Christ in baptism is secondary (*TD* V, pp. 332–3).

Balthasar considers 2 Corinthians 5:14–15 as providing a succinct account of the relationship between the shape of Christian discipleship and the *pro nobis* character of Jesus Christ's death. Paul writes, 'For the love of Christ urges us on, because we are convinced that one has died for all; therefore all have died. And he died for all, so that those who live might live no longer for themselves, but for him who died and was raised for him' (2 Corinthians 5:14–15). The indicative statement 'one has died for all; therefore all have died' entails, according to Balthasar's reading, the imperative 'those who live might live no longer for themselves but for him who for their sake died and was raised'. The imperative cannot be understood or followed without the indicative, and the indicative leads directly, and Balthasar can even say inescapably, to the imperative.

Here Paul concludes that the believer lives not for himself, but for him who died and was raised for the sake of all. Not only does the believer die in baptism by being buried with Christ into his death; the baptized believer, by dying with Christ, also participates in Christ's being raised from the dead by the Father. The believer dies with Christ and is raised with Christ for the purpose of walking in newness of life (Romans 6:4). The life of the disciple is determined both by the indicative of Christ's *pro nobis* death and resurrection, and by the ensuing imperative to die to self and live for Jesus Christ. Balthasar concludes:

> The lives of those who are animated by the *imperative* inherent in the *indicative*, and who are marked sacramentally and existentially, will be governed explicitly by the unity-in-duality of Christ's death and risen life. Their life will be an eschatological life, bearing the imprint of the most radical dying and the most radical turning to eternal life, not just for a fleeting moment, but constantly. (*TD* V, p. 333)

---

26   Ibid., p. 293.

Balthasar, we must point out, does not consider discipleship in the form of martyrdom as exclusively or even primarily concerned with the disciple's actual physical death. He departs from the teaching and practice of Ignatius, Bishop of Antioch, and his single-minded pursuit of martyrdom, marked by the desire for the hastening of his death. Balthasar declares that the Christian must not actively seek death; rather, the Christian must simply display a carefree attitude and 'allow God to place him in a defenseless position'.[27] It is Balthasar's emphasis on *defencelessness* as a requisite mark of Christian martyrdom and discipleship that aligns his views with Barth's stress on Christian love as non-violent love. Christians, according to Balthasar, 'are there [in the world] to bear witness to the love of God and, if they have a mind to, let this love shine through them into the world. Their task is to testify (if necessary by the sacrifice of their own lives) that this love is the eternal life that triumphs over death. They do not seek death, although the desire for martyrdom may not be unknown to them.'[28] The Christian does not seek death, because God is the lord of both life and death, and only God can determine when and how one ought to die. The mark of discipleship in the form of martyrdom is the openness and willingness of the Christian to die out of love for God and for others, if this is in fact what God requires; it is not the dying itself. 'One should not rush into martyrdom', Balthasar writes, 'for who knows what one still has to do for God in this life? But, equally, one may not refuse it when it is inevitably demanded.'[29]

Defencelessness is the principal characteristic of martyrdom according to Balthasar. In speaking about feast days commemorating martyrs, which, we must remember, are days of rejoicing, Balthasar writes, 'Neither the one who celebrates it nor the one whose death it commemorates bears weapons; each is defenseless. And this defencelessness is what really matters.'[30] It must be remembered that this posture of defencelessness is not based upon a distorted form of self-loathing and masochism, nor is it a position reached by human ingenuity and established by a human capacity. Defencelessness is the proper form of Christian existence because it is commanded by God, exemplified in the life and death of Jesus Christ, and grounded in the person of Christ crucified and buried. The disciples' countenance in defencelessness, in turn, must not be solemn resignation; rather, it must be one

---

27 Balthasar, *The Moment of Christian Witness*, p. 138.

28 Ibid., p. 139.

29 Balthasar, *New Elucidations*, p. 289. Balthasar develops this theme of openness and willingness to suffer and die for the sake of Christ without actively pursuing suffering and death in the following: 'Readiness is everything: readiness for engagement with Christ for God's concerns in the world, whether this engagement be a meaningful, active endeavor to further among mankind Christ's principles and his solidarity with the poor and oppressed, or an endurance – not to be simply called passive, since it is, again, active in a different way – in order to cooperate, together with the Crucified, in transforming souls, that is, in their process of purification toward a valid witness. The Christian readiness in both directions, toward action as well as endurance, can be meaningful and total.' Ibid., pp. 296–7.

30 Balthasar, *The Moment of Christian Witness*, p. 136.

of joy. The Christian must be joyful, because he/she lives in the realization that sin and death have been defeated, the kingdom of God has been established on earth as in heaven, and that he/she has been buried with Christ and now walks in newness of life (Romans 6:4).

> Joy in defenselessness, defenselessness without anxiety: in these words a mysterious superiority makes itself felt. Behind the beatitudes of the Sermon on the Mount, with its glorification of the meek, the gentle, the merciful, the peaceful and the lowly – behind the command not to resist or retaliate in the face of persecution lies the idea of joy as the fountain that nourishes all since the resurrection of the Lord ... With the knowledge that heaven is open, the Christian is nourished even in his ordinary day-to-day life by a never-failing fountain, which springs from the very depths of God's nature and wells up in his servants into eternal life (John 4:14).[31]

As was made clear in Chapter two, defencelessness is the defining feature of Balthasar's explication of the descent into hell. Balthasar strongly critiques traditional interpretations of Jesus Christ's descent into hell that employ militaristic imagery and depict Jesus – the harrower of hell – as the armed warrior who defeats his enemies by the violent means of brute force and power. Although Balthasar affirms that Jesus Christ is victorious over sin, hell and the devil in his death and descent into hell, he insists that this victory is won not by violent means, but by Jesus Christ's passive and defenceless solidarity with dead sinners, which is true power – what Balthasar calls 'omnipotent powerlessness'. Jesus Christ does not engage in an armed struggle or combat with his enemies; rather, through the mysterious power of suffering non-violent love, God in Christ defeats sin and death and relegates them to the past. 'What kind of victory was Christ's?' Balthasar asks, 'Ultimately, surely, in the Passion he *no longer* resisted the superior power of evil but allowed it to rage in him, the defenseless One, and so burn itself out' (*TD* IV, p. 484). Jesus Christ's descent into hell, we may conclude, is the clearest exemplification of non-violent enemy-love.

The descent into hell also contributes to an understanding of the mysterious power of non-violent enemy-love insofar as it takes place in the hiddenness and silence of Holy Saturday. The descent into hell teaches us that to the very public display of non-violent love in the crucifixion of Jesus Christ we must add the unseen form of Jesus Christ's non-violent love in his burial and descent into hell. Effective suffering and non-violent enemy-love is not restricted to those cases that are well publicized and honoured for dramatic heroism. Even those instances of overlooked or unknown suffering significantly participate in and bear witness to God's transforming love for the world. Balthasar highlights the essential, and often neglected, role played by silent and unseen suffering.

---

31   Ibid., p. 135.

This brings us to another subject: the invisible and yet world-changing power of the suffering and silent Church, in which suffering purifies and deepens many, transforming them into true representatives of Christianity. This is the case even if the communications media take no note of it and perhaps very few of the Christians who are privileged to live in freedom think gratefully of this invisible representation before God. For it belongs indispensably to the substance of Christian faith to consider the fruitfulness of prayer and suffering for others as possible and real, and by no means to value it less than all the external undertakings that alter the structures of evil.[32]

Non-violent love and action need not be planned public resistance executed with the intention of challenging and disabling societal power structures.[33] Individual and communal forms of suffering and praying for others including the enemy that never gain the spotlight of public attention are also invaluable to God's transforming love and the struggle against evil.

The descent into hell, furthermore, emphasizes the universal scope of God's love and Jesus Christ's saving death. This radical inclusiveness also determines those whom disciples are called to love. Balthasar's understanding of the descent into hell and his conviction that Jesus Christ died for all human beings, which includes the claim that salvation is offered to all human beings, are reciprocally related. His belief that Jesus died for all arises from the Church's confession that Jesus Christ descended into hell, and this conviction also shapes his distinctive interpretation of the descent into hell. 'If Christ has suffered, not only for the elect but for all human beings', Balthasar asserts, 'he has by this very fact assumed their eschatological "No" in regard to the event of salvation which came about in him' (*MP*, p. 172). God's love for the entire world and God's desire that all be saved drives Jesus Christ to the cross and leads him to hell. In assuming the eschatological 'No' that faces human beings, Jesus Christ not only enters into loving solidarity with his enemies; he also shares the ultimate situation even of those who reject him – those whom the bridegroom 'does not know' (Matthew 25:12) and those who have been expelled to the 'outer darkness' (Matthew 22:13).

Although Balthasar does not rule out the possibility that an individual may indeed misuse human freedom and forever resist God's love, he insists that God is free to pursue steadfastly this individual in a non-violent and non-coercive manner. God may do this, and indeed does this in the unique and unsurpassed suffering of

---

32 Balthasar, *New Elucidations*, pp. 295–6.

33 We must also point out that Balthasar does not consider non-violent resistance as the only form of social and political action proper for Christians, nor does he uncritically embrace the practice of non-violence in the social and political arena – for example, he recognizes that often tactics of non-violence are in fact manifestations of power. Balthasar affirms that Jesus Christ's example of non-violent love is not to be restricted to the private and interpersonal realm, yet he acknowledges the complexity of contemporary society and the reality of earthly power structures. He also questions the validity of translating without remainder the non-violent love of God displayed in the passion of Christ into a tactic for achieving mundane political goals. See his discussion of the 'Theodramatic Dimensions of Liberation' in *TD* IV, pp. 476–87.

the abandoned and forsaken Son, whose suffering and loneliness exceed the state of the sinner who is intent on rejecting God's love. This eschatological consequence of Jesus Christ's descent into hell is perhaps the most innovative aspect of Balthasar's exposition of the descent into hell. In a passage that Edward Oakes calls the 'most revolutionary aspect of Balthasar's eschatology', Balthasar writes:

> It remains, however, to consider whether it still is not open to God to encounter the sinner who has turned away from him in the impotent form of the crucified brother who has been abandoned by God, and indeed in such a way that it becomes clear to the one who has turned away from God that: this One beside me who has been forsaken by God (like myself) has been abandoned by God for my sake. Now there can be no more talk of doing violence to freedom if God appears in the loneliness of the one who has chosen the total loneliness of living only for himself (or perhaps one should say: who thinks that is how he has chosen) and shows himself to be as the One who is still lonelier than the sinner.[34]

Though in this passage Balthasar retains his opposition to a guaranteed *apokatastasis*, he states in no uncertain terms that God is free to pursue humanity to the limit, and that although universal salvation is not a certainty, it is a genuine possibility. Universal salvation must not be affirmed as inevitable, but it must not be denied. The gospel demands that we hope for the salvation of all, because God loves all and wills that all shall be saved. The descent into hell demonstrates the depth of God's love for all and is the fitting outcome of his desire that all come to repentance (2 Peter 3:9) and that all be saved and come to the knowledge of the truth (1 Timothy 2:4).[35]

---

34   Balthasar, 'Eschatology in Outline', pp. 456–7.

35   Balthasar identifies two sets of passages in Scripture that pertain to the issue of universal salvation. The first speaks to the real possibility of severe judgment and punishment; the second to the universal scope of God's triumph over everything that opposes God in the redemptive and victorious death of Jesus Christ. Balthasar does not conclude that we ought to ignore the first set, and in turn, deny the real possibility of judgment and punishment with all the severity of hell. At the same time, he insists that the second set of universal passages must not be ignored or altered on the basis of the first set, and it is this practice that he directly addresses. Granting priority to the former set of passages leads to an artificial alteration of passages from the latter set. In this case, the interpreter claims to have firm knowledge that leads him to place restrictions on the universal scope of certain passages. Passages that are inclusive in character become rigidly exclusive. Balthasar critically and sarcastically writes, 'But what about Jesus' triumphant words when he looks forward to the effect of his Passion: "Now shall the ruler of this world be cast out; and I, when I am lifted up from the earth, will draw *all* men to myself" (Jn 12:31f)? Oh, he will perhaps attempt to draw them all but will not succeed in holding them all. "Be of good cheer, I have overcome *the world*" (Jn 16:33). Unfortunately, only half of it, despite your efforts, Lord. "The grace of God has appeared for the salvation of *all* men" (Tit 2:11) – let us say, more precisely, to offer salvation, since how many will accept it is questionable. God does not wish "that any should perish, but that *all* should reach repentance" (2 Pt 3:9). He may well wish it, but unfortunately he will not achieve it . . .' Hans Urs von Balthasar, *Dare We Hope 'That All Men be Saved'? With a Short Discourse on Hell*, trans. by David Kipp and Lothar Krauth (San Francisco: Ignatius Press, 1988), pp. 184–6.

Although Balthasar is often read and criticized for affirming the certainty of universal salvation, declaring hell an impossibility, and neglecting the explicit biblical teaching regarding judgment and punishment, this is not his intention nor is it his practice. Balthasar acknowledges the crucial theological role played by the biblical theme of judgment and the real threat of punishment. The role played by judgment and the threat of punishment, Balthasar insists, is to call the individual into question and is never to be applied to others at the exclusion of oneself. Judgment, punishment and hell must always be seen as real threats that hang over the head of the individual, rather than as realities that will fall exclusively upon the heads of others. 'If the threats of judgment and the cruel, horrifying images of the gravity of the punishments imposed upon sinners that we find in Scripture and Tradition have any point', Balthasar writes, 'then it is surely, in the first instance, to make *me* see the seriousness of the responsibility that I bear along with my freedom.'[36] Balthasar strongly challenges those who comfortably affirm a populated hell and confidently, and, we must say, conveniently, locate themselves outside the walls of this prison of judgment and torment. Balthasar insists that if hell is a real possibility for others, then hell must above all be a real possibility for oneself. Correspondingly, if there is genuine hope for oneself, then there is genuine hope for all others. For Balthasar, declaring judgment and hell as realities primarily and exclusively for others is not only a misreading of Scripture (Romans 2:1–11; 1 Corinthians 4:4–5; Malachi 3:2–3); it also makes the command of New Testament ethic to love all people impossible to fulfil. Balthasar proposes the following thesis regarding this issue of judgment and hell for others and the New Testament mandate to love and live in solidarity with others, 'Whoever reckons with the possibility of even only *one* person's being lost besides himself is hardly able to love unreservedly ... Just the slightest nagging thought of a final hell for others tempts us, in moments in which human togetherness becomes especially difficult, to leave the other to himself.'[37]

The obligation to hope for the salvation of all, which is integrally related to the confession of the descent into hell, gives specific shape to the New Testament ethic of enemy love. It is only by actively hoping for the salvation of all that Christians are able to follow the New Testament mandate to love and pray for all, including and especially one's enemies. Hoping and praying for the salvation of all, along with the eschatological affirmation of Jesus Christ's descent into hell and his 'face to face' encounter with those who reject God's offer of love in the Crucified, furthermore enables the believer to engage specifically in *non-violent* enemy-love – to 'not resist an evildoer' (Matthew 5:38) and to not 'repay evil with evil' (Romans 12:17, 1 Thessalonians 5:15, 1 Peter 3:9). In this knowledge of the eschatological dimension of the descent into hell, moreover, the believer recognizes

---

36   Ibid., p. 211.
37   Ibid.

that God is in control of history and that even if his/her prayer and love for the enemy seem to fail in this life, all hope is not lost.

To put it another way, non-violent enemy-love embodies the conviction that faithfulness to God is a higher virtue than effectiveness, while those who insist on determining which course of action will be most effective readily legitimize violence. Those engaged in non-violence are motivated not by efficiency and effectiveness, but by faithfulness and gratitude to God. The ethical practice of non-violence, however, is not quietistic; rather, it involves the acknowledgement that the disciple's active opposition to evil and evil people is not to be won or lost on the basis of the disciple's own strength, ability and resolve. As Christian disciples oppose evil in a non-violent manner, they participate in the mystery of God's non-violent opposition of evil. Only God is able to overcome evil, yet God has enlisted disciples of Jesus Christ to play a role in this battle and victory.[38]

Balthasar asserts that if we do not hope for the salvation of all people, and instead with professed certainty consign people, individually or collectively, to the pains of hell, then it is impossible to carry out the command to love and pray for all people. We can genuinely love and pray for our enemies only if we can hope for their salvation. And since we must hope for their salvation, because this is God's perfect desire, we are obligated to love and pray for them. Oakes insightfully observes, 'It is, I think, too little noticed how the command to hope for the salvation of all (and it *is* a command: 1 Timothy 2:1–4) is intimately linked with the command to love one's enemies, and that to "know" that some are destined to hell will lead, by a short but inexorable logic, to a diminution of the love one should feel for one's enemies.'[39] The disciple is commanded to offer supplications, prayers, intercessions and thanksgivings for *everyone*, and these activities are right and acceptable in the sight of God because God desires *everyone to be saved*. Furthermore, this salvation for *everyone* is achieved in Jesus Christ – the one mediator between God and humanity – in his life and death, which he offered as a ransom for *everyone* (1 Timothy 2:1–4). The disciples' activity of prayer and love

---

38 'Far from being a Quietist escape', Balthasar writes, 'the imprint of Christ's death involves those who bear it in the battle with evil in its fight "with God himself"; once they have embraced God's cause, evil is their enemy too, though in a "secondary" way. While "only God himself can conquer" the power that strives against him, he nonetheless wants believers to join in the fight, using his weapons. In this constant battle (cf. 1 Cor 15:31) they die daily, renouncing the power to "dispose, control and make choices for themselves," practicing a "renunciation that bears fruit in God."' *TD* V, p. 339.

39 Oakes, *Pattern of Redemption*, p. 308. Balthasar explicitly makes this link when he writes, 'If it is said of God that: "God our Savior ... desires all men to be saved and to come to the knowledge of the truth. For there is one God and there is one mediator between God and man, the man Christ Jesus, who gave himself as a ransom for all" (1 Tim 2:4–5), then this is the reason for the fact that the Church should make "supplications, prayers, intercessions and thanksgivings ... for all men" (1 Tim 2:1), which could not be asked of her if she were not allowed to have at least the hope that prayers as widely directed as these are sensible and might be heard. If, that is, she knew with certainty that this hope was too widely directed, then what is asked of her would be self-contradictory.' Balthasar, *Dare We Hope 'That All Men be Saved'?*, pp. 35–6.

for all people therefore is integrally related to their hope for the salvation of all. Hope, prayer and love are based upon God's desire that all be saved and the fulfilment of this desire in Jesus Christ's sacrificial and substitutionary death.

The practice of non-violent enemy-love contributes to the Church's vocation as a witness to God's love for the whole world. Commenting on the Vatican II document *Lumen Gentium* (Dogmatic Constitution on the Church), Balthasar links the Church's role as the 'resplendence of the glory of Christ for all people' with the command of love for the neighbour, and by implication, love for the enemy.[40] The concern of Vatican II, Balthasar asserts, was 'to direct into the secular world through the Church, which is a divine mystery, the mysterious ray of trinitarian and crucified love, wholly and completely. Let us add that this image of the Church – the mediation of the *whole* love of God to the *whole* world – is what makes possible true love of our neighbor'.[41] So, the Church is called to bear witness to the abundance of God's self-giving love, which is enacted in the cross, the descent into hell and the resurrection of Jesus Christ. Further, the Church is to bear witness to the reality that God's abundant self-giving love is directed to all people, the entire world. This informs the command to love one's neighbour, as it stresses once again that God's love is for all and that there is hope that all will be saved. In the following passage Balthasar brings together the necessity of hoping for the salvation of all, the peculiar shape of Christian love for the neighbour and the significance of Holy Saturday for affirming universal hope and understanding the profound demands of Christian love:

> The barrier must fall that Augustine set up through his concept of double predestination to heaven and hell: that everyone can ultimately hope for himself only. No, on the contrary, I must be able to hope for every brother so much that, in a fictitious *Ernstfall* (decisive moment), if it were a question of whether he or I were to enter into the Kingdom of God, I would – with Paul (Rom 9:3)

– let him go. But in order to know what that means, one would have to have uppermost in mind a theology of Holy Saturday – the descent of Christ into hell – or at least a theology of the dark night of the soul of which John of the Cross gave an experimental description. But who today has time to worry about such things?[42]

Hope for the salvation of all, non-violent love for all and the descent into hell all converge in the believer's willingness to be accursed and cut off from Jesus Christ for the sake of the salvation of others. The believer, Balthasar asserts, must be willing to give up his/her soul for the sake of the other. The disciple must not simply offer his/her life for the sake of a cause or for the sake of another person; the disciple must be willing to offer his/her entire existence, even to the limit of dying a spiritual death, for the sake of others. True Christian discipleship and martyrdom is never self-seeking or self-serving; it is fundamentally a being-for-others.[43] The martyr dies not in order to enhance his/her own future life, but for the sake of others, and in essence for the sake of God and his truth. God grants true life to those who surrender their lives. 'For those who want to save their life will lose it, and those who lose their life for my sake, and for the sake of the gospel, will save it' (Mark 8:35).

Balthasar acknowledges the allusion to Moses' offer to be blotted out of God's book of life in order for the people's sin to be forgiven (Exodus 32:32) in Paul's willingness to be accursed and cut off from Christ for the sake of his brethren. He then insists that these two instances are intelligible only in the light of Jesus Christ's actual death in God-abandonment and his descent into hell. Moses' action anticipates Jesus' death and descent into hell, and Paul offers himself in response to Christ.[44] While both Moses and Paul are spared from having their desire fulfilled, Jesus actually is accursed and anathematized for the sake of others. Jesus Christ sacrificed his soul for the sake of others; therefore, Christian disciples are called to follow Jesus and be willing to relinquish their own salvation for the salvation of others. Salvation is not a possession to be hoarded and guarded tightly. Rather, salvation and, in fact, one's very life are, and forever remain, gifts of God, gifts to

---

42   Ibid., p. 126.

43   Along with the exceptional case of being willing to be cut off from Christ for the sake of the other, we may also point to other everyday forms of renunciation as essential to genuine Christian discipleship. See Barth's insightful treatment of the concrete demands of discipleship, which include the renunciation or relativization of: possessions, fame, force, family and piety. See *CD* IV/2, pp. 546–53.

44   Balthasar supports his interpretation by citing Origen and Gregory Nazianzen as representative of an interpretation held in common in Patristic interpretation. Significantly, he specifically identifies the action of Moses and Paul with Jesus Christ's love for his *enemies*. Balthasar writes, 'Origen compares Romans 9:3 with Exodus 32:32; indeed, he goes beyond that to compare Paul's offer to be accursed with what is said in Galatians 3:13, where Christ becomes a curse for our sake. Gregory Nazianzen (Or 2:55) says the same: Paul is here emulating Christ. *All the Fathers sing the praises of his love of his enemies* [my emphasis].' Balthasar, *Dare We Hope 'That All Men be Saved'?*, p. 206.

which we ought never lay claim and which we must be willing to lose and forfeit for the sake of the lives and salvation of others.

To the examples of Moses and Paul, Balthasar adds the many instances in the history of the Church in which people wish and vow to sacrifice their own salvation for the salvation of others. He writes, 'What sorts of things do we not find in the hidden, shadowy corners of Christian history; what limits are reached in the imploring prayers of Christian mothers for their sons and daughters who have gone astray? What limits to the offering up of self by martyrs or even by simple priests for their enemies or irretrievable charges?'[45] These instances in the Church's history and the cases today, both known and unknown, as well as the prominent examples of Paul and Moses, are intelligible only as they participate in and are determined by the particular concrete event of Jesus Christ's death in God-abandonment and his experience of hell on Holy Saturday. Balthasar answers the questions that he poses above by pointing to Jesus Christ's sacrifice and his being abandoned and forsaken by God for the life of the world. He writes:

> Only God could reveal it [the limits] to us, in inseparable connection with the dying cry of his Son: 'My God, why hast thou forsaken me?' For in this cry – when the Son of God became a 'curse' and was made 'to be sin' for us – all the offerings up of self that seem so insane to us, of Moses and Paul, are caught up, taken in and gone beyond.[46]

The most critical contribution made by the descent into hell to an understanding of Christian love as non-violent enemy-love, therefore, is the extreme limit to which the disciple is called in his/her love and prayer for his/her neighbour and his/her enemy. The disciple is called to an existence of radical solidarity with and being-for-others. Informed by Jesus Christ's descent into hell and his solidarity with God's enemies and those who reject God's love, Christian existence takes the shape of selfless love for others, even to the point of being willing to forfeit intimacy with God in Christ so that others may enjoy this intimacy. This unqualified selfless love for others is perfect love, for, as the descent into hell demonstrates, this is precisely how Jesus Christ loved and loves all humanity.[47]

---

45   Ibid., p. 207.
46   Ibid., p. 208.
47   In his elevation of Paul's offer in Romans 9 as the prime example for the shape of Christian love, Balthasar not only uses the Patristic Fathers as support; he also cites Luther and Luther's claim that Paul's offer is 'evidence of consummate love'. Ibid., p. 207.
    Luther makes at least two significant points in his commentary on Romans 9:3. First, he explains how Paul's offer to be accursed and cut off from Christ for the sake of his brethren demonstrates Paul's love both for Christ and for the Jews. Second, he demonstrates how Paul's love is thoroughly selfless love. Luther does this by comparing those who find these words by Paul both puzzling and offensive with those who consider these words as 'most beautiful and testimonies of a perfect example'. Luther writes, 'The words "I could wish, etc." are a most excellent and entirely apostolic way of speaking here of love both toward Christ and toward the Jews. For from the great love for Christ he hopes for great glory from the Jews for Christ.' Those for whom Paul's words are strange and foolish love God, Luther

Conclusion: the descent into hell, Christian love and discipleship

Our examination of the respective treatments of the relationship between the passion of Jesus Christ and the Christian discipleship articulated by Barth and Balthasar clearly demonstrates how these positions complement each other in valuable and significant ways. In delineating these elements of the relationship between the passion of Christ and discipleship, we will reiterate the commonalities between Barth and Balthasar and will also highlight the distinctive mark made by the confession of the descent into hell.

The first element is that Christian discipleship is essentially the embodiment of non-violent love for the enemy. Both Barth and Balthasar view Jesus Christ's passion as the manifestation and enactment of Jesus' love for humanity, who are sinners and his enemies. Both Balthasar and Barth recognize God's abundant love for humanity – sinners and enemies – in Jesus Christ's passion, as well as the transformative power of this love to change enemies into faithful covenant partners.

The descent into hell makes two contributions to the affirmation that God's love is non-violent love for the enemy and that discipleship should therefore take the form of non-violent enemy-love. First, the descent into hell amplifies the affirmation that God loves all human beings and that Jesus Christ died for all human beings. Included in this 'all' are sinners, God's enemies, and, further, those who reject God's offer of love. The message of the descent into hell, Balthasar asserts again and again, is that Jesus Christ suffered and died for all human beings, not only for the elect, and as a result he 'assumed their eschatological "No" in regard to the event of salvation which came about in him' (*MP*, p. 172). Second, the descent into hell demonstrates even more clearly than does the cross the non-violent character of God's love for and opposition to his enemies. Balthasar emphasizes consistently the 'defencelessness' of Jesus Christ in the descent into hell and his utter passivity in his solidarity with the dead. It is this posture of defencelessness that marks Jesus Christ's descent into hell and which, in turn, ought to mark true Christian discipleship – the perfect example being Christian martyrdom.

The second element requires that Christian discipleship, understood as the ethic of non-violent enemy-love, must be considered not as a human possibility, but as a possibility only insofar as the disciple participates in God's eternal non-violent love through fellowship with Jesus Christ crucified and buried. Both Barth and Balthasar insist that the disciple's love is a sharing in God's love for the world and

---

claims, with a 'covetous love, that is, because of their salvation and eternal rest or because of their escape from hell, and not for the sake of God Himself, but for their own sakes'. Those who welcome these words, in contrast, love God with a radical selfless love. These people 'freely offer themselves to the entire will of God, even to hell and eternal death, if that is what God wills, so that His will may be fully done. Therefore they seek absolutely nothing for themselves.' Martin Luther, *Luther's Works* volume 25, *Lectures on Romans*, ed. Hilton Oswald and trans. Jacob A. O. Preus (St Louis, MO: Concordia Publishing House, 1972), pp. 380–1.

is effective only because God's love is effective. Both also recognize that an essential aspect of this love and of discipleship is a participation in Jesus Christ's crucifixion, burial and resurrection. Notably, Barth and Balthasar connect Christian discipleship as non-violent enemy-love to a particular interpretation of the passion of Jesus Christ, that is, one that emphasizes that vicarious character of this passion. Discipleship is marked by a radical being-for-others as it is a response to and a participation in the *pro nobis* life and passion of Jesus Christ. Both also affirm the similarity and critical dissimilarity between the suffering of the Christian and the *pro nobis* suffering of Jesus Christ. However, whereas Barth leans toward the dissimilarity, Balthasar attempts to explore the similarity. Related to this is the category 'witness'. Barth consistently uses the term witness to describe the disciple and his activities. The disciple, by engaging in the practice of non-violent love for the enemy, bears witness to Jesus Christ. Balthasar affirms, in agreement with Barth, that the disciple does not draw attention to his own abilities or powers, yet he will go further than Barth and speak of the disciple as not only bearing witness to Jesus Christ and to God's love for the world, but as being Jesus Christ in the world and mediating God's love to the world. The issue here may be seen as an issue of ecclesiology and the distinction between the Church as herald or witness, and the Church as sacrament. Unfortunately, an examination of this distinction between Barth and Balthasar lies beyond the scope of this study.

The descent into hell adds two qualifications to this element. First, the eschatological ramifications that follow from Balthasar's treatment of the descent into hell, i.e., the possibility of postmortem conversion, strengthen the call to prayer for the enemy as well as non-violent love for the enemy. The descent into hell demonstrates that even if one's prayer and non-violent solidarity with others seemingly fails in this life, God in Jesus Christ will bring this prayer and solidarity to fruition. Second, the descent into hell, which is hidden in the burial of Christ and audible only in the silence of Holy Saturday, validates the importance of all instances in which individuals patiently endure oppression and in suffering pray for their enemies, especially those instances held out of the spotlight and far from the centre of public attention.

The third element addresses the extent of what is required of discipleship as non-violent enemy-love and is a direct result of Balthasar's understanding of the descent into hell. True Christian love as non-violent love and as informed by the descent into hell is utterly selfless. The disciple loves in an unrestricted manner and with absolutely no concern for self-interest. Christian love must exhibit the willingness on the part of the disciple to love and exist in solidarity with others, even to the point of being willing to forfeit his whole existence for the sake of the life and salvation of the other. Christian love must take this form because it must be shaped by the descent into hell, which is a manifestation of the length to which Jesus Christ goes in his salvific existence in which he is purely for others. Jesus Christ hazards his own existence and experiences the pains of hell out of love for the Father and love for all humanity. In grateful response to this pure selfless love, the disciple too must be willing to hazard his/her whole existence for the sake of God and for the sake of the other.

Given the extent to which the descent into hell specifically and profoundly shapes Christian identity and discipleship, manifests the identity and being of God, and contributes powerfully to a rich and comprehensive interpretation of Jesus Christ's passion, we can conclude that the descent into hell should not be considered an accidental and unfortunate intrusion into the Church's confession, which should therefore be excised from the teaching and confession of the Church. It is clear that the descent into hell is not of mere historical interest; rather, it is bears acute contemporary relevance.

By focusing on the function of the descent into hell in Barth's soteriology, we see the details of his reflection on the gravity of Jesus Christ's suffering and death, which takes place for us, on our behalf and in our place. This suffering and death is in solidarity with all human suffering and death, but it is also unique. Jesus alone suffers the fullness of spiritual death as he alone bears the weight of God's wrath and dies forsaken and abandoned by God. This human experience of the second death and hell, moreover, is taken into the divine life and marks God's victory over death and hell. By placing Barth in conversation with Balthasar, the importance of Balthasar's far-reaching and innovative reflection on the theological significance of the descent into hell to enhance and challenge Barth's treatment of the descent into hell is brought to light. Balthasar challenges Barth and those who locate themselves in his heritage to think further about the distinction between Good Friday and Jesus' death on the cross, which is marked by his cry of abandonment and forsakenness, and the silence of the grave and Holy Saturday, when the corpse of Jesus lies in the tomb. At the same time, it is evident that Barth's theological rigour and restraint offer a needed challenge to some of Balthasar's speculative flights and provocative assertions regarding the inner life of God and Jesus Christ's descent into hell.

In sum, the Church must not discard the descent into hell from its confession and teaching. As Barth and Balthasar demonstrate, the descent into hell enhances our understanding of the salvific significance of Jesus Christ's passion as attested in Scripture. Further, it reveals and manifests the abundant and absolute love of the triune God. Finally, the descent into hell profoundly informs an understanding of the New Testament mandate to love and pray for all people, especially one's enemies, and gives shape to the demands of Christian discipleship. These demands, however, are not unjust restrictions or met by human achievements; rather, they give rise to true freedom in which the disciple is enabled to live and die selflessly, for God and for others, in intimate fellowship and partnership with Jesus Christ (Galatians 2:19–20; Romans 14:7–8), the One who lived, died, descended into hell and was resurrected on our behalf and in our place, for us and for our salvation.

Bibliography

Aulén, Gustav. *Christus Victor: A Historical Study of the Three Main Types of the Idea of the Atonement.* Translated by A. G. Hebert. New York: Macmillan Publishing Co., 1969.

Balthasar, Hans Urs von. *Convergences: To the Sources of Christian Mystery.* Translated by E. A. Nelson. San Francisco: Ignatius Press, 1983.

—— *Credo: Meditations on the Apostles' Creed.* Translated by David Kipp. New York: Crossroad, 1990.

—— *Dare we Hope 'That All Men be Saved'? With a Short Discourse on Hell.* Translated by David Kipp and Lothar Krauth. San Francisco: Ignatius Press, 1988.

—— *Does Jesus Know Us? Do We Know Him?* Translated by Graham Harrison. San Francisco: Ignatius Press, 1983.

—— *Explorations in Theology*, volume I, *The Word Made Flesh.* Translated by A. V. Littledale with Alexander Dru. San Francisco: Ignatius Press, 1989.

—— *Explorations in Theology*, volume IV, *Spirit & Institution.* Translated by Edward T. Oakes, S.J. San Francisco: Ignatius Press, 1995.

—— *First Glance at Adrienne von Speyr.* Translated by Antje Lawry and Sergia Englund, O.C.D. San Francisco: Ignatius Press, 1981.

—— *The Glory of the Lord: A Theological Aesthetics*, volume VII, *Theology: The New Covenant.* Edited by John Riches and translated by Brian McNeil, C.R.V. Edinburgh: T. & T. Clark; San Francisco: Ignatius Press, 1989.

—— *Heart of the World.* Translated by Erasmo S. Leiva. San Francisco: Ignatius Press, 1979.

—— *The Moment of Christian Witness.* Translated by Richard Beckley. San Francisco: Ignatius Press, 1994.

—— *Mysterium Paschale: The Mystery of Easter.* Translated by Aidan Nichols, O.P. Edinburgh: T. & T. Clark, 1990.

—— *New Elucidations.* Translated by Sister Mary Theresilde Skerry. San Francisco: Ignatius Press, 1986.

—— *Theo-Drama: Theological Dramatic Theory*, volume II, *The Dramatis Personae: Man in God.* Translated by Graham Harrison. San Francisco: Ignatius Press, 1990.

—— *Theo-Drama: Theological Dramatic Theory*, volume III, *The Dramatis Personae: The Person in Christ.* Translated by Graham Harrison. San Francisco: Ignatius Press, 1992.

—— *Theo-Drama: Theological Dramatic Theory*, volume IV, *The Action.* Translated by Graham Harrison. San Francisco: Ignatius Press, 1994.

—— *Theo-Drama: Theological Dramatic Theory*, volume V, *The Last Act.* Translated by Graham Harrison. San Francisco: Ignatius Press, 1998.

—— *The Way of the Cross.* Translated by Rodelinde Albrecht and Maureen Sullivan. New York: Herder and Herder, 1969.

—— *You Crown the Year with Your Goodness: Sermons Through the Liturgical Year.* Translated by Graham Harrison. San Francisco: Ignatius Press, 1989.

Balthasar, Hans Urs von, and Ratzinger, Joseph. *Two Say Why: 'Why I am Still a Christian'*, by Hans Urs von Balthsar, and *'Why I am Still in the Church'*, by Joseph Ratzinger. Translated by John Griffiths. London: Search Press; Chicago: Franciscan Herald Press, 1973.

Barth, Karl. *Church Dogmatics.* Edited by G. W. Bromiley and T. F. Torrance. Edinburgh: T. & T. Clark, 1936–75.

—— *Church Dogmatics*, volume I, part 1. The Doctrine of the Word of God, Prolegomena. 2nd Edition. Translated by G. W. Bromiley. Edinburgh: T. & T. Clark, 1975.

—— *Church Dogmatics*, volume I, part 2. The Doctrine of the Word of God, Prolegomena. Translated by G. T. Thomson and H. Knight. Edinburgh: T. & T. Clark, 1956.

—— *Church Dogmatics*, volume II, part 1. The Doctrine of God. Translated by T. H. L. Parker, W. B. Johnson, H. Knight and J. L. M. Haire. Edinburgh: T. & T. Clark, 1957.

—— *Church Dogmatics*, volume II, part 2. The Doctrine of God. Translated by G. W. Bromiley, J. C. Campbell, Ian Wilson, J. Strathearn McNab, H. Knight and R. A. Stewart. Edinburgh: T. & T. Clark, 1957.

—— *Church Dogmatics*, volume III, part 2. The Doctrine of Creation. Translated by H. Knight, G. W. Bromiley, J. K. S. Reid and R. H. Fuller. Edinburgh: T. & T. Clark, 1960.

—— *Church Dogmatics*, volume IV, part 1. The Doctrine of Reconciliation. Translated by G. W. Bromiley. Edinburgh: T. & T. Clark, 1956.

—— *Church Dogmatics*, volume IV, part 2. The Doctrine of Reconciliation. Translated by G. W. Bromiley. Edinburgh: T. & T. Clark, 1958.

—— *Church Dogmatics*, volume IV, part 3, first half. The Doctrine of Reconciliation. Translated by G. W. Bromiley. Edinburgh: T. & T. Clark, 1961.

—— *Church Dogmatics*, volume IV, part 3, second half. The Doctrine of Reconciliation. Translated by G. W. Bromiley. Edinburgh: T. & T. Clark, 1962.

—— *Church Dogmatics*, volume IV, part 4. The Doctrine of Reconciliation. Translated by G. W. Bromiley. Edinburgh: T. & T. Clark, 1969.

—— *Credo: A Presentation of the Chief Problems of Dogmatics with Reference to the Apostle's* [sic] *Creed*. Translated by James Strathearn McNab. London: Hodder & Stoughton, 1936.

—— *Dogmatics in Outline*. Translated by G. T. Thomson. New York: Harper & Row, Harper Torchbooks, 1959.

—— *The Faith of the Church: A Commentary on the Apostles' Creed According to Calvin's Catechism*. Edited by Jean-Louis Leuba and translated by Gabriel Vahanian. New York: Meridian Books, 1958.

—— 'Die Vorstellung vom Descensus Christi ad Inferos in der kirchlichen Literatur bis Origenes'. In *Vorträge und kleinere Arbeiten 1905–1909*. Edited by Hans-Anton Drewes and Hinrich Stoevesandt, pp. 244–312. Zurich: TVZ, 1992.

Calvin, John. *The Institutes of the Christian Religion*. Edited by John T. McNeill and translated by Ford Lewis Battles. 2 volumes. Philadelphia: Westminster Press, 1960.

Cunningham, Mary Kathleen. *What is Theological Exegesis? Interpretation and Use of Scripture in Barth's Doctrine of Election*. Valley Forge, PA: Trinity Press International, 1995.

Grudem, Wayne. 'He Did Not Descend into Hell: A Plea for Following Scripture Instead of the Apostles' Creed'. *Journal of the Evangelical Theological Society* 34 (1991): pp. 103–13.

Hunsinger, George. 'The Politics of the Nonviolent God: Reflections on René Girard and Karl Barth'. *Scottish Journal of Theology* 51 (1998): pp. 61–85.

Hunt, Anne. *The Trinity and the Paschal Mystery: A Development in Recent Catholic Theology*. Collegeville, MN: The Liturgical Press, 1997.

Kerr, Fergus. 'Adrienne von Speyr and Hans Urs von Balthasar'. *New Blackfriars* 79 (1998): pp. 26–32.

—— 'The Doctrine of the Atonement: Recent Roman Catholic Theology'. *Epworth Review* 22 (1995): pp. 19–26.

Lewis, Alan E. *Between Cross and Resurrection: A Theology of Holy Saturday*. Grand Rapids, MI: Wm. B. Eerdmans Co., 2001.

Louth, Andrew. 'The Place of *Heart of the World* in the Theology of Hans Urs von Balthasar'. In *The Analogy of Beauty*. Edited by John K. Riches, pp. 147–63. Edinburgh: T. & T. Clark, 1986.

McCormack, Bruce L. 'For Us and For Our Salvation: Incarnation and Atonement in the Reformed Tradition'. *Studies in Reformed Theology and History*. Volume 1, Number 2 (Spring 1993).

—— 'Grace and Being: The Role of God's Gracious Election in Karl Barth's Theological Ontology,' in *The Cambridge Companion to Karl Barth*. Edited by John Webster, pp. 92–110. Cambridge: Cambridge University Press, 2000.

—— 'Historical Criticism and Dogmatic Interest in Karl Barth's Theological Exegesis of the New Testament'. In *Biblical Hermeneutics in Historical Perspective: Studies in Honor of Karlfried Froehlich on His Sixtieth Birthday*. Edited by Mark S. Burrows and Paul Rorem, pp. 322–38. Grand Rapids, MI: Wm. B. Eerdmans Co., 1991.

McIntosh, Mark A. *Christology from Within: Spirituality and the Incarnation in Hans Urs von Balthasar*. Notre Dame, IN: University of Notre Dame Press, 1996.

Mansini, Guy. 'Balthasar and the Theodramatic Enrichment of the Trinity'. *The Thomist* 64 (2000): pp. 499–519.

Molnar, Paul. 'The Function of the Trinity in Moltmann's Ecological Doctrine of Creation'. *Theological Studies* 51 (1990): pp. 673–97.

—— 'The Function of the Immanent Trinity in the Theology of Karl Barth: Implications for Today'. *Scottish Journal of Theology* 42 (1989): pp. 367–99.

—— 'Toward a Contemporary Doctrine of the Immanent Trinity: Karl Barth and the Present Discussion'. *Scottish Journal of Theology* 49 (1996): pp. 311–57.

Moltmann, Jürgen. *The Crucified God: The Cross of Christ as the Foundation and Criticism of Christian Theology*. Translated by R. A. Wilson and John Bowden. Minneapolis: Fortress Press, 1993.

—— *The Future of Creation: Collected Essays*. Translated by Margaret Kohl. Philadelphia: Fortress Press, 1979.

—— *The Trinity and the Kingdom: The Doctrine of God*. Translated by Margaret Kohl. Minneapolis: Fortress Press, 1993.

—— *The Way of Jesus Christ: Christology in Messianic Dimensions*. Translated by Margaret Kohl. Minneapolis: Fortress Press, 1993.

Oakes, Edward T. *Pattern of Redemption: The Theology of Hans Urs von Balthasar*. New York: Continuum, 1994.

O'Donnell, John J. *The Mystery of the Triune God*. London: Sheed & Ward, 1988.

O'Hanlon, Gerard. *The Immutability of God in the Theology of Hans Urs von Balthasar*. Cambridge: Cambridge University Press, 1990.

Otto, Randall E. '*Descendit in inferna*: A Reformed Review of a Creedal Conundrum'. *The Westminster Theological Journal* 52 (1990): pp. 143–50.

Gene Outka. *Agape: An Ethical Analysis*. New Haven and London: Yale University Press, 1972.

—— 'Following at a Distance: Ethics and the Identity of Jesus'. In *Scriptural Authority and Narrative Interpretation*. Edited by Garrett Green, pp. 144–60. Philadelphia: Fortress Press, 1987.

Root, Michael. 'Dying He Lives: Biblical Image, Biblical Narrative and the Redemptive Jesus'. *Semeia* 30 (1985): pp. 155–69.

—— 'The Narrative Structure of Soteriology'. *Modern Theology* 2 (1986): pp. 145–58.

Saward, John. *The Mysteries of March: Hans Urs von Balthasar on the Incarnation and Easter*. Washington, DC: The Catholic University of America Press, 1990.

Thompson, John. 'Barth and Balthasar: An Ecumenical Dialogue'. In *The Beauty of Christ: An Introduction to the Theology of Hans Urs von Balthasar*. Edited by Bede McGregor, O.P. and Thomas Norris, pp. 171–92. Edinburgh: T. & T. Clark, 1994.

—— *Modern Trinitarian Perspectives*. New York: Oxford University Press, 1994.

Thompson, William M. *The Struggle for Theology's Soul: Contesting Scripture in Christology*. New York: Crossroad, 1996.

Torrance, J. B. 'The Priesthood of Jesus'. In *Essays in Christology for Karl Barth*. Edited by T. H. L. Parker, pp. 153–73. London: Lutterworth Press, 1956.

Webster, John. 'Atonement, History and Narrative'. *Theologische Zeitschrift* 42 (1986): pp. 115–31.

Williams, Rowan. 'Balthasar and Rahner'. In *The Analogy of Beauty*. Edited by John Riches, pp. 11–34. Edinburgh: T. & T. Clark, 1986.

Index